"The noble head is high, and one foot raised."

The Bearded Collie

by Chris Walkowicz

Edited by
William W. Denlinger and R. Annabel Rathman

Cover Design by
Bob Groves

Alpine
PUBLICATIONS
Loveland, Colorado

DEDICATION

Dedicated to my mother, Myrtle Nelson Ippen, who taught me to care—and to dream.

"If you don't have a dream . . . ."

Author Chris Walkowicz and friends. Photo by Rich Johnson.

Library of Congress Cataloging-in-Publication Data

Walkowicz, Chris.
 The bearded collie / by Chris Walkowicz ; edited by William W. Denlinger and R. Annabel Rathman.
    p.   cm.
  Originally published : Fairfax, Va. : Denlinger's Publishers, 1987.
  ISBN 0-931866-81-2
  1. Bearded collie. I. Denlinger, William Watson, 1924- II. Rathman, R. Annabel. III. Title.
[SF429.B32W35 1995]
636.7'37--dc20   95-43164
                                                      CIP

Copyright 1995 by Alpine Publications, Inc.
Copyright 1986 by William Denlinger.

All rights reserved. No part of this book may be used or reproduced in any manner whatsoever without written permission from the publisher, except in the case of brief quotations embodied in critical reviews. For permission, write to Alpine Publications, Inc., P. O. Box 7027, Loveland, CO 80537.

This book is available at special quantity discounts for breeders and for club promotions, premiums, or educational use. Write for details.

1 2 3 4 5 6 7 8 9 0

Printed in the United States of America.

Contents

A Beardie Is   6
Bearded Collie   6
Abbreviations   7
The Beardie Mystique   9
The Official Standard for the
    Bearded Collie   13
Interpretation of the Standard   17
Selecting Your Bearded Collie   23
Bringing Your Dog Home   27
Nutrition   31
Maintaining the Dog's Health   35
Grooming   41
Manners for the Family Dog   47
Genetics   51
Breeding and Whelping   57
History of the Bearded Collie   61
    Clubs   64
        Rescuing Beardies   64
Influential American Kennels
        and Breeders   67
Canadian Kennels and Dogs   71
Show and Obedience Competition   75
Junior Handlers and Junior
        Showmanship   81
Herding Trials   85
    Training   85
        Herding-Certified Beardies   87
Winners   89
    BIS Winners   89
    All-Time Top Sire and Dam   90
    Group Placement Winners   90
    BCCA National Specialty Show
        Winners   94
    "Select" Beardies   95
    International Specialty Show Winners   96
    Westminster Kennel Club Show Winners   97
    Santa Barbara Kennel Club
        Show Winners   98
    AKC Centennial Show Winners (1984)   98
    Top-Achieving Obedience Dogs   100
    Shuman System Records   101
    Top Obedience Dogs   101
Great Producers   103
    Register of Merit Titleholders   107
    R.O.M.X. Sires   107
    R.O.M. Sires   107
    R.O.M.X. Dams   107
    R.O.M. Dams   107
    BCCA Annual Top Producers   109
The First Decade—Champions of Record   111
"Owd Bob"   124
Pedigrees   125

Reproduced on the front cover of this book is a photograph of Parchment Farm's Annie Laurie, owned by Beth Tilson. Reproduced on the back cover are photographs of Canadian Ch. Brandylind's Classy Chamois, Canadian C.D., owned by Linda Smith; Ch. Classical State of Affairs, owned by Bea Sawka and Jean Henderson; and Ch. Birkhill's Ebony Dexter, owned by Jean Henderson.

A BEARDIE IS . . . .

A Beardie is a dog of almost overpowering friendliness, extremely active, boisterous, an expert in escapology, a dog with a loud bark who is not afraid to use it. It is not a dog for the house proud or car proud or the fanatical gardener or for parents of nervous children or for those who are forced to leave it in the house all day, but for anyone who is prepared to train it and control it, to exercise it and to look after its coat, to put up with mud, sand or worse that it will bring into the house and can keep it occupied, there is no breed which will provide more faithful companionship or greater entertainment.

Major James G. Logan
Glengorm Bearded Collies

BEARDED COLLIE

"He was a mongrel collie of the old Highland stock, known as 'beardies,' and his towzled (sic) head, not unlike an extra shaggy Dandie Dinmont's was set upon a body of immense length, girth and muscle. His manners were atrocious to all except his master, and local report accused him of every canine vice except worrying sheep."

"John MacNab," by John Buchan, 1924
Description of The Bluidy Mackenzie

When serialized on British television in 1975, Mackenzie was played by Bredon Quarry, notably knocking his master off stepping stones into a river, refusing to follow his master's friend into a car, and chasing a villain into a lake.

Abbreviations

The following abbreviations are used in text and listings in this book.

AKC—American Kennel Club. The registry body of breeds recognized in the United States; the governing body of shows and registrations.

Am./Can./Ber./Mex. Ch.—Championships in all countries specified, i.e., Am.—American; Can.—Canadian; Ber.—Bermudian; Mex.—Mexican.

(B)—Bitch.

BCCA—Bearded Collie Club of America; the parent club of all Beardie clubs and owners.

BC Number—The initials BC followed by a number signify that the dog is certified free of hip dysplasia by the Orthopedic Foundation for Animals, Inc. (OFA).

BIS—Best in Show. The winner chosen from the Group winners as the best dog or bitch shown that day.

BOB—Best of Breed. The dog or bitch chosen as best from all class dogs and champions competing in the breed that day.

BOS—Best of Opposite Sex. The best from the sex opposite that chosen BOB.

BOW—Best of Winners, i.e., the best of the WD and WB.

C.C.—Challenge Certificate, awarded in England. It is necessary to obtain three in order to win the title of champion. In England, champions and class dogs compete together for the CC.

C.D.—Companion Dog. The first title awarded in obedience competition to a dog with the specified number of passing scores in Novice classes.

C.D.X.—Companion Dog Excellent. The next title awarded in progression for qualifying scores in Open classes.

Ch.—Champion of Record, title awarded by AKC upon winning fifteen points, with two major wins.

(D)—Dog.

H.C.—Herding Certified, having passed the Herding Instinct test.

H. Ch.—Herding Champion.

HIT—High in Trial; highest scoring dog in obedience trial.

HSD—Highest Scoring Dog for the day in obedience competition.

O.T.Ch.—Obedience Trial Champion, pronounced "OTCH." A dog that has won the required points and First Place awards specified in current Obedience Regulations.

R.O.M.—Register of Merit. An award for breeding excellence.

R.O.M.I.—Register of Merit for progeny passing Herding Instinct tests.

R.O.M.X.—Register of Merit Excellent. Outstanding producer.

RWB—Reserve Winners Bitch. Awarded to the bitch deemed second best in the classes. If, for any reason, the WB is disqualified, the RWB will be awarded the championship points.

RWD—Reserve Winners Dog. Awarded to the male deemed second best in the classes. If, for any reason, the WD is disqualified, the RWD will be awarded the championship points.

Sch. A.D.—Schutzhund title, awarded to dogs that have passed the required tests.

T.D.—Tracking Dog. This title is awarded for running a qualifying track.

T.D.X.—Tracking Dog Excellent. An advanced degree of tracking.

T.T.—Temperament Test, certification for dogs that have met the required standards.

U.D.—Utility Dog. The title awarded for the specified number of passing scores in Utility competition, the most advanced and difficult of the obedience classes. This title may be combined with the T.D. and shown as the U.D.T.

WB—Winners Bitch. The female chosen as best in the classes. Awarded championship point(s), depending on the number of bitches in competition.

WD—Winners Dog. The male chosen as best in the classes. Awarded championship point(s), depending on the number of males in competition.

Ch. Lord of the Unicorn finishing his championship. Owners, Pam and Therese Gaffney.

The Beardie Mystique

When a body meets a Beardie comin' through the rye—or any place—you can be sure of a rousing good time. Bearded Collies, known as Beardies by their devoted fans, are delightfully full of curiosity, persistence, playfulness, and surprises.

Possibly because the Beardie was so recently domesticated to the pet and show world, the dog still retains his natural instincts—more so than many other breeds.

A Beardie often takes his leisure beneath coffee tables, sofas, and chairs. This is the den instinct. A Beardie refuses to believe he could become too large to fit under his favorite sofa, which normally happens when he passes from puppyhood into adulthood. (For females this may occur for the first time during pregnancy.) Beardie "limbos" under the object of his affections to his normal den, littered with all of his precious belongings, but discovers to his horror that he is unable to emerge. The chair bumps and thumps, and Beardie squeaks, then screeches in dismay, while the owner rushes to the rescue. When Beardie darts out, he gives the object a look of disbelief and distaste, and refuses to honor it with his attention ever again. He finds another place to make his den.

Children, other dogs, and—of necessity—you, are herded. *Why,* she looks at you with utter innocence, *if there are no sheep, I must make do with what I have.* She herds you to the door. She herds you in. She herds you out. She herds her puppies. No danger of a lost Beardie babe. In fact, Beardies are such good babysitters, it is claimed one was a model for Nana in Peter Pan.

Left alone, a Beardie will find ways to entertain himself. He is not choosy as to what is proper or improper entertainment. He just might decide that a table leg looks more toothsome than his chewbone, or that the garden provides a quick way to make himself cool by digging in the mud, or a place for the amusing pastime of uprooting plants, and quickly dusting his coat with ground-in dirt.

Unusually intelligent, the Beardie's natural independence and his tendency to make decisions give rise to his persistence. In their native Scottish Highlands, Beardies were required to work out of the owners' sight, and so they had to be astute and able to make their own judgments. Today's owners must be on their toes in order to remain the alpha party in the relationship and not allow the dog to become boss.

The "Beardie bounce." Sweet Briar. Owners, Bob and Jo Ann Frey.

A Beardie is stubborn about new routines, tending to ride the tide with the familiar, balking at the new—unless it's he who is choosing another direction. A dominant, firm, but gentle hand will turn the tide in just a couple of sessions. It is definitely easier to train a Beardie to adapt to a new experience, such as crating, relaxing on a grooming table, or gaiting on a leash, when he is small enough to be controlled with ease.

A Beardie is outgoing and loving, even when visitors are not interested in his attentions. He loves without question, and will not thrive as a neglected kennel dog. If you are thoughtless enough to upset your Beardie, he will mope. He will crawl into his den and must be coaxed out. Or he might turn his back on you, refusing to grace you with his usual adoring expression.

Ch. Arcadia's Jonny Walker and his baby.

A typical puppy.

Beardies are popular dogs for commercials.

Whether it is a minor trespass, such as a bath or a scolding, or a major offense, such as leaving him alone for a day, the Beardie forgives your wrongs quickly. With your gentle pleas for forgiveness, he will once again award you his attention. If you, being only human, are not as quick to forgive *his* straying from the path, he will sigh and gaze mournfully at you from beneath his crown of hair until you succumb to his charisma.

Like his country's natives, a Beardie is hard-working, steady, confident, independent, and friendly. He also can be bossy, in order to achieve his own way, and selfish about his belongings, or even everyone else's belongings. A Beardie will empty a toy basket, removing the toys one by one, until he has the entire collection in his den. One owner tells of a game she plays with her Beardie. She removes one object from the hoard and places it back in the basket. When he rushes to retrieve the toy, she removes another, and this continues until owner or Beardie gives out—usually the owner, she admits.

Our own Beardie ruler, Bryn Mawr, becomes a bustling burst of motion when we add another dog to the household. The menagerie normally consists of one "retired" German Shepherd female and Bryn in the house, with the kennel dogs taking turns. Bryn manages quite well. She allows the *grande dame* peace unless the old lady has the nerve to chew on a bone. Grandma is dominant and the youngster must give in, but Bryn saves face by voicing her objections to the invasion. Meanwhile, she keeps the visiting kennel dog well in line and in place. It's a different story if a fourth dog enters the system— whether it's a puppy being housebroken, an expectant dam, or a dog being prepared for a show. Bryn becomes a whirlwind, running to bark at Grandma over "her" bone, darting to the intruder to remind him just who is boss here, then to remove a knotted sock from the possession of the visiting kennel dog—all emphasized by her "woof!" Little wonder she was awarded the nickname of P.B., which stands for "Pain in the . . . ."

Physical punishment is a detriment when training a Beardie, for it wounds his pride. He either melts into a totally useless lump of abject misery, or becomes a stubborn, immovable beastie.

A Beardie is always ready for a romp and inclusion in family activities, for he is not just a dog, but a member of the family. A Beardie is content in any surroundings— apartment, luxurious mansion, or vast acreage—so long as he has his people.

Note the lithe ease of a Beardie moving freely, tirelessly, trotting with no strain, yet with movement frequently broken by the "Beardie bounce" from the sheer joy of being alive.

To wrap up the Beardie mystique, a Beardie is affectionate, energetic, intelligent, steady, forgiving, stubborn, greedy, winsome—in short, almost human.

The den instinct.

Beardies love children.

Ch. Lochengar Never Surrender. Owners, Lochengar.

LEFT: GOOD HEAD.

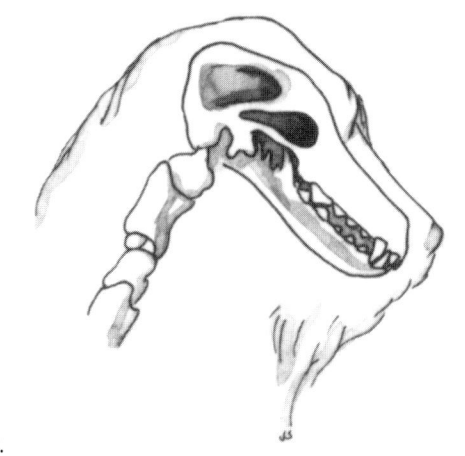

RIGHT: PROPER SCISSORS BITE.

LEFT: OVERBITE.

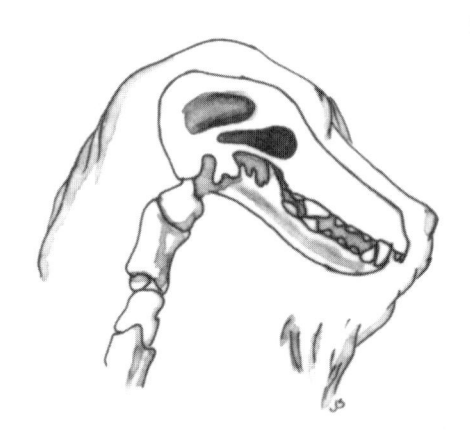

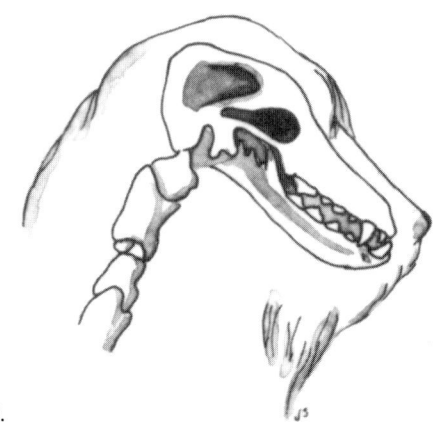

RIGHT: UNDERBITE.

CORRECT FRONT.

CORRECT FRONT.

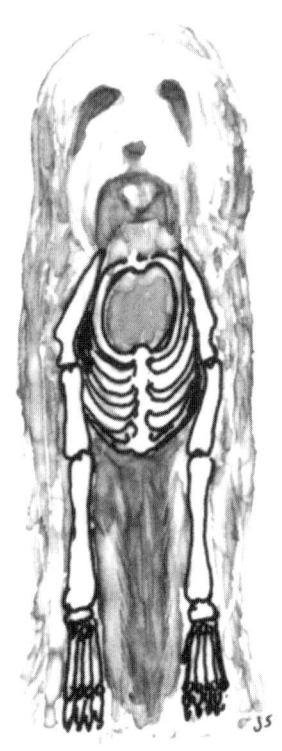

CORRECT REAR.

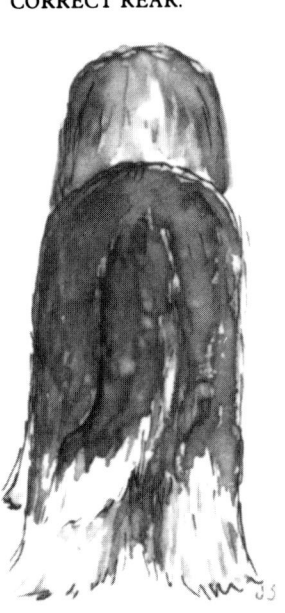

CORRECT REAR.

The Official Standard for the Bearded Collie

Characteristics—The Bearded Collie is hardy and active, with an aura of strength and agility characteristic of a real working dog. Bred for centuries as a companion and servant of man, the Bearded Collie is a devoted and intelligent member of the family. He is stable and self-confident, showing no signs of shyness or aggression. This is a natural and unspoiled breed.

General Appearance—The Bearded Collie is a medium sized dog with a medium length coat that follows the natural lines of the body and allows plenty of daylight under the body. The body is long and lean, and though strongly made, does not appear heavy. A bright inquiring expression is a distinctive feature of the breed. The Bearded Collie should be shown in a natural stance.

Head—The head is moderate to the size of the dog. The skull is broad and flat; the stop is moderate; the cheeks are well filled beneath the eyes; the muzzle is strong and full; the foreface is equal in length to the distance between the stop and occiput. The nose is large and squarish. A snipy muzzle is to be penalized. *(See Color section for pigmentation.)*

Eyes: The eyes are large, expressive, soft and affectionate, but not round nor protruding, and are set widely apart. The eyebrows are arched to the sides to frame the eyes and are long enough to blend smoothly into the coat on the sides of the head. *(See Color section for eye color.)*

Ears: The ears are medium sized, hanging and covered with long hair. They are set level with the eyes. When the dog is alert, the ears have a slight lift at the base.

Teeth: The teeth are strong and white, meeting in a scissors bite. Full dentition is desirable.

Neck—The neck is in proportion to the length of the body, strong and slightly arched, blending smoothly into the shoulders.

Forequarters—The shoulders are well laid back at an angle of approximately forty-five degrees; a line drawn from the highest point of the shoulder blade to the forward point of articulation approximates a right angle with a line from the forward point of articulation to the point of the elbow. The top of the shoulder blades lie in against the withers, but they slope outwards from there sufficiently to accommodate the desired spring of ribs. The legs are straight and vertical, with substantial, but not heavy, bone and are covered with shaggy hair all around. The pasterns are flexible without weakness.

Body—The body is longer than it is high in an approximate ratio of five to four, length measured from point of chest to point of buttocks, height measured at the highest point of the withers. The length of the back comes from the length of the ribcage and not that of the loin. The back is level. The ribs are well sprung from the spine but are flat at the sides. The chest is deep, reaching at least to the elbows. The loins are strong. The level back line blends smoothly into the curve of the rump. A flat croup or a steep croup is to be severely penalized.

Hindquarters—The hind legs are powerful and muscular at the thighs with well bent stifles. The hocks are low. In normal stance, the bones below the hocks are perpendicular to the ground and parallel to each other when viewed from the rear; the hind feet fall just behind a perpendicular line from the point of the buttocks when viewed from the side. The legs are covered with shaggy hair all around.

Tail: The tail is set low and is long enough for the end of the bone to reach at least to the point of the hocks. It is normally carried low with an upward swirl at the tip while the dog is standing. When the dog is excited or in motion, the curve is accentuated and the tail may be raised but is never carried beyond a vertical line. The tail is covered with abundant hair.

Feet—The feet are oval in shape with the soles well padded. The toes are arched and close together, and well covered with hair including between the pads.

Coat—The coat is double with the undercoat soft, furry and close. The outercoat is flat, harsh, strong and shaggy, free from woolliness and curl, although a slight wave is permissible. The coat falls naturally to either side but must never be artificially parted. The length and density of the hair are sufficient to provide a protective coat and to enhance the shape of the dog, but not so profuse as to obscure the natural lines of the body. The dog should be shown as naturally as is consistent with good grooming but the coat must not be trimmed in any way. On the head, the bridge of the nose is sparsely covered with hair which is slightly longer on the sides to cover the lips. From the cheeks, the lower lips and under the chin, the coat increases in length towards the chest, forming the typical beard. An excessively long, silky coat or one which has been trimmed in any way must be severely penalized.

Color—

Coat: All Bearded Collies are born either black, blue, brown or fawn, with or without markings. With maturity, the coat color may lighten, so that a born black may become any shade of gray from black to slate to silver, a born brown from chocolate to sandy. Blues and fawns also show shades from dark to light. Where white occurs, it only appears on the foreface as a blaze, on the skull, on the tip of the tail, on the chest, legs and feet and around the neck. The white hair does not grow on the body behind the shoulder nor on the face to surround the eyes. Tan markings occasionally appear and are acceptable on the eyebrows, inside the ears, on the cheeks, under the root of the tail, and on the legs where the white joins the main color.

Pigmentation: Pigmentation on the Bearded Collie follows coat color. In a born black, the eye rims, nose and lips are black, whereas in the born blue, the pigmentation is a blue-gray color. A born brown dog has brown pigmentation and born fawns a correspondingly lighter brown. The pigmentation is completely filled in and shows no sign of spots.

Eyes: Eye color will generally tone with the coat color. In a born blue or fawn, the distinctively lighter eyes are correct and must not be penalized.

Size—The ideal height at the withers is 21-22 inches for adult dogs and 20-21 inches for adult bitches. Height over and under the ideal is to be severely penalized. The express objective of this criterion is to insure that the Bearded Collie remains a medium sized dog.

Gait—Movement is free, supple and powerful. Balance combines good reach in forequarters with strong drive in hindquarters. The back remains firm and level. The feet are lifted only enough to clear the ground, giving the impression that the dog glides along making minimum contact. Movement is lithe and flexible to enable the dog to make the sharp turns and sudden stops required of the sheep dog. When viewed from the front and rear, the front and rear legs travel in the same plane from the shoulder and hip joint to pads at all speeds. Legs remain straight, but feet move inward as speed increases until the edges of the feet converge on a center line at a fast trot.

Serious faults:
—*snipy muzzle*
—*flat croup or steep croup*
—*excessively long, silky coat*
—*trimmed or sculptured coat*
—*height over or under the ideal*

Note. A first Standard for the Bearded Collie was approved October 12, 1976. The revised Standard shown above was approved August 9, 1978.

American and Canadian Ch. Bendale Special Lady, C.D.X.

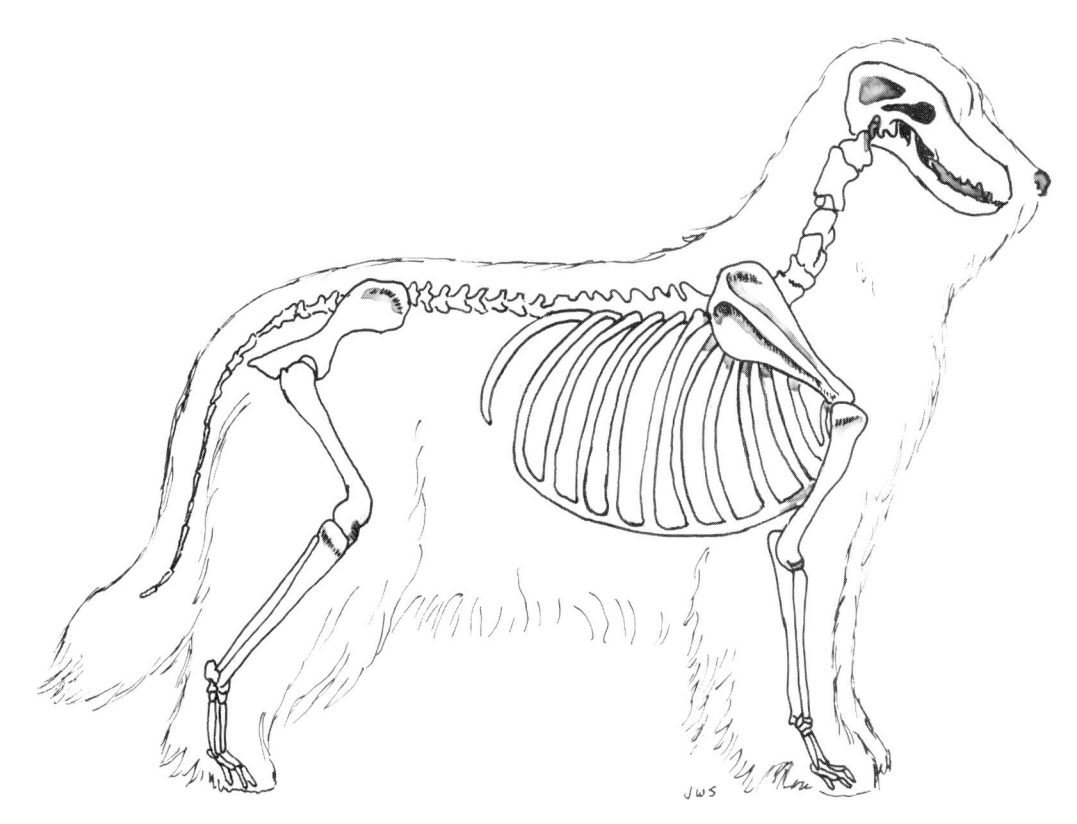

CORRECT SKELETAL STRUCTURE.

PROPER COAT AND MARKINGS.

Ch. Ha'Penny Moon Shadow. Owners, Robert Greitzer and J. Richard Schneider.

Interpretation of the Standard

A Standard, which describes the ideal dog of a particular breed, is proposed by the national parent club of the breed and then approved by The American Kennel Club. The Standard forms the basis for judging in the conformation ring. The American Bearded Collie Standard is similar to the English Standard, with a few alterations and clarifications.

People interested in showing or breeding their Beardies should be cognizant of the Standard and the reasons for its requirements. In addition, buyers who wish to obtain a quality Beardie would be wise to study the Standard prior to making their purchase.

As with all breeds, debate and proposals to amend the Standard occur. Current suggestions call for disqualification of dogs that are predominantly white or that deviate more than one inch from the size requirement. There also is encouragement for acceptance of the level bite, to correspond with the Canadian and British Standards. Whether or not these suggestions are accepted will be decided in time. Changes in the Standard should serve only to make our Beardies closer to the ideal, not to make allowances for incorrect dogs or to eliminate competition.

Fortunately, the Standard, like the Bible, is open to individual interpretation. If not, the same dog would win every exhibition, and the rest of us could sit at home. The Standard does, however, give us an ideal for which we should endeavor to breed.

The Standard appears in italics below, with my interpretation immediately following each section.

Characteristics—The Bearded Collie is hardy and active, with an aura of strength and agility characteristic of a real working dog. Bred for centuries as a companion and servant of man, the Bearded Collie is a devoted and intelligent member of the family. He is stable and self-confident, showing no signs of shyness or aggression. This is a natural and unspoiled breed.

A strong, sturdy dog that is ready at all times to join his master in any sport or job, the Beardie exhibits a sound temperament. He should be neither meek nor rowdy when asked to perform his duty, whether herding, exhibiting, or making friends. He is both sensitive and sensible.

Although temperaments vary from bold, effusive, happy, and completely self-possessed to a mild and gentle sweetness, a Beardie that is painfully shy or overly aggressive is not a typical Beardie. Such a dog should not be perpetuated by breeding.

General Appearance—The Bearded Collie is a medium sized dog with a medium length coat that follows the natural lines of the body and allows plenty of daylight under the body. The body is long and lean, and though strongly made, does not appear heavy. A bright inquiring expression is a distinctive feature of the breed. The Bearded Collie should be shown in a natural stance.

The Beardie should be a natural dog with no artificiality. An identifying feature is the winsome expression, so perfectly captured in "Owd Bob." The expression seems to demand a response. He should appear to be sturdy and yet have grace and charm. When not at play, the dog should have a certain nobility.

The ideal Bearded Collie should be healthy, spirited, friendly, and attractive. He should have good body proportion, should be longer than he is tall, and his size should be somewhere in the middle of the total dog population.

The Standard stresses several times that the breed is natural, and it is hoped that breeders, exhibitors, and judges will continue to allow the dog to be natural. Trimming, other than for purposes of cleanliness (around the genitals), is not the "natural state." Beardies have a part in the coat, which can be encouraged with disciplined combing, not with the tooth end of the comb or a knitting-needle. In other words, the rough, tousled-looking tyke should appear as one. He should not be unbathed or unbrushed, but neither should he be doused with softening conditioners or have an artificially altered coat.

Head—The head is in proportion to the size of the dog. The skull is broad and flat; the stop is moderate; the cheeks are well filled beneath the eyes; the muzzle is strong and full; the foreface is equal in length to the distance between the stop and occiput. The nose is large and squarish. A snipy muzzle is to be penalized.

The head should be strong and large enough at adulthood to fill the hand. Ideally it is in proportion to the body and exhibits good bone, with a flat skull. The stop is obvious, making the head wedge-shaped. The muzzle is highly important—full, with a strong underjaw. Bad muzzles often hide bad mouths.

Eyes: The eyes are large, expressive, soft and affectionate, but not round nor protruding, and are set widely apart. The eyebrows are arched to the sides to frame the eyes and are long enough to blend smoothly into the coat on the sides of the head.

An endearing look of charm and mischief should invite your touch. A closer look at the large eyes will reveal intelligence. Eyes that do not match coat color do not exhibit the lovely "inquiring expression." Eyebrows are brushed up and forward, but should not obscure the eyes.

Ears: The ears are medium sized, hanging and covered with long hair. They are set level with the eyes. When the dog is alert, the ears have a slight lift at the base.

The ears should be set just below the top of the skull, at the edge, and lifted when alert. Lighter ear leather lifts more easily than heavy ears. Low-set Spaniel-type or Setter-type ears do not lift. Ears should be folded either across the flap, or lengthwise like the old type.

Teeth: The teeth are strong and white, meeting in a scissors bite. Full dentition is desirable.

Though the level bite frequently is seen, the scissors bite is preferred. The original American Standard stated level bites were acceptable. Both the Canadian and English Standards accept the level bite, and with the importation of dogs from those countries, the level bite is difficult to eradicate from the breed.

Neck—The neck is in proportion to the length of the body, strong, and slightly arched, blending smoothly into the shoulders.

Forequarters—The shoulders are well laid back at an angle of approximately forty-five degrees; a line drawn from the highest point of the shoulder blade to the forward point of articulation approximates a right angle with a line from the forward point of articulation to the point of the elbow. The top of the shoulder blades lie in against the withers, but they slope outwards from there sufficiently to accommodate the desired spring of ribs. The legs are straight and vertical, with substantial, but not heavy, bone and are covered with shaggy hair all around. The pasterns are flexible without weakness.

Movement reveals the shoulder construction. Too short an upper arm restricts proper movement, which should be easy, long-striding, and flowing.

The front legs should be long and straight, not curved, pinched in, or turned out at the elbows. The pasterns should be at a slight angle to the leg, giving spring in motion. They should not be flat or broken down, nor upright like a Terrier's.

Body—The body is longer than it is high in an approximate ratio of five to four, length measured from point of chest to point of buttocks, height measured at the highest point of the withers. The length of the back comes from the length of the ribcage and not that of the loin. The back is level. The ribs are well sprung from the spine but are flat at the sides. The chest is deep, reaching at least to the elbows. The loins are strong. The level back line blends smoothly into the curve of the rump. A flat croup or a steep croup is to be severely penalized.

Longer than he is tall, the dog should not appear square. The ribcage is long, with ribs slanted backwards, giving added length to the body and plenty of room for the heart and lungs. Length of ribcage allows for quick, easy turns, whereas length of loin weakens the back. The ribcage should be rounded, becoming flatter below the elbows.

The topline is level, and does not sag. It is not high in the rear, nor extremely slanted in a natural stance. The topline smooths into a croup angled about thirty degrees, curving smoothly into the tail. This allows the dog the agility to perform top-of-your-head leaps. The body should be well filled out, not heavy or thin.

The entire body is put together to enable the dog to work in rough terrain, rocks, and hills.

Hindquarters—The hind legs are powerful and muscular at the thighs with well bent stifles. The hocks are low. In normal stance, the bones below the hocks are perpendicular to the ground and parallel to each other when viewed from the rear; the hind feet fall just behind a perpendicular line from the point of buttocks when viewed from the side. The legs are covered with shaggy hair all around.

Tail: The tail is set low and is long enough for the end of the bone to reach at least the point of the hocks. It is normally carried low with an upward swirl at the tip while the dog is standing. When the dog is excited or in motion, the curve is accentuated and the tail may be raised but is never carried beyond a vertical line. The tail is covered with abundant hair.

Angulation of the hindquarters, ideally, is equal to that of the shoulders. A long stifle provides the powerful rear drive. A slight "hocking in" during puppyhood should straighten with maturity.

The tail exhibits the dog's attitude and a happy dog tends to carry his tail higher than a complacent or dispirited dog. This is true particularly in puppies. As an adult, when at work—such as in the ring—the tail should not be curled above the topline.

Feet—The feet are oval in shape with the soles well padded. The toes are arched and close together, and well covered with hair including between the pads.

The feet should not be spread. The hair between the pads protects the feet.

Coat—The coat is double with the undercoat soft, furry, and close. The outercoat is flat, harsh, strong and shaggy, free from woolliness and curl, although a slight wave is permissible. The coat falls naturally to either side but must never be artificially parted. The length and density of the hair are sufficient to provide a protective coat and to enhance the shape of the dog, but not so profuse as to obscure the natural lines of the body. The dog should be shown as naturally as is consistent with good grooming but the coat must not be trimmed in any way. On the head, the bridge of the nose is sparsely covered with hair which is slightly longer on the sides to cover the lips. From the cheeks, the lower lips and under the chin, the coat increases in length towards the chest, forming the typical beard. An excessively long, silky coat or one which has been trimmed in any way must be severely penalized.

Proper coat texture in Beardies is highly important. The coat is thick and springy. The undercoat is visible, often lighter in color and softer in texture. The coat should be neither too short nor too long. The puppy coat is fuller than the adult coat, which comes in between eighteen and twenty-four months.

A Beardie with too little coat would suffer from the damp and chill climate in its natural environment. Too much coat would become entangled and torn on the brush. Occasionally a smooth-coated Beardie is whelped. The difference in the coat will be obvious by four to five weeks. Instead of the bristly, whiskery look around the face, the hair will be sleek and lie close to the skull, much like the coat of a Shetland Sheepdog or a Border Collie. Smooth-coated Beardies should be placed in pet homes. Most breeders sell them on "neuter contracts," meaning that the buyer must agree to have the pet neutered.

The coat is distinctive. The Beardie should not be as woolly as the Old English Sheepdog, nor as conditioned as the Afghan, nor parted precisely like the Tibetan Terrier. When the breed was first recognized, many people judged a Beardie entirely by its coat. Thankfully, for the most part this has changed to judging the entire dog. The coat is but one component.

Color—

Coat: All Bearded Collies are born either black, blue, brown or fawn, with or without white markings. With maturity, the coat may lighten, so that a born black may become any shade of gray from black to slate to silver, a born brown from chocolate to sandy. Blues and fawns also show shades from dark to light. Where white occurs, it only appears on the foreface as a blaze, on the skull, on the tip of the tail, on the chest, legs and feet and around the neck. The white hair does not grow on the body behind the shoulder nor on the face to surround the eyes. Tan markings occasionally appear and are acceptable on the eyebrows, inside the ears, on the cheeks, under the root of the tail, and on the legs where the white joins the main color.

Pigmentation: Pigmentation on a Bearded Collie follows coat color. In a born black, the eye rims, nose and lips are black, whereas in the born blue, the pigmentation is a blue-gray color. A born brown dog has brown pigmentation and born fawns a correspondingly lighter brown. The pigmentation is completely filled in and shows no sign of spots.

Eyes: Eye color will generally tone with the coat color. In a born blue or fawn, the distinctively lighter eyes are correct and must not be penalized.

White, when it appears, should occur only in the Irish pattern—collar, forelegs and chest, rear feet to the hocks, muzzle, tip of tail, and blaze up the middle of the face. The blaze can reach to the collar. The Standard could be worded better by changing placement of the comma, to read: "on the foreface, as a blaze on the skull," removing the erroneous impression that white may not be on the beard, but may cover the entire skull. White may appear in lesser amounts, even to self-colored (solid color with no markings). Most breeders do not register, or they require neutering of, puppies that show white markings surrounding the eyes or on the ears. The same practice follows with body mismarks. White appearing much

Ch. Gaymardon's Yorktown Yankee. Owners, Gaymardon.

Ch. Arcadia's Country Music, C.D., H.C. Owner, Betty Brask.

19

above the hocks on the *outside* of the rear legs or beyond the shoulder in large amounts is not desirable. This preference dates back to the time of stock dogs. A white dog was ignored by the sheep as being one of the flock. In addition, it was difficult to keep the dog clean.

Many Beardies carry a fading gene, and their colors lighten as they mature, with the lightest coloration occurring at the age of one year. Color tone (or shade) is not as important as pigmentation. Eye rims, nose, and lips should be completely colored to correspond with coat. Skin under the white portions of hair may be pink or pink spotted, which is sometimes noticeable on the bridge of the muzzle.

Size—The ideal height at the withers is 21-22 inches for adult dogs and 20-21 inches for adult bitches. Height over and under the ideal is to be severely penalized. The express objective of this criterion is to insure that the Bearded Collie remains a medium sized dog.

Dogs and bitches may mature at slightly over or under the Standard. Though the Standard sets forth the ideal, minor discrepancies of size are not as important as body proportion. Height is measured at the top point of the withers. It is important that the dog remain a size that permits agility. In the 1912 British Standard, size was specified as twenty to twenty-four inches for dogs with bitches slightly shorter. The medium size of the dog allows it to move swiftly and gather its charges.

Gait—Movement is free, supple and powerful. Balance combines good reach in forequarters with strong drive in hindquarters. The back remains firm and level. The feet are lifted only enough to clear the ground, giving the impression that the dog glides along making minimum contact. Movement is lithe and flexible to enable the dog to make the sharp turns and sudden stops required of the sheep dog. When viewed from the front and rear, the front and rear legs travel in the same plane from the shoulder and hip joint to pads at all speeds. Legs remain straight, but feet move inward as speed increases until the edges of the feet converge on a center line at a fast trot.

Half or more of the Beardie's composition can be judged in its movement. Proper movement denotes proper conformation and even serves as evidence of ideal temperament. Movement should not be sluggish or lethargic, nor uncontrollable. Moving at a trot, the dog appears an attractive picture, moving easily and not tiring.

The German Shepherd is the only breed that has a comparable gait, with suspended movement, all four feet being off the ground at times. But whereas the German Shepherd's gait signifies nobility, the Beardie's is magical. You expect him to take off in flight on invisible wings.

The last sentence of this section presents a rather humorous picture of the legs remaining in place, while the feet disconnect or turn inward. What actually is meant, of course, is that the dog single-tracks as it picks up speed.

Serious faults:
—snipy muzzle
—flat croup or steep croup
—excessively long, silky coat
—trimmed or sculptured coat
—height over or under the ideal

Bilateral cryptorchids (dogs with neither testicle descended) and unilateral cryptorchids, commonly called monorchids (dogs with only one testicle descended), are disqualified in all breeds by The American Kennel Club. Bilateral cryptorchids are sterile. Although monorchids can sire puppies, they should not be used for breeding purposes because they can pass on the condition genetically.

Everything in the Standard describes the ideal working dog. The dog should be in condition to do the work for which the breed was developed, whether or not it is required to do so in its individual situation. For instance, the proper coat is not to be deemed correct for aesthetic purposes, but for protection from inclement weather.

Ch. Glen Eire Dendarra Charity, Ch. Glen Eire Molly Brown, and Ch. Glen Eire Good Gracious. Owner, Anne Dolan.

Selecting Your Bearded Collie

The first requirement before selecting a dog of any breed is to know yourself and your lifestyle. A Beardie is not for everybody. If you prefer a dull, plodding, listless dog that is submissive to your every command, don't have a Beardie. If you prefer life in a rocking chair, don't own a Beardie. If you plan to chain your dog in the back yard, *don't* buy a Beardie. But if you have decided to join your life with that of a Beardie, that is only the *first* decision.

Do you want a puppy or an adult?

"A puppy, of course!" is the initial response. Just as with human adoptions, most people want to share their whole life with the new family member and wish to start with an infant. For people in some situations, however, the answer might be an adult dog. When you buy an adult, what you see is what you get. Breeders occasionally have adults available. Sometimes they must free up kennel space, or have a dog that they had wished to show, but could not. Now and then, they have a dog that is no longer being shown or used in their breeding program and are looking for a good retirement home for the dog. The advantages of purchasing an adult dog are several: obtaining a dog that is housebroken, trained, has had inoculations, and is over the "uglies" and the chewing stage. An adult dog is less likely to evidence congenital problems later on. If the new owner works away from home all day, has previously experienced the delight of puppies, and/or wishes to avoid the toddler stage, an older dog just might be the right answer.

Do you want a male or a female?

There is a size difference—males, on the average, are an inch taller and ten pounds heavier than females. There are advantages and disadvantages to each sex. Males often carry more coat. They do not have heat cycles. Males attract more attention in the ring. Females are the foundation for breeding kennels. Females have the choice of mates.

Although true of some breeds, Beardies do not differ in personality according to sex. Males are just as affectionate and obedient. Females are just as playful and ready for a romp. There will be no sexual promiscuity with either sex if watched properly and/or neutered.

Do you want show or pet quality?

Some buyers say they want a "show puppy," but don't want to pay show price and don't intend to show. Since breeders establish their reputations by having their best puppies shown, it is natural for them to prefer that a pup with show quality potential not spend his days sitting in someone's back yard. Breeders charge more for these pups, and with the sale may include guarantees against show faults.

Other prospective buyers say they want a pet quality puppy, then become upset when the pup doesn't go out and shake the show world by the nape of the neck. A false statement of intent is unfair to the dog, the breeder, and the buyer. Be honest with yourself and with the breeder. If a good pet and companion is your priority, it does not matter if show attitude, angles, or coat is lacking. A pet is as lovable as a show dog. When buyers believe they want a "pick" puppy, their intent is usually for a pet that is pretty. No one, except the owner or the vet, will know if it is missing a tooth or a testicle. That pup will be just as much fun, just as affectionate, and just as good in the obedience ring.

What type of personality do you prefer?

Naturally, you want a sound dog that does not bite people or cringe when approached. Temperaments, though, range from noisy to quiet, boisterous to docile, submissive to dominant, quick and eager to complacent and inactive, and more—or less—intelligent than the owner!

Do you plan to breed?

If so, the decision of sex is settled. A breeder should always start with a good female, the best affordable. It is no time to scrimp. As the female develops, the best male for her may be chosen. If you start with a male, you don't have the choice; the females must come to you—and sometimes they don't!

To learn all the intricacies of choosing your new companion, read books, attend shows, visit kennels, talk to breeders, even in other breeds. You can obtain the names of reliable sources through your local dog clubs, the Bearded Collie Club of America, The American Kennel Club, veterinarians, other breeders, and shows.

Buy your puppy from a breeder who is reputable, has a clean kennel and healthy dogs, is willing to guarantee the dog, and exhibits a certain hard-to-define but unmistakable rapport with the dogs. Look for a special caress, an adoring look from a dog, a love that is demonstrated, not verbally spouted. The best breeder is not necessarily the one most touted by ads and financial backing. The best is not necessarily *not* that breeder either. Study statistics and facts.

Before deciding on your puppy, look at several. Most breeders allow their puppies to go to new homes at eight to twelve weeks of age. By this age they have had their first shots, have been wormed if necessary, and are at their peak period of adjustment. Do not try to talk a breeder into selling earlier. Good reasons for not doing so include sibling socialization, immunizations, and development of personalities and bodies.

Ch. Classical's Silver Cloud. Owners, Bea and Kevin Sawka.

Do the pups appear healthy and friendly? If they are not, you can only go downhill. A poor start means a poor—and early—finish.

Look at the pedigree. Although titles do not necessarily guarantee a good dog, the puppy's ancestors should have several breed and/or obedience titles, indicating soundness.

Look at the sire and dam. Ask to see health records. The breeder should provide medical records of inoculations and worming, AKC registration papers, a pedigree, and instructions on feeding. Does the breeder offer guarantees against congenital defects? Are prices on a par with those of other breeders? Price is not indicative of quality. The most expensive (or on the contrary, the cheapest) is not necessarily the best (or worst).

Always choose a puppy that is sound in temperament. You want a companion that is going to be around for many years and is physically and mentally healthy. Puppies should be pudgy until twelve weeks, have healthy, furry coats, and be friendly and playful.

Choosing a Show Prospect

Show prospects may be selected, with some degree of success and hope, at twelve weeks. Variables can change, but by this age markings, coat, orchidism in males, and certain other hereditary features can be predicted. Although a crystal ball may be necessary to foresee how a Beardie's size and bite will change, some educated "guesstimation" is possible at this age.

The only way to be positive that you have bought a show dog is to obtain one that has reached maturity and has already begun proving his prowess in the show ring. Frequently, buyers don't want to wait that long, nor do many breeders, so most people are willing to take a gamble with puppies. Even though puppies go through awkward growth spurts, and Beardies experience horrid coat stages, a good quality puppy usually will return to the promise he exhibited at eight to ten weeks.

If you want a show prospect, choose one that has a free-flowing natural gait, and an attitude that shows confidence and sparkle. A bold, outgoing temperament is a must. Though individual personalities may vary, the pup should be friendly. In Bearded Collies, it is also important to find one that has proper coat texture and markings. The coat should be thick and fairly harsh.

Avoid the occasional smooth coat that appears to lie sleekly against the body. The face should be whiskery, with mustache and beard already forming. Dogs with smooth coats should be placed as pets on a spay/neuter contract.

Color is unimportant except for personal preference and, along with markings, should be the last consideration. As long as the puppy is not a "mismark" (see "The Bearded Collie Standard," pages 13-14, and "Interpretation of the Standard," pages 19-20, it does not matter how much or how little white markings the puppy has. More important by far are personality and body structure.

White Bearded Collies are not shown nor used for breeding in England and Canada, and by few owners in the United States. Since there are many lovely puppies correct in color and markings, there is no need to choose a poorly marked puppy for showing and for use in building a breeding kennel.

Some people choose a favorite color first, are stubborn about it, and thus wind up with a dog they don't even like—because it is too boisterous, or it has a genetic history of dysplasia or paranoid shyness. However, if it comes

Ch. Mistiburn's Mistletoe at six months. Owners, Ralph and Irene Carson.

down to a choice between two, Beardies do offer coats of many colors. So a preference can be stated to the breeder.

Although the eventual adult shades are not obvious in puppyhood, the puppy that fades or "grays out" first is likely to develop the lightest adult coat. Graying is first noticeable around the eyes.

Look for a head that appears square. Heads develop into their future promise at about five weeks. The skull should be broad and fairly flat. Look for good breadth of muzzle, which should be about the same length as the skull, ending in a blunt nose. Mouth faults often correspond with faulty muzzles. The teeth should meet in a scissors bite. A lower jaw that has teeth set straight across, rather than rounded, seems to change less as the puppy matures. Beardie bites sometimes "go off" between four to nine months of age, but those that were good from birth to eight weeks have a good chance of again becoming correct.

Ears should be triangular, and set on the edge of the skull, not on top. The eyes should be large, and their color should correspond with the coat color. Desirable expression is a must.

The front legs should be straight, with feet tightly formed and oval. Fronts suffer many changes in Beardie puppies. To determine whether a front is likely to remain straight, pick up a paw. A bone turned at the pastern often remains permanently curved, rather than straight. Rear hocks should drop squarely, without turning inward.

Find a male that has obvious secondary sex characteristics and a female that is totally feminine. Bone should never be fine nor should the chest be shallow.

Look for a slightly arched neck, with the shoulder blades well laid back. A level topline flowing into a gently sloping croup is desirable, because it enables the Beardie to fulfill his breed potential of herding sheep in rough hill country.

The ribcage should be long, rounded deeply, then flat below the elbow, accompanied by a short loin. Thighs should be muscular, with well-bent stifles and hocks. The tail is preferably low-set and long.

If you are acquiring your first puppy, try to take a knowledgeable person along to help you decide which pup has the best show potential. Choose a breeder who has a reputation for being honest and for breeding quality show dogs.

Be prepared to transport your puppy home in comfort. A dog crate is the wisest choice, and will keep him safe and confined. Take newspapers and towels in case he should become carsick.

Make an appointment with your veterinarian within the first two days after bringing your dog home, and bring records the breeder has provided. It is wise to have a stool check for worms at this time, because, although the breeder may have wormed them, many puppies become reinfested during the time they remain with the litter.

"Pick a peck of puppies." Bred by Buehrigs.

Piebald body mismarks.

A "rainbow" litter. Jande Bearded Collies.

"Pals."

Introduce to the grooming table—but one at a time, please. Parchment Farm Beardies.

Bringing Your Dog Home

If you have spent several weeks deciding on your new dog, you have had enough time to prepare. Bring your dog home to comfortable new quarters and to the right equipment.

A Beardie does equally well as a kennel or house dog, so long as he has **plenty** of personal attention. Socialization of the puppy should include determining whether the individual progresses better in the house or is content in the kennel. Most prefer the house—wouldn't you?

The puppy must have shelter, food, and exercise. If he lives inside, he must have a kennel run or a fenced yard, or be walked on leash for exercise. If he lives outside, he needs some type of confinement and a doghouse to protect him from the elements. A doghouse satisfies his denning instinct, giving him a place of protection and privacy. Indoors, a dog crate will do the same.

Crates are an aid in housebreaking, for Beardies are neat creatures and your puppy will become embarrassed if he soils himself. He will be housebroken quickly if trained properly. Start a puppy into the crate with a little boost of encouragement, saying something like "crate" or "kennel." Soon you can just tap the crate, tell him, and in he hops and settles down for a nap. Feeding a puppy in a crate will establish the place as the dog's own.

A crate also serves to control the dog when you are not present. His den speeds housebreaking and eliminates destruction of your house. When he sleeps and eats in the crate, he soon welcomes it as his home. The young one may test you a bit at first with plaintive cries, pleading to join you. If families survive the first night of Beardie yodels, the pup settles into his new home quickly.

When the pup begins his bid for attention, assure him that he is okay, but that you expect him to behave himself and be quiet. If the plea becomes stronger, so should the commands. Beardies are sound sensitive, and if the first few scoldings do not quite nip the protest in the beginning, a resounding thump on the crate accomplishes wonders.

The praise of crates cannot be sung high enough or long enough. Beardies yearn for a den for protective surroundings of their own. If you have five Beardies and five crates, each will go to its own when it is time for bed, or feeding, or privacy. Beardies often learn to swing open the door and to close it after themselves, if an owner doesn't answer their summons. Crates also provide ideal post-surgical confinement.

Beardies are creatures of habit, and as one breeder relates, each of her dogs has its own place to be fed. Every night each dog is waiting in its own space, and when visitors return, they go to "their" spot. She says this is true even of pups that left at eight weeks and return for a visit a year or two later.

Shipping crates, which can be purchased through airlines or pet supply stores, make good dens and allow the dog privacy, and allow you peace of mind. Metal crates with pans will also serve the purpose. Once you are certain the puppy will not "goof" when confined, you can replace shredded newspaper with a soft rug.

A size "400" shipping crate is spacious for a pup and is adequate for an adult Beardie as well. While traveling, the best protection for your Beardie is a crate. Motels welcome dogs confined to crates.

The puppy must receive plenty of exercise. Walk him often so he can relieve himself. Play with him, instead of expecting him to entertain himself. Both of you will enjoy it more, and he will be less likely to amuse himself with trouble.

The English believe in daily natural exercise, taking long walks once or twice a day over hill and dale. For most people in America, this is impractical. Some breeders may have to travel miles to find such terrain. Not only is free exercise inconvenient for most owners, but also it is prohibited by laws. Accident avoidance requires keeping the dog on leash. Therefore, we often must resort to roadwork by bicycle or car to keep our Beardies in a hard-muscled condition.

Even if your dog is fortunate enough to have his own play yard or pen, take him on walks for exercise. After all, one of the reasons you got a dog was to enjoy the companionship. This means, of course, that you will need a leash and collar. Since Beardies are long-coated dogs, use a collar that will not break the coat. It is not necessary for the dog to wear a collar indoors.

Choose a leash that is comfortable for you when handling the dog. Most Beardie owners select a nylon show lead with a slip collar attached, or a leather leash clipped to a nylon collar. Chain leashes wreak havoc with the owner's hands.

Among your first purchases must be *dog food* and *bowls* for food and water. Plastic bowls do not hold up to the dog that finishes his meal by tossing the bowl in the air and playing catch with it. Stainless steel bowls are most durable. Flat-bottomed bowls do not tip as easily as rounded bowls. Of course, dishes should be washed each day.

Choose a good quality, *nutritious dog food*. This can be mixed with canned food or fresh meat. The dry food is sufficient, but (as with all of us), a little meat is an inducement to clean the plate. Meat alone is not a satisfactory diet nor is it good for the teeth. Dry food helps

From "hopeless" puppy coat (above)

keep teeth clean. To aid the effort, a large *knucklebone* keeps teeth free of tartar and does not splinter. Dogs take to the bone with gusto. Fresh water should be available to your dog at all times, and is vital in extreme heat.

A *brush* and *comb* are musts with the long-coated Beardie. Obtain the proper tools for the Beardie coat, so that it will not be damaged. A good quality boar bristle brush or pin brush is preferable. A comb with medium teeth for combing down to the roots, should be obtained.

Only *pet shampoos* should be used for giving baths. Shampoos are not interchangeable between dog and master. Your shampoo destroys the natural oils in the dog's coat. A Beardie's outer coat should be harsh. Therefore, do not use softeners or conditioners unless the coat has been damaged. A shampoo made especially for white dogs enhances the Beardie's lovely white markings, and does not detract from the darker areas of the coat.

Your pet should have a few toys to play with. It is better to encourage him to teethe on them, rather than have him chew on your slippers or the table leg. Hard rubber balls, resilient nylon bones, frisbees, and knucklebones are the best chew toys. Bones should be large enough so they cannot be swallowed, and tough enough so they will not splinter.

The home-made variety of toys are not as durable, but are inexpensive. (We all know kids who discard the expensive toy and play with the box for homemade entertainment.) Wash out an empty plastic bottle (one that held about a liter), or a bleach jug, and watch the puppy bat it around the yard. Fill it with harmless noisemakers, such as doggie treats, and it's even more fun for the dog. Knotted socks can be used for tug of war and as toss toys.

Beardies are jealous of their toys and chewbones. If you have more than one dog, let each relish his treats in privacy to avoid confrontations.

Children love Beardies, and vice-versa, but both must be taught how to behave. They should be gentle in their play, though it may be—and probably will be—boisterous. Play should not include kicking, hitting, or biting—by either party.

Most new owners tend to talk too much when training their Beardie. They say, "Oh, no! Don't do that, Bonnie! Stop that this instant. That's my new shoe and now it's ruined. Whatever am I going to do with you? You're a naughty girl!" A simple, loud "NO!" would suffice, and the simple instruction also would be better understood.

Beardies often are sound-sensitive. They should be acclimated to normal household noises—banging pots, slamming doors, yelling children, and vacuum cleaners. If your Beardie becomes upset at a loud noise, such as that from firecrackers, try to calm him, and crate him if necessary.

Keep a record of your dog's illnesses, weight, and inoculations (and heat cycle if your Beardie is a female). Then, if your dog becomes ill, you will be able to provide your veterinarian with complete information.

to grand adult (below). Ch. Jaseton Princess Argonetta. Owners, Richard and Linda Nootbaar.

Canadian Ch. Brandylind's Classy Chassis, Canadian and American C.D., in her baseball outfit.

Ch. Crisch Midnight Bracken, age four months, and K. C. Schaefer, two years.

Ch. Classical Super Natural. Owners, Bea and Kevin Sawka.

Ch. Arcadia's Marcy of Rich-Lin, C.D., R.O.M. Owners, Teresa Viernow and Chris Walkowicz.

29

Ch. Tudor Lodge Koala at Crisch, R.O.M. Owner, Chris Schaefer.

Nutrition

The main food elements required by dogs are proteins, fats, and carbohydrates. Vitamins A, B complex, D, and E are essential, as are ample amounts of calcium and iron. Nine other minerals are required in small amounts but are amply provided in almost any diet, so there is no need to be concerned about them.

The most important nutrient is protein and it must be provided every day of the dog's life, for it is essential for normal daily growth and replacement of body tissues burned up in daily activity. Preferred animal protein products are beef, mutton, horse meat, and boned fish. Visceral organs—heart, liver, and tripe—are good but if used in too large quantities may cause diarrhea. (Bones in large amounts have the same effect.) Some veterinarians feel that pork is undesirable, while others consider lean pork acceptable so long as it is well cooked. Bacon drippings often are recommended for inclusion in the dog's diet, but this is a matter best discussed with your veterinarian since the salt in the bacon drippings might prove harmful to a dog that is not in good health. The "meat meal" used in some commercial foods is made from scrap meat processed at high temperatures and then dried. It is not quite so nutritious as fresh meat, but in combination with other protein products, it is an acceptable ingredient in the dog's diet.

Cooked egg and raw egg yolk are good sources of protein, but raw egg white should not be fed since it may cause diarrhea. Cottage cheese and milk (fresh, dried, and canned) are high in protein, also. Puppies thrive on milk and it is usually included in the diet until the puppy is about three months of age, but when fed to older dogs it may cause diarrhea. Soybean meal, wheat germ meal, and dried brewers yeast are vegetable products high in protein and may be used to advantage in the dog's diet.

Vegetable and animal fats in moderate amounts should be used, especially if a main ingredient of the diet is dry or kibbled food. Fats should not be used excessively or the dog may become overweight. Generally, fats should be increased slightly in the winter and reduced somewhat during warm weather.

Carbohydrates are required for proper assimilation of fats. Dog biscuits, kibble, dog meal, and other dehydrated foods are good sources of carbohydrates, as are cereal products derived from rice, corn, wheat, and ground or rolled oats.

Vegetables supply additional proteins, vitamins, and minerals, and by providing bulk are of value in overcoming constipation. Raw or cooked carrots, celery, lettuce, beets, asparagus, and tomatoes, and cooked spinach may be used. They should always be chopped or ground well and mixed with the other food. Various combinations may be used, but a good home-mixed ration for the mature dog consists of two parts of meat and one each of vegetables and dog meal (or cereal product).

Dicalcium phosphate and cod-liver oil are added to puppy diets to ensure inclusion of adequate amounts of calcium and Vitamins A and D. Indiscriminate use of dietary supplements not only is unjustified but also may be harmful, and many breeders feel that their over-use may lead to excessive growth as well as to overweight at maturity. Also, kidney damage in adult dogs has been traced to over-supplementation of the diet with calcium and Vitamin D. Too much calcium may lead to parathyroid imbalance and increased risk of torsion.

Foods manufactured by well-known and reputable food processors are nutritionally sound and are offered in sufficient variety of flavors, textures, and consistencies that most dogs will find them tempting and satisfying. Canned foods are usually "ready to eat," while dehydrated foods in the form of kibble, meal, or biscuits may require the addition of water or milk. Dried foods containing fat sometimes become rancid, so to avoid an unpalatable change in flavor, the manufacturer may not include fat in dried food but recommend its addition at the time the water or milk is added.

Candy and other sweets are taboo, for the dog has no nutritional need for them and if he is permitted to eat them, he usually will eat less of foods he requires. Also taboo are fried foods, highly seasoned foods, and extremely starchy foods, for the dog's digestive tract is not equipped to handle them.

Frozen foods should be thawed completely and warmed at least to lukewarm, while hot foods should be cooled to lukewarm. Food should be in a fairly firm state, for sloppy food is difficult for the dog to digest.

Whether meat is raw or cooked makes little difference, so long as the dog is also given the juice that seeps from the meat during cooking. Bones provide little nourishment, although gnawing bones helps make the teeth strong and helps to keep tartar from accumulating on them. Beef bones, especially large knuckle bones, are best. Fish, poultry, and chop bones should never be given to dogs since they have a tendency to splinter and may puncture the dog's digestive tract.

Clean, fresh, cool water is essential and an adequate supply should be available twenty-four hours a day from the time the puppy is big enough to walk. Especially during hot weather, the drinking pan should be emptied and refilled at frequent intervals.

"Sizing up the competition." Photo by Delores A. Kuenning.

Ch. Benji O'Braemoor. Owner, Virginia Parsons.

When weaning puppies, we use uncultured yogurt or buttermilk, which have natural supplies of lactobacillus. This ingredient controls stomach upset and counteracts any reaction to medication or antibiotics. Young puppies are fed three times a day, cutting back to twice at about four to six months. At about one year they may be fed once or twice a day, according to your preference and theirs. By limiting his intake, your dog will indicate to you when he is ready to have his feedings decreased.

Puppies usually are weaned by the time they are six weeks old, so when you acquire a new puppy ten to twelve weeks old, he will already have been started on a feeding schedule. The breeder should supply exact details as to number of meals per day, types and amounts of food offered, etc. It is essential to adhere to this established routine, for drastic changes in diet may produce intestinal upsets. In most instances, a combination of dry meal, canned meat, and the plastic wrapped hamburger-like products provide a well-balanced diet. For a puppy that is too fat or too thin, or for one that has health problems, a veterinarian may recommend a specially formulated diet, but ordinarily, the commercially prepared foods can be used.

The amount of food offered at each meal must gradually be increased and by five months the puppy will require about twice what he needed at three months. However, the puppy should not be allowed to become too fat. Obesity has become a major health problem for dogs, and it is estimated that forty-one percent of American dogs are overweight. It is essential that weight be controlled throughout the dog's lifetime and that the dog be kept in trim condition—neither too fat nor too thin—for many physical problems can be traced directly to overweight. If the habit of overeating is developed in puppyhood, controlling the weight of the mature dog will be much more difficult.

A mature dog usually eats slightly less than he did as a growing puppy. For mature dogs, one large meal a day is usually sufficient, although some owners prefer to give two meals. As long as the dog enjoys optimum health and is neither too fat nor too thin, the number of meals a day makes little difference.

The amount of food required for mature dogs will vary. With canned dog food or home-prepared foods (that is, the combination of meat, vegetables, and meal), the approximate amount required is one-half ounce of food per pound of body weight. Most manufacturers of commercial foods provide information on packages as to approximate daily needs of various breeds.

For most dogs, the amount of food provided should be increased slightly during the winter months and reduced somewhat during hot weather when the dog is less active.

Foods can be made more appealing when a dog loses its appetite from illness, summer heat, or advanced age. Try warming the food, adding meat or gravy, or sprinkling with a dash of garlic. Stir in his favorite tidbits. If the dog refuses to eat solids, coax him with bouillons so he does not become dehydrated. Not only are bouillons and soups nourishing but they make the dog thirsty, causing him to drink more water.

As a dog becomes older and less active, he may become too fat. Or his appetite may decrease so he becomes too thin. It is necessary to adjust the diet in either case, for the dog will live longer and enjoy better health if he is maintained in trim condition. The simplest way to decrease or increase body weight is by decreasing or increasing the amount of fat in the diet. Protein content should be maintained at a high level throughout the dog's life.

If the older dog becomes reluctant to eat, it may be necessary to coax him with special food he normally relishes. Warming the food will increase its aroma and usually will help to entice the dog to eat. If he still refuses, rubbing some of the food on the dog's lips and gums may stimulate interest. It may be helpful also to offer food in smaller amounts and increase the number of meals per day. Foods that are highly nutritious and easily digested are especially desirable for older dogs. Small amounts of cooked, ground liver, cottage cheese, or mashed, hard-cooked eggs should be included in the diet often.

American and Canadian Ch. Jande's Winsome Winnie. Owners, Jan and DeArle Masters.

Ch. Silverleaf Autumn Harvest with Crisch Panda of Briery Knob and Briery Knob Highland Wind.

Before a bitch is bred, her owner should make sure that she is in optimum condition—slightly on the lean side rather than fat. The bitch in whelp is given much the same diet she was fed prior to breeding, with slight increases in amounts of meat, liver, and dairy products. Beginning about five weeks after breeding, she should be fed two meals per day rather than one, and the total daily intake increased. (Some bitches in whelp require as much as fifty percent more food than they consume normally.) She must not be permitted to become fat, for whelping problems are more likely to occur in overweight dogs. Cod-liver oil and dicalcium phosphate should be provided until after the puppies are weaned.

The stud dog used only occasionally for breeding will not require a special diet, but he should be well fed and maintained in optimum condition. A dog used frequently may require a slightly increased amount of food. But his basic diet will require no change so long as his general health is good and his flesh is firm and hard.

Eight-week-old pups. Braemoor.

Rogues Hollow Tweed, H.Ch. Owners, Mari Shaffer and Sue Holm.

Maintaining the Dog's Health

In dealing with health problems, simple measures of preventive care are always preferable to cures—which may be complicated and costly. Many of the problems which afflict dogs can be avoided quite easily by instituting good dog-keeping practices in connection with feeding and housing.

Proper nutrition is essential in maintaining the dog's resistance to infectious diseases, in reducing susceptibility to organic diseases, and, of course, in preventing dietary deficiency diseases.

Cleanliness is essential in preventing the growth of disease-producing bacteria and other micro-organisms. All equipment, especially water and food dishes, must be kept immaculately clean. Cleanliness is also essential in controlling external parasites, which thrive in unsanitary surroundings.

Symptoms of Illness

Symptoms of illness may be so obvious there is no question that the dog is ill, or so subtle that the owner isn't sure whether there is a change from normal or not. **Loss of appetite, malaise** (general lack of interest in what is going on), **and vomiting** may be ignored if they occur singly and persist only for a day. However, in combination with other evidence of illness, such symptoms may be significant and the dog should be watched closely. **Abnormal bowel movements,** especially diarrhea or bloody stools, are causes for immediate concern. Urinary abnormalities may indicate infections, and bloody urine is always an indication of a serious condition. When a dog that has long been housebroken suddenly becomes incontinent, a veterinarian should be consulted, for he may be able to suggest treatment or medication that will be helpful.

Fever is a positive indication of illness and consistent deviation from the normal temperature range of 100 to 102 degrees is cause for concern. Have the dog in a standing position when taking his temperature. Coat the bulb of a rectal thermometer with petroleum jelly, raise the dog's tail, insert the thermometer to approximately half its length, and hold it in position for two minutes. Clean the thermometer with rubbing alcohol after each use and be sure to shake it down.

Fits, often considered a symptom of worms, may result from a variety of causes, including vitamin deficiencies, or playing to the point of exhaustion. A veterinarian should be consulted when a fit occurs, for it may be a symptom of serious illness.

Persistent coughing is often considered a symptom of worms, but may also indicate heart trouble—especially in older dogs.

Stary coat—dull and lackluster—indicates generally poor health and possible worm infestation. **Dull eyes** may result from similar conditions. Certain forms of blindness may also cause the eyes to lose the sparkle of vibrant good health.

Vomiting is another symptom often attributed to worm infestation. Dogs suffering from indigestion sometimes eat grass, apparently to induce vomiting and relieve discomfort.

Accidents and Injuries

Injuries of a serious nature—deep cuts, broken bones, severe burns, etc.—always require veterinary care. However, the dog may need first aid before being moved to a veterinary hospital.

A dog injured in any way should be approached cautiously, for reactions of a dog in pain are unpredictable and he may bite even a beloved master. A muzzle should always be applied before any attempt is made to move the dog or treat him in any way. The muzzle can be improvised from a strip of cloth, leash, or even heavy cord, looped firmly around the dog's jaws and tied under the lower jaw. The ends should then be extended back of the neck and tied again so the loop around the jaws will stay in place.

A stretcher for moving a heavy dog can be improvised from a rug or a board, and preferably two people should be available to transport it. A small dog can be carried by one person simply by grasping the loose skin at the nape of the neck with one hand and placing the other hand under the dog's hips.

Burns from chemicals should first be treated by flushing the coat with plain water, taking care to protect the dog's eyes and ears. A baking soda solution can then be applied to neutralize the chemical further. If the burned area is small, a bland ointment should be applied. If the burned area is large, more extensive treatment will be required, as well as veterinary care.

Burns from hot liquid or hot metals should be treated by applying a bland ointment, provided the burned area is small. Burns over large areas should be treated by a veterinarian.

Electric shock usually results because an owner negligently leaves an electric cord exposed where the dog can chew on it. If possible, disconnect the cord before touching the dog. Otherwise, yank the cord from the dog's mouth so you will not receive a shock when you try to help him. If the dog is unconscious, artificial respiration and stimulants will be required, so a veterinarian should be consulted at once.

Fractures require immediate professional attention. A broken bone should be immobilized while the dog is transported to the veterinarian but no attempt should be made to splint it.

Poisoning is more often accidental than deliberate, but whichever the case, symptoms and treatment are the same. If the poisoning is not discovered immediately, the dog may be found unconscious. His mouth will be slimy, he will tremble, have difficulty breathing, and possibly go into convulsions. Veterinary treatment must be secured immediately.

If you find the dog eating something you know to be poisonous, induce vomiting immediately by repeatedly forcing the dog to swallow a mixture of equal parts of hydrogen peroxide and water. Delay of even a few minutes may result in death. When the contents of the stomach have been emptied, force the dog to swallow raw egg white, which will slow absorption of the poison. Then call the veterinarian. Provide him with information as to the type of poison, and follow his advice as to further treatment.

Some chemicals are toxic even though not swallowed, so before using a product, make sure it can be used safely around pets.

Severe bleeding from a leg can be controlled by applying a tourniquet between the wound and the body, but the tourniquet must be loosened at ten minute intervals. Severe bleeding from head or body can be controlled by placing a cloth or gauze pad over the wound, then applying firm pressure with the hand.

To treat minor cuts, first trim the hair from around the wound, then wash the area with warm soapy water and apply a mild antiseptic such as tincture of metaphen.

Shock is usually the aftermath of severe injury and requires immediate veterinary attention. The dog appears dazed, lips and tongue are pale, and breathing is shallow. The dog should be wrapped in blankets and kept warm, and if possible, kept lying down with his head lower than his body.

Bacterial and Viral Diseases

Coronavirus causes an intestinal disease similar in symptoms to the more familiar parvovirus. Like parvovirus, coronavirus can be vectored (carried on and transmitted) by items such as clothing and brushes—not only by contact. The percentage of fatality is less than for parvovirus, but it still is dangerous. A preventive vaccine is available.

Distemper takes many and varied forms, so it is sometimes difficult for even experienced veterinarians to diagnose. Distemper was the number one killer of dogs until the widespread use of the preventive vaccine. Although it is not unknown in older dogs, its victims usually are puppies. While some dogs do recover, permanent damage to the brain or nervous system is often sustained. Symptoms may include lethargy, diarrhea, vomiting, reduced appetite, cough, nasal discharge, inflammation of the eyes, and a rise in temperature. If distemper is suspected, a veterinarian must be consulted at once, for early treatment is essential. Effective preventive measures lie in inoculation. Shots for temporary immunity should be given all puppies within a few weeks after whelping, and the annual inoculations should be given as soon thereafter as possible.

Infectious hepatitis in dogs affects the liver, as does the human form, but apparently is not transmissible to man. Symptoms are similar to those of distemper, and the disease rapidly reaches the acute state. Since hepatitis is often fatal, prompt veterinary treatment is essential. Effective vaccines are available and should be provided all puppies.

Leptospirosis is caused by a micro-organism often transmitted by contact with rats, or by ingestion of food contaminated by rats. The disease can be transmitted to man, so anyone caring for an afflicted dog must take steps to avoid infection. Symptoms include vomiting, loss of appetite, diarrhea, fever, depression and lethargy, redness of eyes and gums, and sometimes jaundice. Since permanent kidney damage may result, veterinary treatment should be secured immediately. An effective vaccine is available as a preventive measure.

Parvovirus is a highly contagious and often fatal intestinal disease characterized by severe vomiting and diarrhea (often bloody), a high temperature, and rapid dehydration. Although usually preceded by lethargy and loss of appetite, the onset is sudden, and veterinary treatment must be sought at the first sign of symptoms. A preventive vaccine affords protection but, of course, must be given before symptoms appear.

Rabies is a disease that is always fatal—and it is transmissible to man. It is caused by a virus that attacks the nervous system and is present in the saliva of an infected animal. When an infected animal bites another, the virus is transmitted to the new victim. It may also enter the body through cuts and scratches that come in contact with saliva containing the virus.

All warm-blooded animals are subject to rabies and it may be transmitted by foxes, skunks, squirrels, horses, and cattle as well as dogs. Anyone bitten by a dog (or other animal) should see his physician immediately, and health and law enforcement officials should be notified. Also, if your dog is bitten by another animal, consult your veterinarian immediately.

In most areas, rabies shots are required by law. Even if not required, all dogs should be given anti-rabies vaccine, for it is an effective preventive measure.

Dietary Deficiency Diseases

Rickets afflicts puppies not provided sufficient calcium and Vitamin D. Symptoms include lameness, arching of neck and back, and a tendency of the legs to bow. Treatment consists of providing adequate amounts of dicalcium phosphate and Vitamin D and exposing the dog to sunlight. If detected and treated before reaching an advanced stage, bone damage may be lessened somewhat, although it cannot be corrected completely.

Osteomalacia, similar to rickets, may occur in adult dogs. Treatment is the same as for rickets, but here, too, prevention is preferable to cure. Permanent deformities resulting from rickets or osteomalacia will not be inherited, so once victims recover, they can be used for breeding.

External Parasites

Fleas, lice, mites, and ticks can be eradicated in the dog's quarters by regular use of one of the insecticide sprays with a four to six weeks' residual effect. Bedding, blankets, and pillows should be laundered frequently and treated with an insecticide. Treatment for external parasites varies, depending upon the parasite involved.

Fleas may be controlled by sprays or dips and medications such as Proban® and Pro Spot®. A combination program of regularly treating the premises and the dog is effective. Penetrating the heavy coat with a veterinary-recommended spray assists in flea control. (Some do yellow the coats, so test-spray a small section.) Spraying all areas where the dog lives is recommended as well. For heavy infestations, dips are the most efficacious.

Your veterinarian can advise you about the use of the flea-killing pill (Proban®) or drop (Pro Spot®). Collars may be an aid for small, smooth-coated dogs, but are not a sufficient preventive measure for Beardies.

Some dogs are allergic to fleas and develop angry sores. Other dogs may be sensitive to treatments. Work with your veterinarian on flea control.

Lice may be eradicated by applying dips formulated especially for this purpose to the dog's coat. A fine-toothed comb should then be used to remove dead lice and eggs, which are firmly attached to the coat.

Mites live deep in the ear canal, producing irritation to the lining of the ear and causing a brownish-black, dry type of discharge. Plain mineral oil or ear ointment should be swabbed on the inner surface of the ear twice a week until mites are eliminated.

Ticks may carry Rocky Mountain spotted fever, so, to avoid possible infection, they should be removed from the dog only with tweezers and should be destroyed by burning (or by dropping them into insecticide). Heavy infestation can be controlled by sponging the coat daily with a solution containing a special tick dip.

Among other preparations available for controlling parasites on the dog's body are some that can be given internally. Since dosage must be carefully controlled, these preparations should not be used without consulting a veterinarian.

Internal Parasites

Internal parasites, with the exception of the tapeworm, may be transmitted from a mother dog to the puppies. Infestation may also result from contact with infected bedding or through access to a yard where an infected dog relieves himself. The types that may infest dogs are roundworms, whipworms, tapeworms, hookworms, and heartworms. All cause similar symptoms: a generally unthrifty appearance, stary coat, dull eyes, weakness and emaciation despite a ravenous appetite, coughing, vomiting, diarrhea, and sometimes bloody stools. Not all symptoms are present in every case, of course.

A heavy infestation with any type of worm is a serious matter and treatment must be started early and continued until the dog is free of the parasite, or the dog's health will suffer seriously. Death may even result.

Promiscuous dosing for worms is dangerous and different types of worms require different treatment. So if you suspect your dog has worms, ask your veterinarian to make a microscopic examination of the feces, and to prescribe appropriate treatment if evidence of worm infestation is found.

Heartworms were once thought to be a problem confined to the southern part of the United States but they have become an increasingly common problem in the Midwest and other areas. The larva is transmitted from dog to dog through the bite of the mosquito, and eight to nine months may elapse from the time the dog is bitten until the heartworm is mature. Once they have entered the bloodstream, heartworms mature in the heart, where they interfere with heart action. Symptoms include lethargy, chronic coughing, and loss of weight. Having the dog's blood examined microscopically is the only way the tiny larvae (called microfilaria) can be detected. Eradication of heartworms is extremely difficult, so a veterinarian well versed in this field should be consulted. But prevention is better. Consult your veterinarian about types and dosages of preventive medication. Whatever the choice, use it, for heartworms *kill*.

Hookworms are found in puppies as well as adult dogs. When excreted in the feces, the mature worm looks like a thread and is about three-quarters of an inch in length. Eradication is a serious problem in areas where the soil is infested with the worms, for the dog may become reinfested after treatment. Consequently, medication usually must be repeated at intervals, and the premises— including the grounds where the dog exercises—must be treated and must be kept well drained.

If you suspect that a puppy may have hookworms, check its gums and tongue. If the puppy is heavily infested, the worms will cause anemia and the gums and tongue will be a very pale pink color. If the puppy is anemic, the veterinarian probably will prescribe a tonic in addition to the proper worm medicine.

Roundworms are the most common of all the worms that may infest the dog, for most puppies are born with them or become infested with them shortly after birth. Roundworms vary in length from two to eight inches and can be detected readily through microscopic examination of the feces. At maturity, upon excretion, the roundworm will spiral into a circle, but after it dies it resembles a cut rubber band. Roundworms may also be found in stools or vomitus.

Tapeworms require an intermediate host, usually the flea or the louse, but they sometimes are found in raw fish, so a dog can become infested by swallowing a flea or a louse, or by eating infested fish.

A complete tapeworm can be two to three feet long. The head and neck of the tapeworm are small and threadlike, while the body is made up of segments like links of a sausage, which are about half an inch long and flat. Segments of the body separate from the worm and will be found in the feces or will hang from the coat around the anus and when dry will resemble dark grains of rice.

The head of the tapeworm is imbedded in the lining of the intestine where the worm feeds on the blood of the dog. The difficulty in eradicating the tapeworm lies in the fact that most medicines have a laxative action which is too severe and which pulls the body from the head so the body is eliminated with the feces, but the implanted head remains to start growing a new body. An effective medication is a tablet which does not dissolve until it reaches the intestine where it anesthetizes the worm to loosen the head before expulsion.

Whipworms are more common in the eastern states than in states along the West Coast, but whipworms may infest dogs in any section of the United States. Whipworms vary in length from two to five inches and are tapered in shape so they resemble a buggy whip—which accounts for the name.

At maturity, the whipworm migrates into the caecum, where it is difficult to reach with medication. A fecal examination will show whether whipworms are present, so after treatment, it is best to have several examinations made in order to be sure the dog is free of them.

Skin Problems

Skin problems usually cause persistent itching. However, **follicular (demodectic) mange** does not usually do so but is evidenced by moth-eaten-looking patches, especially about the head and along the back. **Sarcoptic mange** produces severe itching and is evidenced by patchy, crusty areas on body, legs, and abdomen. Any evidence suggesting either should be called to the attention of a veterinarian. Both require extensive treatment and sarcoptic mange may be contracted by humans.

Allergies are not readily distinguished from other skin troubles except through laboratory tests. However, dog owners should be alert to the fact that various coat dressings and shampoos, or simply bathing the dog too often, may produce allergic skin reactions.

Eczema is characterized by extreme itching, redness of the skin and exudation of serous matter. It may result from a variety of causes, including allergies, and the exact cause in a particular case may be difficult to determine. Consult your veterinarian about treatment.

Other Health Problems

Clogged anal glands cause intense discomfort, which the dog may attempt to relieve by scooting himself along the floor on his haunches. These glands, located on either side of the anus, secrete a substance that enables the dog to expel the contents of the rectum. If they become clogged, they may give the dog an unpleasant odor and when neglected, serious infection may result. Contents of the glands can be easily expelled into a wad of cotton, which should be held under the tail with the left hand. Then, using the right hand, pressure should be exerted with the thumb on one side of the anus, the forefinger on the other. The normal secretion is brownish in color, with an unpleasant odor. The presence of blood or pus indicates infection and should be called to the attention of a veterinarian.

Eye problems of a minor nature—redness or occasional discharge—may be treated with a few drops of boric acid solution (two percent) or salt solution (1 teaspoonful table salt to 1 pint sterile water). Cuts on the eyeball, bruises close to the eyes, or persistent discharge should be treated only by a veterinarian.

Ch. Jande's Lucky Tri, C.D., and Gaymarden's High Roads Honey. Owners, Bruce and Janet Buehrig.

Heat exhaustion is a serious (and often fatal) problem caused by exposure to extreme heat. Usually it occurs when a thoughtless owner leaves the dog in a closed vehicle without proper shade and ventilation. Even on a day when outside temperatures do not seem excessively high, heat builds up rapidly to an extremely high temperature in a closed vehicle parked in direct sunlight or even in partial shade. Many dogs (and young children) die each year from being left in an inadequately ventilated vehicle. To prevent such a tragedy, an owner or parent should never leave a dog or child unattended in a vehicle even for a short time.

During hot weather, whenever a dog is taken for a ride in an air-conditioned automobile, the cool air should be reduced gradually when nearing the destination, for the sudden shock of going from cool air to extremely hot temperatures can also result in shock and heat exhaustion.

Symptoms of heat exhaustion include rapid and difficult breathing and near or complete collapse. After removing the victim from the vehicle, first aid treatment consists of sponging cool water over the body to reduce temperature as quickly as possible. Immediate medical treatment is essential in severe cases of heat exhaustion.

Care of the Ailing or Injured Dog

A dog that is seriously ill, requiring surgical treatment, transfusions, or intravenous feeding, must be hospitalized. One requiring less complicated treatment is better cared for at home, but it is essential that the dog be kept in a quiet environment. Preferably his bed should be in a room apart from family activity, yet close at hand, so his condition can be checked frequently. Clean bedding and adequate warmth are essential, as are a constant supply of fresh, cool water, and foods to tempt the appetite.

Special equipment is not ordinarily needed, but the following items will be useful in caring for a sick dog, as well as in giving first aid for injuries:

petroleum jelly   tincture of metaphen
rubbing alcohol   cotton, gauze, and adhesive tape
mineral oil   burn ointment
rectal thermometer   tweezers
hydrogen peroxide   boric acid solution (two percent)

If special medication is prescribed, it may be administered in any one of several ways. A pill or small capsule may be concealed in a small piece of meat, which the dog will usually swallow with no problem. A large capsule may be given by holding the dog's mouth open, inserting the capsule as far as possible down the throat, then holding the mouth closed until the dog swallows. Liquid medicine should be measured into a small bottle or test tube. Then, if the corner of the dog's lip is pulled out while the head is tilted upward, the liquid can be poured between the lips and teeth, a small amount at a time. If he refuses to swallow, keeping the dog's head tilted and stroking his throat will usually induce swallowing.

"The road home."

Liquid medication may also be given by use of a hypodermic syringe without a needle. The syringe is slipped into the side of the mouth and over the rise at the back of the tongue, and the medicine is "injected" slowly down the throat. This is especially good for medicine with a bad taste, for the medicine does not touch the taste buds in the front part of the tongue. It also eliminates spills and guarantees that all the medicine goes in.

Foods offered the sick dog should be particularly nutritious and easily digested. Meals should be smaller than usual and offered at more frequent intervals. If the dog is reluctant to eat, offer food he particularly likes and warm it slightly to increase the aroma and thus make it more tempting.

Exercise is essential to good health.

"The final touch."

The finished product. Ch. Walkoway's Sherlock Holmes. Owner, Dr. Rick Tuck.

Grooming

It is best to acquaint the Beardie with grooming procedures while he is a puppy. Grooming the Beardie is more than a nicety—it is a necessity. A Beardie that is ungroomed is unattractive, unkempt, unhealthy, and unhappy. If neglected, he must be clipped or shaved.

There are advantages to a regular grooming schedule, and your puppy should be groomed at least once a week; however, overcombing should be avoided because it causes the undercoat to become sparse. Properly, dead coat is removed with a brush and comb, and your Beardie then will not shed unsightly clumps of hair about the house.

As soon as you acquire your puppy, introduce him to the grooming tools, table, and routine. The breeder should begin using the brush lightly at five or six weeks, accustoming him to the touch. By eight weeks, begin using the comb.

Minimum basic tools include a brush, comb with medium teeth, dog shampoo especially for white coats, and whitener product. The brush should be a good quality bristle or pin brush. The Mason Pearson is a favorite. A slicker brush should not be used except when the dog is shedding, because it tears the coat. When the dog is shedding, a rake or "moulting" comb will aid the process of removing the dead hair. The comb should have a handle for extra grip and comfort.

The shampoo for white coats may be used on the entire coat or just on the white portions, with a regular shampoo used on the rest. Cornstarch, baby powder, or chalk is rubbed into the damp white portions of the coat. This causes temporary whitening, which may be desirable when showing your dog. After the product is rubbed into the coat, all traces *must* be brushed out before the dog enters the ring. Many owners prefer to use detangling agents and anti-static spray for ease in combing.

Grooming not only keeps your dog attractive, but also aids discovery of skin problems. The skin and coat many times reveal the first symptoms of a deeper problem. Calluses or cracked pads can be softened with a dab of petroleum jelly.

Care of the coat. If you have broken routine, and matting has become a problem, be very patient. Be prepared to spend a lengthy time repairing the damage you have allowed to occur. Unless the dog is extremely grimy, brushing should be done prior to bathing, for the water sets the tangles and makes them more difficult or even impossible to remove.

The coat is not fully mature until nearly three years of age. During that time, you will note many stages of color, length, and fullness of undercoat. The knowledgeable person can estimate the age of a young Beardie by its coat.

Puppies appear straggly and scruffy when losing coat. Some lose it from the front to the rear, at times appearing to be two different dogs. Others lose their undercoats in handfuls, appearing to have a shorter coat than they did when they were junior pups. Some dogs lose the coat from the part toward the feet, heightening a lanky, teenage-look.

Grooming sessions average one-half to three-quarters of an hour once a week. Certain complications lengthen the process, including complete grubbiness, a bout of diarrhea, or loss of the puppy coat. The most difficult stage during which to groom a Beardie is about one year of age, when the dog begins shedding the profuse puppy coat. Grooming sessions should then be increased to every day or two, speeding up the process and stimulating new hair growth.

The only trimming that should be done is around the genitals and anus for hygienic purposes. The Standard spells out that it is a no-no to do any sculpturing of the coat for conformation show exhibiting.

Certainly, pet owners may elect to trim the coat for the ease and comfort of the dog. Many breeders and exhibitors trim the coats of dogs that no longer are being shown, adapting a Schnauzer-type or Airedale-type clip.

Ticks and fleas. Look for ticks and fleas as you groom your dog. You can usually feel ticks by running your fingertips lightly through the coat. Check for ticks inside the ears, including the little pocket at the upper edge. Tweezers can be used to remove a tick. Be sure to remove all of it—don't leave the tick's head embedded in the skin.

A technique for finding fleas is to stroke the coat with a fine-toothed comb toward the dog's stomach, where the hair is sparser. Then quickly turn the dog on his side or back, or stand him on his hind legs, to see if you have flushed a flea into the open. If you spot one, press a moistened fingertip on it to render it less mobile, then pick it off and crush it.

Some dogs have bad reactions to being dipped for fleas, so this method should be used only with caution. Brewer's yeast in the diet may repel fleas.

If you use a flea spray, choose one that actually kills fleas rather than merely stuns them and causes them to drop off. The label on the can or bottle should make this distinction clear. Work spray well into the coat, to the skin. When spraying, use rubber gloves to keep the insecticide off your skin, and a respiratory mask to keep it out of your lungs. Also, avoid using the spray in such a way that it will enter the dog's lungs or get in his eyes. Wash your hands with soap after applying flea spray to your dog's coat. No Beardie owner can be overly cautious about preventing

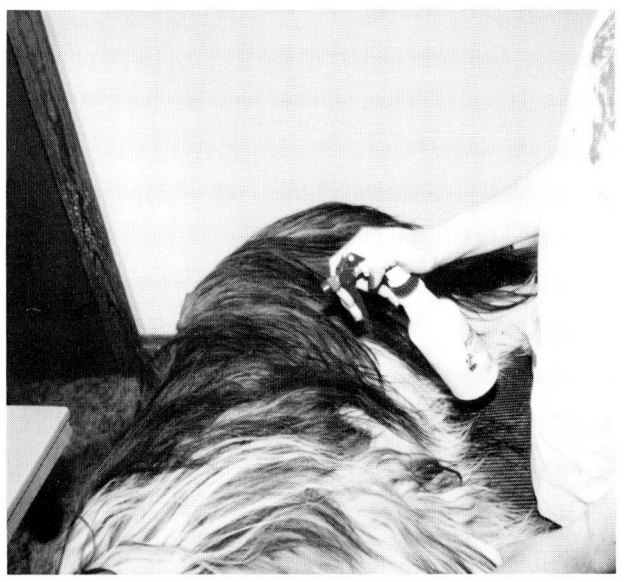

Always spray before brushing.

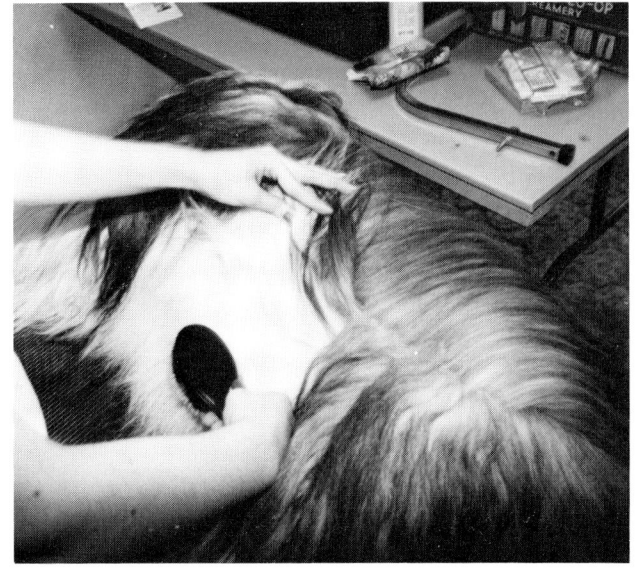

Line brushing.

Working out a mat.

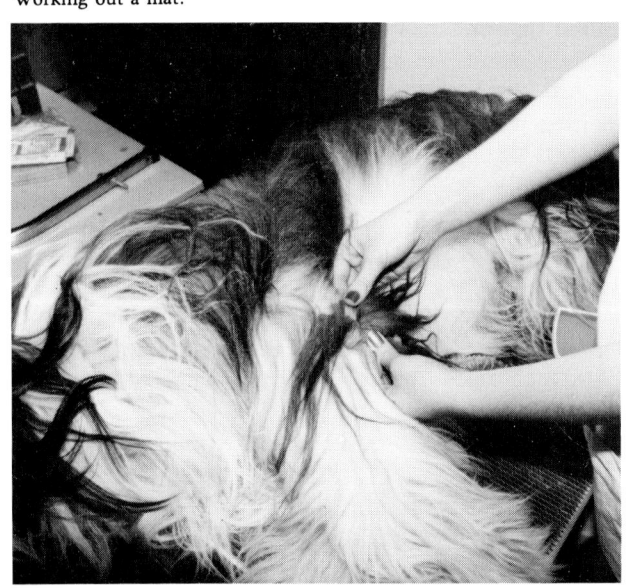

Line brushing.

42

and controlling fleas. A Beardie "going after" a mild infestation of fleas can accomplish six month's damage to its coat within two weeks.

Show Grooming. Have the dog lying on his side, and dampen the coat by spraying with water or grooming lotion. Spray as needed to keep the coat damp, but not wet. If desired, rub whitener into the coat.

Start with the head. Brush the coat up or hold it up with your hands, giving fullness to the coat when you brush it down. With one hand, part a small section and brush through the hair. Use the comb as required for smoothing the coat. This is called "line brushing" and allows you to reach to the skin to eliminate all tangles. The object is to groom the coat thoroughly, without breaking it.

Work back to the tail; then do the other side. The dog soon learns the command "over," "flipside," or whatever term you use. Don't forget the belly and underside of the legs. Pay special attention to the feet, the area under the forearm next to the brisket, and areas behind the ears and elbows.

If the mats do not untangle easily with the comb, use a "detangler" lotion. Spray a bit on and rub it in, working the mat out with your fingers and the end tooth of the comb, or with a "rake."

The coat should be groomed down from the part. The part is encouraged with brushing from the time the dog is a wee pup. It is unnecessary, in fact forbidden, to part the coat artificially with an instrument such as that used on the Maltese or Tibetan Terrier.

The hair between the pads of the feet should not be ignored. It must be kept clean and combed. Walking on rough surfaces curbs the hair growth.

At this time, have the dog stand, and touch up the chest, neck, and other hard-to-reach parts of the body. Brush the hair on top of the head back, the mustache down and forward, and the beard forward. A final swish, and he's ready to go. Your Beardie shakes, and all falls naturally into place.

Kennel owners who keep their Beardies in runs sometimes need to take extra steps to keep the dogs in show condition. Large kennels often trim their retired dogs for ease in grooming. One owner shared a secret in kenneling show dogs: use eight-foot-wide runs, rather than the usual four-foot runs. This eliminates much of the "kennel running," and the breaking of coat caused by a wagging tail thumping against a fence.

For footing inside the kennel runs, one suggestion is rough concrete, because Beardies love to muck about in gravel, the muddier the better. An alternate surfacing material is heavy-gauge expanded metal, with a diamond-shape mesh of about one inch. Four-foot by eight-foot pieces are available, and they can be placed on cinder blocks and boards, elevating the dogs, thus allowing wastes to pass through.

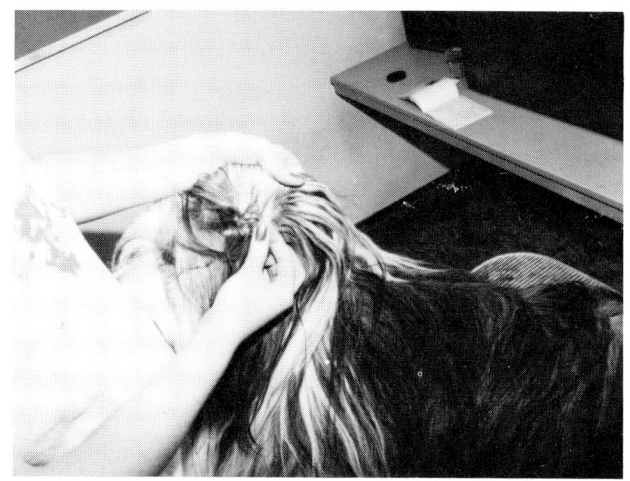

Plucking hair from the ears.

Combing the beard.

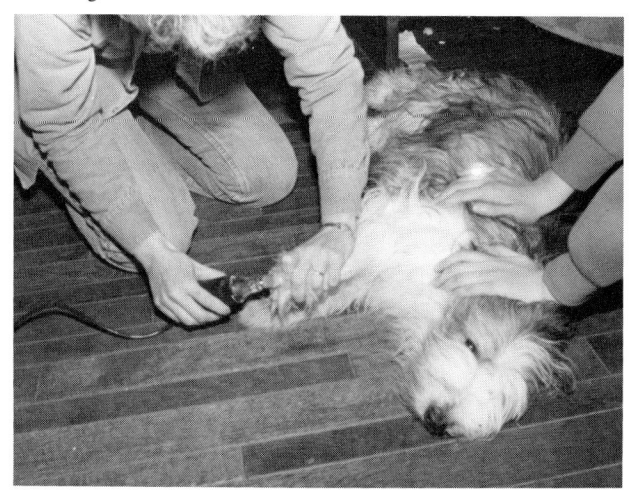

Grinding nails.

If the Beardie's white becomes yellowed, groomers recommend the following treatment: Dilute one ounce of Clairol's Born Blonde #351 Silent Snow, with nine ounces of very hot water. Shake thoroughly and squirt onto the white. Leave five minutes and rinse. Follow with Roux Classic Silver #49 White Blaze, according to directions.

Another solution used is one part chlorine bleach to five parts water. Apply the bleach mixture before rinsing the shampoo from the white. Allow it to remain five minutes, then rinse. A small area should be tested to be certain further yellowing does not occur from the bleach.

To control staining, particularly around the mouth and feet, most breeders use a method similar to the following: Make a mixture of equal parts of cornstarch and Fuller's Earth (or grooming chalk) and store in a covered bowl. About twice a week, wet the stained areas with water or a product such as Pro-Line Self Rinse Plus. Put some of the mixture in a tin pan. Holding the pan under the beard or foot, brush the mixture into the coat, forming a soft paste. Let it harden and dry (about twenty minutes), then brush it out.

Exhibitors prefer bathing their Beardie a few days before a dog show, so that the coat will not be softened at show time. A conditioner for harsh coats may be used if weather or constant grooming warrants it. For dogs that are being shown (and groomed) extensively, or for a winter-time bath substitute, spray the coat with distilled water or a non-oily coat dressing. Dust grooming powder all over. When dry, brush out all the powder.

Remember, a "natural" dog does not mean an ungroomed dog.

Nails. Too many pet owners neglect their dog's nails. If the dog doesn't keep his nails worn down through extensive exercise on hard surfaces—and he probably won't—the nails should be clipped or filed every week or so. When a dog is in a natural stance, his nails should not reach the ground. Over-long nails cause a dog to walk on the back of his feet. This is unnatural and uncomfortable for the dog, and causes his feet to splay. Unclipped nails, especially dewclaws, eventually curl under as they grow, sometimes even circling back and piercing the skin.

Caring for the nails is not difficult and doesn't require much time if done regularly at reasonable intervals. Nails can be clipped with nail trimmers. Once they have been cut back, a few strokes every few days with a file should keep them at a proper length.

To clip or file nails, place the dog on the grooming table, lift the paw slightly forward and upward, and hold it gently but firmly in a natural position. When filing or clipping the dog's nails, a right-handed groomer should stand on the dog's right side, facing the dog, and hold the nail firmly with the thumb and finger of the left hand. Thus the right hand will address the nails from the front.

Care must be taken not to cut the nail so short that the blood vessel in the quick, which forms the bottom half of the stem of the nail, is severed, causing bleeding as well as pain to the dog. One can avoid cutting into the quick by clipping off only the tip of the over-long nail, cutting just outside the point at which the nail, underneath, begins to hook downward.

As a further precaution against cutting the quick, one can angle the clipper slightly forward, so that more is taken off from the top of the nail than from the bottom, where the quick is.

Should you accidentally draw blood, apply an antiseptic, such as hydrogen peroxide, then squeeze the end of the nail between your fingers for a moment or two. Usually, the blood will clot quickly and bleeding will cease. A styptic powder can be purchased from a pet supply shop. If the label carries the warning "for external use only," it would be well to prevent your dog from licking the nail after the powder has been applied—which he probably will want to do.

Most dogs are uneasy about having their nails clipped. They accept filing much more readily. A file can be obtained from a pet supply shop, or an ordinary bastard file from the hardware store can be used. A file that is used for sharpening rotary lawnmower blades is a suitable size and texture for Bearded Collies.

To file a nail, stroke diagonally upward and inward across the upper edge of the nail, to avoid the quick. Downward strokes across the nail's tip may also be used. With an electric nail grinder, it is possible to shorten the nail more than with trimmers. The grinder is handled in much the same way as the file. (Although many dogs are not fond of the buzz, they become acclimated, if not enthusiastic.) The end of the nail is smoother than when a clipper is used, and the grinder is a convenience to owners of several dogs. Care must be taken that the coat does not become entangled around the grinding disk.

Clipping nails.

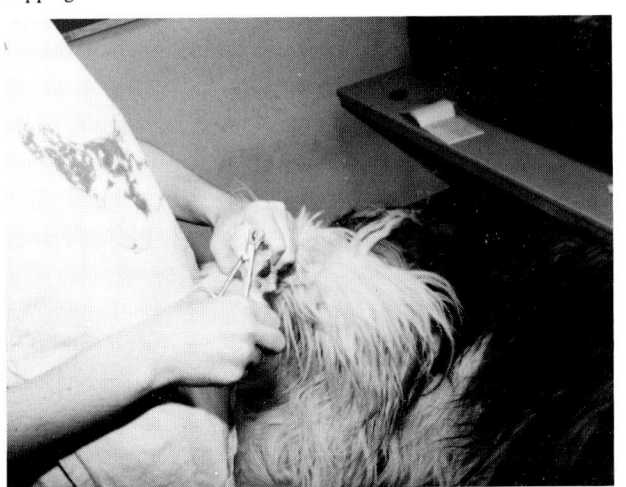

Eyes. Many dogs have a slight accumulation of mucus in the inside corner of the eyes when they awaken. A mild salt solution (one teaspoon of table salt to a pint of warm water) can be sponged around the eye to remove the matter. It can also be removed with a piece of damp paper tissue or cotton, care being taken not to touch the eyeball.

Ears. Check the inside of the ears frequently. Pluck excess hair from inside the ear. Using a swab, you can remove dirt and wax from the folds of the upper ear, after softening with an oil-base solvent that you can obtain from your veterinarian. Do not attempt to probe the ear canal: you might pierce the eardrum and cause permanent damage. This delicate task should be left to the veterinarian.

Teeth. Pet owners too often neglect their dog's teeth. The result is eventual dental trouble that might have been avoided with preventive care.

Brush or wipe your dog's teeth regularly. Frequently giving him a marrow bone or hard biscuit to chew will help to keep his teeth clean but will not help enough to prevent accumulation of tartar.

To clean your dog's teeth, hold his head firmly, press the lips apart, then rub the teeth gently with a damp cloth, a gauze pad, or a child's toothbrush, on which a generous pinch or two of baking soda has been placed. A mild salt solution can also be used. Another alternative dentifrice is a meat-flavored toothpaste made especially for dogs and available at a pet shop or from a veterinarian. Dogs love it!

Your dog's teeth should be cleaned frequently. Don't neglect the back teeth just because they are harder to reach. Periodically, as necessary, have your veterinarian do a thorough cleaning.

Bathing. Beardie pups, being what they are, create a few occasions when it is necessary to bathe them, or at least parts of them. Use a shampoo made for dogs with harsh coats. Do not use a softening shampoo or a conditioner unless the coat is damaged. There are several dog shampoos formulated especially to remove stains from white coats. Shampoo the white areas of the Beardie's coat first, and do not rinse until the rest of the coat is done. Scrub thoroughly to get through the dense coat.

Your Bearded Collie could accidentally acquire some offensive odor, or get some undesirable substance in his coat, making a bath inevitable. In such an emergency, the following common-sense guidelines should be useful.

The dog should be permitted to relieve himself before the bath.

Assemble the necessary equipment for the bath beforehand. This includes a tub large enough for a Bearded Collie to stand in. If the tub has a drain, so much the better, for it will permit the water to flow out continuously, and the dog will not be kept standing in water throughout the bath.

A rubber mat should be placed in the bottom of the tub

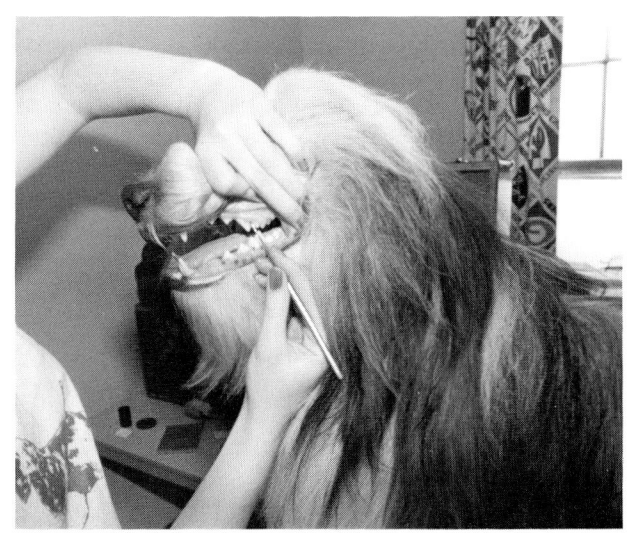

Cleaning teeth with a scaler.

to prevent the dog from slipping. A small hose with a spray nozzle is ideal for wetting and rinsing the coat. If such a hose is not available, a pail should be provided for bath and rinse water. A cup for dipping water, dog shampoo, a small bottle of mineral or olive oil, and a supply of absorbent cotton should be placed nearby, as well as a supply of heavy towels, a washcloth, and the dog's combs and brushes.

Bath water and rinse water should be cool to lukewarm in temperature. To avoid getting water in the dog's ears, place a small amount of absorbent cotton in each.

With the dog standing in the tub, wet his body with the hose and spray nozzle or by using the cup to pour water over him. Be very careful not to splash his head, or get water or shampoo in his eyes. Should you accidentally do so, place a few drops of mineral or olive oil in the inner corner of the eye to give relief.

When the dog is thoroughly wet, put a small amount of shampoo on his back and work the lather into the coat with a gentle, squeezing action. Wash the entire body, then use the hose and spray (or cup and pail) to rinse the dog.

Dip the washcloth into clean water, wring it out enough that it won't drip, then wash the dog's head, taking care to avoid the eyes.

Remove the cotton from the dog's ears and sponge them gently, inside and out. Shampoo should never be used inside the ears. If the ears are extremely soiled, sponge them clean with cotton saturated with mineral or olive oil.

Quickly wrap a towel around the dog, remove him from the tub, and towel him as dry as possible. Act quickly, for once he is out of the tub he instinctively will shake himself, giving you an impromptu bath if you are not careful.

While the hair is slightly damp, use a clean comb or brush to remove any tangles.

"STAY!"

Manners for the Family Dog

Although each dog has personality quirks and idiosyncrasies that set him apart as an individual, dogs in general have two characteristics that can be utilized to advantage in training. The first is the dog's strong desire to please, which has been built up through centuries of association with man. The second lies in the innate quality of the dog's mentality. It has been proved conclusively that while dogs have reasoning power, their learning ability is based on a direct association of cause and effect, so that they willingly repeat acts that bring pleasant results and discontinue acts that bring unpleasant results. Hence, to take fullest advantage of a dog's abilities, the trainer must make sure the dog understands a command, and then reward him when he obeys and correct him when he does wrong.

Commands should be as short as possible and should be repeated in the same way, day after day. Saying "Heel," one day, and "Come here and heel," the next will confuse the dog. *Heel, sit, stand, stay, down,* and *come* are standard terminology, and are preferable for a dog that may later be given advanced training.

Tone of voice is important, too. For instance, a coaxing tone helps cajole a young puppy into trying something new. Once an exercise is mastered, commands given in a firm, matter-of-fact voice give the dog confidence in his own ability. Praise, expressed in an exuberant tone, will tell the dog quite clearly that he has earned his master's approval. On the other hand, a firm "No" indicates with equal clarity that he has done wrong.

Rewards for good performance may consist simply of praising lavishly and petting the dog, although many professional trainers use bits of food as rewards. Tidbits are effective only if the dog is hungry, of course. And if you smoke, you must be sure to wash your hands before each training session, for the odor of nicotine is repulsive to dogs. On the hands of a heavy smoker, the odor of nicotine may be so strong that the dog is unable to smell the tidbit.

Correction for wrong-doing should be limited to repeating "No" in a scolding tone of voice, to shaking the dog by the nape of the neck, or to confining the dog to his bed. Spanking or striking the dog is taboo—particularly using sticks, which might cause injury, but the hand should never be used either. For herding as well as some obedience work, the hand is used to signal the dog. Dogs that have been punished by slapping have a tendency to cringe whenever they see a hand raised and consequently do not respond promptly when the owner's intent is not to punish but to signal.

Some trainers recommend correcting the dog by whacking him with a rolled-up newspaper. The idea is that the newspaper will not injure the dog but that the resulting noise will condition the dog to avoid repeating the act that seemingly caused the noise. Many authorities object to this type of correction, for it may result in the dog's becoming "noise-shy"—a decided disadvantage with show dogs which must maintain poise in adverse, often noisy, situations.

To be effective, correction must be administered immediately, so that in the dog's mind there is a direct connection between his act and the correction. You can make voice corrections under almost any circumstances, but you must never call the dog to you and then correct him, or he will associate the correction with the fact that he has come and will become reluctant to respond. If the dog is at a distance and doing something he shouldn't, go to him and scold him while he is still involved in wrong-doing. If this is impossible, ignore the offense until he repeats it. Then correct him properly.

Especially while a dog is young, he should be watched closely and stopped before he gets into mischief. All dogs need to do a certain amount of chewing, so to prevent your puppy's chewing something you value, provide him with his own balls and toys. Never allow him to chew cast-off slippers and then expect him to differentiate between cast-off items and those you value. Nylon stockings, wooden articles, and various other items may cause intestinal obstructions if the dog chews and swallows them, and death may result. Rubber and plastic toys may also be harmful if they are of types the dog can bite through or chew into pieces and then swallow. So it is essential that the dog be permitted to chew only on bones or toys he cannot chew up and swallow.

Serious training for obedience should not be started until a dog is a year old. But basic training in house manners should begin the day the puppy enters his new home. A puppy should never be given the run of the house but should be confined to a box or small pen except for play periods when you can devote full attention to him. The first thing to teach the dog is his name, so that whenever he hears it, he will immediately come to attention. Whenever you are near his box, talk to him, using his name repeatedly. During play periods, talk to him, pet him, and handle him, for he must be conditioned so he will not object to being handled by a veterinarian, show judge, or family friend. As the dog investigates his surroundings, watch him carefully and if he tries something he shouldn't, reprimand him with a scolding "No!" If he repeats the offense, scold him and confine him to his box, then praise him. Discipline must be prompt, consistent, and always followed with praise. Never tease the dog, and never allow others to do so. Kindness and understanding are essential to a pleasant, mutually rewarding relationship.

When the puppy is two to three months old, secure a flat, narrow leather collar and have him start wearing it (never use a harness, which will encourage tugging and pulling). After a week or so, attach a light leather leash to the collar during play sessions and let the puppy walk around, dragging the leash behind him. Then start holding the end of the leash and coaxing the puppy to come to you. He will then be fully accustomed to collar and leash when you start taking him outside while he is being housebroken.

Housebreaking can be accomplished in a matter of approximately two weeks provided you wait until the dog is mature enough to have some control over bodily functions. This is usually at about four months. Until that time, the puppy should spend most of the day confined to a penned area or room, with the floor covered with several thicknesses of newspapers so that he may relieve himself when necessary without damage to floors.

Either of two methods works well in housebreaking—the choice depending upon where you live. If you live in a house with a readily accessible yard, you will probably want to train the puppy from the beginning to go outdoors. If you live in an apartment without easy access to a yard, you may decide to train him first to relieve himself on newspapers and then when he has learned control, to teach the puppy to go outdoors.

If you decide to train the puppy by taking him outdoors, arrange some means of confining him indoors where you can watch him closely—in a small penned area or a crate, or tied to a short leash (five or six feet). Dogs are naturally clean animals, reluctant to soil their quarters, and confining the puppy to a limited area will encourage him to avoid making a mess.

A young puppy must be taken out often, so watch your puppy closely and if he indicates he is about to relieve himself, take him out at once. If he has an accident, scold him and take him out so he will associate the act of going outside with the need to relieve himself. Always take the puppy out within an hour after meals—preferably to the same place each time—and make sure he relieves himself before you return him to the house. Restrict his water for two hours before bedtime and take him out just before you retire for the night. When you wake in the morning, take him out again.

For paper training, set aside a particular room and cover a large area of the floor with several thicknesses of newspapers. Confine the dog on a short leash and each time he relieves himself, remove the soiled papers and replace them with clean ones.

As his control increases, gradually decrease the paper area, leaving part of the floor bare. If he uses the bare floor, scold him mildly and put him on the papers, letting him know that there is where he is to relieve himself. As he comes to understand the idea, increase the bare area until papers cover only space equal to approximately two full newspaper sheets. Keep him using the papers, but begin taking him out on a leash at the times of day that he habitually relieves himself. Watch him closely when he is indoors and at the first sign that he needs to go, take him outdoors. With this method too, restrict the puppy's water for two hours before bedtime.

Using either method, the puppy will be housebroken in an amazingly short time. Once he has learned control he will need to relieve himself only four or five times a day.

Informal obedience training, started at the age of about six to eight months, will provide a good background for any advanced training you may decide to give your dog later. The collar most effective for training is the metal chain-link (fur saver) variety. The correct size for your dog will be about one inch longer that the measurement around the largest part of his head. The chain must be slipped through one of the rings so the collar forms a loop. The collar should be put on with the loose ring at the right of the dog's neck, the chain attached to it coming over the neck and through the holding ring, rather than under the neck. Since the dog is to be at your left for most of the training, this makes the collar most effective.

The leash should be attached to the loose ring, and should be either webbing or leather, six feet long and a half inch to a full inch wide. When you want your dog's attention, or wish to correct him, give a light, quick pull on the leash, which will momentarily tighten the collar about the neck. Release the pressure instantly, and the correction will have been made. If the puppy is already accustomed to a leather collar, he will adjust easily to the training collar. But before you start training sessions, practice walking with the dog until he responds readily when you increase tension on the leash.

Set aside a period of fifteen minutes, once or twice a day, for regular training sessions, and train in a place where there will be no distractions. Teach only one exercise at a time, making sure the dog has mastered it before going on to another. It will probably take at least a week for the dog to master each exercise. As training progresses, start each session by reviewing exercises the dog has already learned, then go on to the new exercise for a period of concerted practice. When discipline is required, make the correction immediately, and always praise the dog after corrections as well as when he obeys promptly. During each session stick strictly to business. Afterwards, take time to play with the dog.

The first exercise to teach is heeling. Have the dog at your left. Start walking, and just as you put your foot

Genetics

Genetics, the science of heredity, deals with the processes by which physical and mental traits of parents are transmitted to offspring. For centuries, man has been trying to solve these puzzles, but only in the last two hundred years have scientists made significant progress.

During the eighteenth century, Kolreuter, a German scientist, made revolutionary discoveries concerning plant sexuality and hybridization but was unable to explain just how hereditary processes work. In the middle of the nineteenth century, Gregor Johann Mendel, an Augustinian monk, experimented with the ordinary garden pea and made other discoveries of major significance. He found that an inherited characteristic was inherited as a complete unit, and that certain characteristics predominated over others. Next, he observed that the hereditary characteristics of each parent are contained in each offspring, even when they are not visible, and that "hidden" characteristics can be transferred without change in their nature to the grandchildren, or even later generations. Finally, he concluded that although heredity contains an element of uncertainty, some things are predictable on the basis of well-defined mathematical laws.

Unfortunately, Mendel's published paper went unheeded, and when he died in 1884 he was still virtually unknown to the scientific world. But other researchers were making discoveries, too. In 1900, three different scientists reported to learned societies that much of their research in hereditary principles had been proved years before by Gregor Mendel and that findings matched perfectly.

Thus, hereditary traits were proved to be transmitted through the chromosomes found in pairs in every living being, one of each pair contributed by the mother, the other by the father. Within each chromosome have been found hundreds of smaller structures, or genes, which are the actual determinants of hereditary characteristics. Some genes are dominant and will be seen in the offspring. Others are recessive and will not be outwardly apparent, yet can be passed on to the offspring to combine with a similar recessive gene of the other parent and thus be seen. Or they may be passed on to the offspring, not be outwardly apparent, but be passed on again to become apparent in a later generation.

Once the genetic theory of inheritance became widely known, scientists began drawing a well-defined line between inheritance and environment. More recent studies show some overlapping of these influences and indicate a combination of the two may be responsible for certain characteristics. For instance, studies have proved that extreme cold increases the amount of black pigment in the skin and hair of the "Himalayan" rabbit, although it has little or no effect on the white or colored rabbit. Current research also indicates that even though characteristics are determined by the genes, some environmental stress occurring at a particular period of pregnancy might cause physical change in the embryo.

Long before breeders had any knowledge of genetics, they practiced one of its most important principles—selective breeding. Experience quickly showed that "like begets like," and by breeding like with like and discarding unlike offspring, the various individual breeds were developed to the point where variations were relatively few. Selective breeding is based on the idea of maintaining the quality of a breed at the highest possible level, while minimizing whatever defects are prevalent. It requires that only the top dogs in a litter be kept for later breeding, and that inferior specimens be eliminated from the breeding program.

In planning any breeding program, the first requisite is a definite goal—that is, to have clearly in mind a definite picture of the type of dog you wish eventually to produce. To attempt to breed perfection is to approach the problem unrealistically. But if you don't breed for improvement, it is preferable that you not breed at all.

As a first step, you should select a bitch that exemplifies as many of the desired characteristics as possible and mate her with a dog that also has as many of the desired characteristics as possible. If you start with mediocre pets, you will produce mediocre pet puppies. If you decide to start with more than one bitch, all should closely approach the type you desire, since you will then stand a better chance of producing uniformly good puppies from all. Breeders often start with a single bitch and keep the best bitches in every succeeding generation.

Experienced breeders look for "prepotency" in all breeding stock—that is, the ability of a dog or bitch to transmit traits to most or all of its offspring. While the term is usually used to describe the transmission of good qualities, a dog may also be prepotent in transmitting faults. To be prepotent in a practical sense, a dog must possess many characteristics controlled by dominant genes. If desired characteristics are recessive, they will be apparent in the offspring only if carried by both sire and dam. Prepotent dogs and bitches usually come from a line of prepotent ancestors, but the mere fact that a dog has exceptional ancestors will not necessarily mean that he himself will produce exceptional offspring.

A single dog may sire a tremendous number of puppies, whereas a bitch can produce only a comparatively few litters during her lifetime. Thus, a sire's influence may be very widespread as compared to that of a bitch. But in evaluating a particular litter, it must be remembered that the bitch has had as much influence as has had the dog.

Inbreeding, line-breeding, outcrossing, or a combination of the three are the methods commonly used in selective breeding.

Inbreeding is the mating together of closely related animals, such as father-daughter, mother-son, or brother-sister. Although some breeders insist such breeding will lead to the production of defective individuals, it is through rigid inbreeding that all breeds of dogs have been established. Controlled tests have shown that any harmful effects appear within the first five or ten generations, and that if rigid selection is exercised from the beginning, a vigorous inbred strain will be built up.

Line-breeding also is the mating together of individuals related by family lines. However, matings are made not so much on the basis of the dog's and bitch's relationship to each other, but instead, on the basis of their relationship to a highly admired ancestor, with a view to perpetuating that ancestor's qualities. Line-breeding constitutes a long-range program and cannot be accomplished in a single generation.

Outcrossing is the breeding together of two dogs that are unrelated in family lines. Actually, since breeds have been developed through the mating of close relatives, all dogs within any given breed are related to some extent. There are few breedings that are true outcrosses, but if there is no common ancestor within five generations, a mating is usually considered an outcross.

Experienced breeders sometimes outcross for one generation in order to eliminate a particular fault, then go back to inbreeding or line-breeding. Neither the good effects nor the bad effects of outcrossing can be truly evaluated in a single mating, for undesirable recessive traits may be introduced into a strain, yet not show up for several generations. Outcrossing is better left to experienced breeders, for continual outcrossing results in a wide variation of type and great uncertainty as to the results that may be expected.

Bearded Collies are born black, brown, blue, or fawn, with or without white markings. More white than that preferred in the Standard labels a dog as a "mismark." At birth, the blacks and browns appear shinier and richer in color than the diluted blue and fawn colored dogs. Breeders first observing browns sometimes have a problem deciding whether to register them as browns or fawns, for many shades of brown are possible. This is especially true before the nose pigmentation fills in. Tips passed on by experienced breeders suggest that fawns are almost "champagne" color, that dilutes appear more plush, and seem silver-tipped. One breeder insists that colors often segregate in the whelping box!

The most common color is black, and the most common marking is the "Irish pattern": White appearing on the chest, neck, front legs, mustache and beard, belly, tip of tail, and rear legs to hocks. There also may be a blaze that appears between the eyes over the top of the skull to the collar.

This pattern is acceptable in lesser, but not greater, amounts for a show prospect. A "mismark" technically is considered to be any dog having white on the body between the shoulder and outer rear legs much above the hocks. Extreme mismarks have piebald markings, large patches of white on the body or white around the eyes. These dogs usually are sold as companions, with a spay-neuter contract.

Many lovely dogs have white creeping onto the turn of the stifle, or a wider collar. Some of these are exhibited and do well in the ring. In other words, while this is not *recommended*, it is *accepted* by many people. The extension of the markings beyond the preferred areas, i.e., a streak, is controlled by modifiers of the white pattern recessive. Full white markings have nothing to do with the white factor, for that is the result of a different gene.

Dogs with fuller white markings or "creeping white," including white on the inner legs above the hocks, are likely to produce other dogs with fuller white markings. However, they do not seem to produce a greater percentage of mismarks.

Results of breeder surveys indicate that the head markings and body markings are controlled by different genes. The mismark gene, which causes the piebald or parti-colored appearance on the body or head, is recessive. The only way of stating with certainty that a dog is free of the white factor is by test breeding. Geneticists agree this is proven only by breeding to a mismark or to three different animals known to produce mismarks.

Test breedings have shown us that a white-factored bitch bred to a white-factored dog does not necessarily produce a litter with all white-factored or mismarked puppies. However, the majority of the progeny will carry the white factor as a recessive.

A hair or two of white in the body area often sheds out and comes in black. Some breeders have noted the same occurrence with white patches on the edge of the ear. At this point, test breedings have not been performed to show whether these pups are actually white-factored or produce like-marked progeny.

Breeders have reported that body mismarks do not seem to have a connection to inherited or color-related health problems, such as those associated with double merles. Blindness or deafness can be associated with mismarked heads.

A note here on the merling factor—blues are not to be mistaken for merles, which occur in browns, reds, and blues. A description of merled Beardies appeared in *Our Dogs* in 1896, and "blue merle" Beardies were noted in

Scotland in 1898. They may still be found among the working dogs in Scotland. The merle coloring is easily recognized, for it appears washed out, with color appearing in random blotches. There is a mottled or dappled appearance. In "The Shepherd's Fire," Scottish artist Sir George Pirie depicted a blue merled Beardie by the fire, with a white puppy also in the picture.

The merles, however, seem to have been overlooked during the registration process, and since the merle is a dominant (one of the parents *must* be a merle), we do not see them today in dogs of purebred registered stock.

Looking back in a foundation pedigree, we note that Britt of Bothkennar was by Jock out of Mootie, a blue merle. Mootie had more than fifty puppies by Jock. One, at least (Nell), was a blue merle, who did have a number of litters by registered dogs. From that point, recording blue merle coloring of registered stock appears to have ceased.

The eye color should correspond with the coat. Blacks should have dark brown eyes, browns should have medium brown eyes, blues should have blue-gray to gray eyes, and fawns should have lighter brown eyes.

Pigmentation on eye rims, nose, and lips should match coat color and be well filled in. Pups whose pigment fills in the fastest usually have less problems with fading pigment or later producing progeny with fading pigment. Fading pigment may occur when pink spots appear on the nose, lips, and occasionally the eye rims. Afflicted dogs also may develop some pink patches on areas of the skin. Fading pigment can be a hereditary problem. However, it also may be a temporary condition resulting from stress, especially at times of great hormonal changes such as during puberty or from the administering of anesthesia or some medications. If the problem continues or becomes more obvious, it must be considered in planning a breeding.

Tan markings may be carried on all Beardie colors, though usually distinct only on blues and blacks. Tan may appear as a spot on the cheek, above the eyes, on the elbows, and under the tail. The easiest time to check for tan markings is at birth, by looking at the vent (under the tail). Such markings may be difficult to discern at maturity. Unfortunately, few owners show the tan color on a pedigree or on the registration application, making it difficult to trace the inheritance of tan markings.

Black is dominant over the other colors. The separate dilutant gene causes a genetic black to be born a blue or a genetic brown to be born a fawn. A simple breakdown of the color genes in Beardies follows:

Dominant	**Recessive**
Black	Brown
Non-dilution	Dilution
Non tan markings	Tan markings
Fading	Non-fading

Genes for self color vs. proper markings vs mismarked whites. There are modifiers for all these genes as well.

The fading factor, which is a dominant characteristic, often becomes apparent as early as eight weeks. Although some Beardies do not fade, those born black frequently fade to slate; brown to beige; fawn to champagne; and blue to silver. Pups that "gray out" the earliest often mature as the lightest color.

Colors lighten until about fifteen months, then once again darken to their adult color at the age of two. Some breeders believe, however, that the Beardie color continues to change until the veteran coat comes in, about the age of seven or even later! Continue to look for changes as long as the ears are a different shade from the rest of the coat.

Beardie colors correlate with those of the Doberman Pinscher, so Beardie breeders wishing more complete information will profit from the genetic studies of that breed. A simplified explanation follows:

There are genes for the four basic colors (black, brown, blue, and fawn), plus white; another gene for either fading or non-fading; a gene for either white markings or self-color; and a gene for tan markings.

There are modifiers for intensity of color; modifiers for the amount of white markings on the body; modifiers for the extent of white markings on the head; and modifiers for skin pigmentation.

Justin and his Missus. Owners, Deanna and Arnold Einbinder.

Ch. Rich-Lin's Rising Son.

Black is dominant over brown, blue, and fawn.

Nondilutants (black and brown) are dominant over blue and fawn.

Tri-color is recessive.

Any color Beardie can produce any other color Beardies depending on the recessive genes the dog and its chosen mate carry.

Two serious defects that are believed heritable—subluxation (hip dysplasia) and orchidism—should be zealously guarded against, and afflicted dogs and their offspring should be eliminated from breeding programs. Hip dysplasia is a condition of the hip joint where the bone of the socket is eroded and the head of the thigh bone is also worn away, causing lameness which becomes progressively more serious until the dog is unable to walk. Orchidism is the failure of one or both testicles to develop and descend properly. When one testicle is involved, the term "monorchid" is used. When both are involved, "cryptorchid" is used colloquially. A cryptorchid is almost always sterile, whereas a monorchid is usually fertile. There is evidence that cryptorchidism "runs in families" and that a monorchid transmits the tendency through bitch and male puppies alike.

Through the years, many misconceptions concerning heredity have been perpetuated. Perhaps the most widely perpetuated is the idea evolved hundreds of years ago that somehow characteristics were passed on through the mixing of the blood of the parents. We still use terminology evolved from that theory when we speak of bloodlines, or describe individuals as full-blooded, despite the fact that the theory was disproved more than a century ago.

Also inaccurate and misleading is any statement that a definite fraction or proportion of an animal's inherited characteristics can be positively attributed to a particular ancestor. Individuals lacking knowledge of genetics sometimes declare that an individual receives half his inherited characteristics from each parent, a quarter from each grandparent, an eighth from each great-grandparent, etc. Thousands of volumes of scientific findings have been published, but no simple way has been found to determine positively which characteristics have been inherited from which ancestors, for the science of heredity is infinitely complex.

Any breeder interested in starting a serious breeding program should study several of the books on canine genetics and breeding and whelping that are currently available. Excellent works covering these subjects are *Meisen Breeding Manual,* by Hilda Meisenzahl, and *The Standard Book of Dog Breeding,* by Dr. Alvin Grossman—both published by the publisher of this book—and *Successful Dog Breeding,* by Chris Walkowicz and Bonnie Wilcox D.V.M.

"Pretty as a picture."

Ch. Rich-Lin's Molly of Arcadia, R.O.M.X., top-producing dam. Owners, Jim and Diann Shannon.

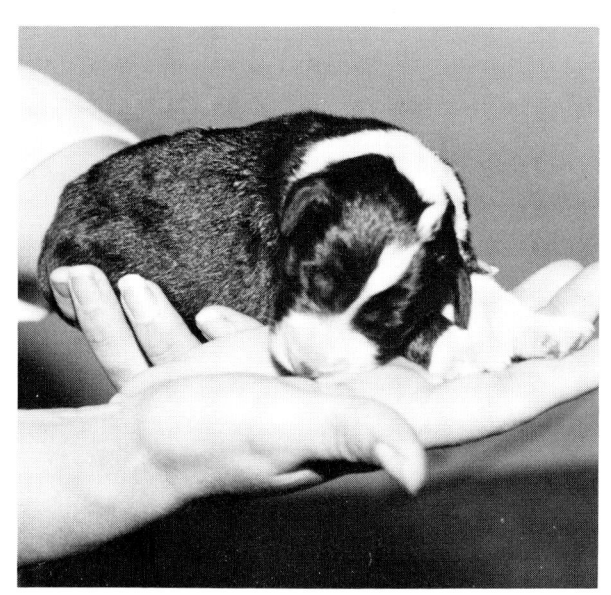

A healthy, well-marked newborn.

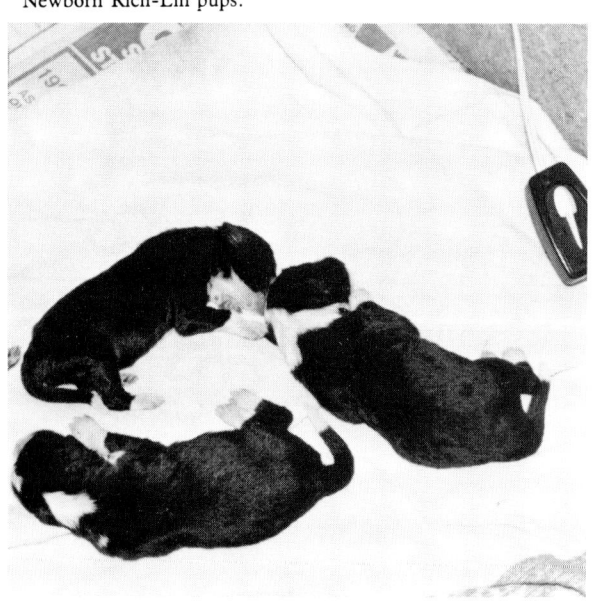

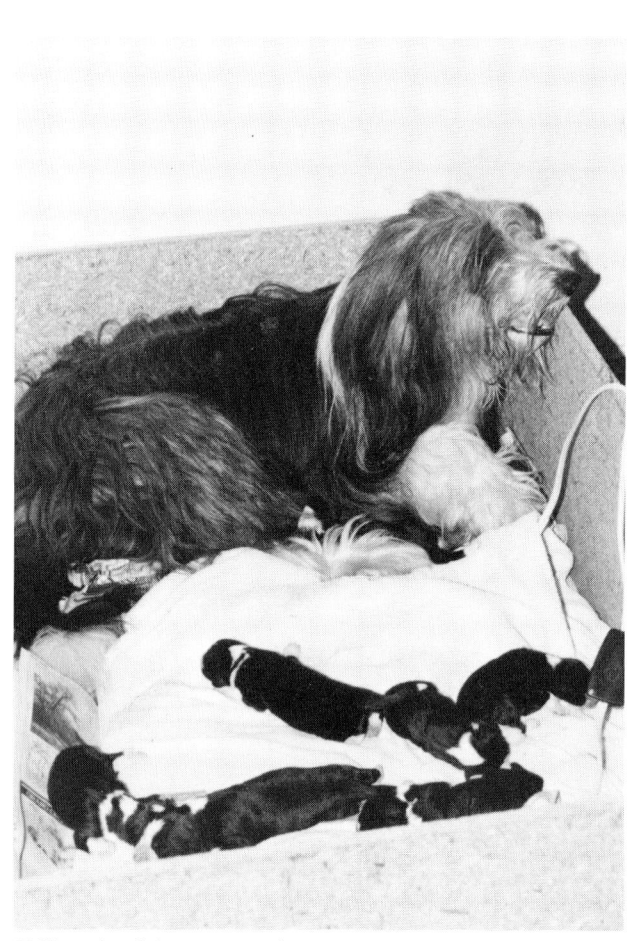

Newborn Rich-Lin pups.

Taking a break between puppies.

Breeding and Whelping

The reproductive ability of a bitch begins when she comes into season the first time at the age of eight to ten months. Thereafter, she will come in season at roughly six-month intervals. Her maximum fertility builds up from puberty to full maturity and then declines until a state of total sterility is reached in old age. Just when this occurs is hard to determine, for the fact that an older bitch shows signs of being in season doesn't necessarily mean she is still capable of reproducing.

The length of the season varies from eighteen to twenty-one days. The first indication is a pronounced swelling of the vulva with coincidental bleeding (called "showing color") for about the first seven to nine days. The discharge gradually turns to a creamy color, and it is during this phase (estrus), from about the tenth to fifteenth days, that the bitch is ovulating and is receptive to the male. The ripe, unfertilized ova survive for about seventy-two hours. If fertilization does take place, each ovum attaches itself to the walls of the uterus, a membrane forms to seal it off, and a foetus develops from it.

Following the estrus phase, the bitch is still in season until about the twenty-first day and will continue to be attractive to males, although she will usually fight them off as she did the first few days. Nevertheless, to avoid accidental mating, the bitch must be confined for the entire period. Virtual imprisonment is necessary, for male dogs display uncanny abilities in their efforts to reach a bitch in season.

The odor that attracts the males is present in the bitch's urine, so it is advisable to take her a good distance from the house before permitting her to relieve herself. To help eliminate problems completely, your veterinarian can prescribe a preparation that will disguise the odor but will not interfere with breeding when the time is right. Many fanciers use such preparations when exhibiting a bitch in the conformation ring and find that nearby males show no interest whatsoever. But it is not advisable to permit a bitch to run loose when she has been given a product of this type, for during estrus she will seek the company of male dogs and an accidental mating may still occur.

A potential brood bitch, regardless of breed, should have good bone, ample breadth and depth of ribbing, and adequate room in the pelvic region. Unless a bitch is physically mature—well beyond the puppy stage when she has her first season—breeding should be delayed until her second or a later season. Furthermore, even though it is possible for a bitch to conceive twice a year, she should not be bred oftener than once a year. A bitch that is bred too often will age prematurely and her puppies are likely to lack vigor. Beardies should not be bred until they are at least eighteen months of age, preferably two years, allowing them time to mature physically *and* mentally.

Two or three months before a bitch is to be mated, her physical condition should be considered carefully. If she is too thin, provide a rich, balanced diet plus the regular exercise needed to develop strong, supple muscles. Daily exercise on the leash is as necessary for the too-thin bitch as for the too-fat one, although the latter will need more exercise and at a brisker pace, as well as a reduction of food, if she is to be brought to optimum condition. A prospective brood bitch must have had all her annual shots as well as rabies vaccination. And a month before her season is due, a veterinarian should examine a stool specimen for worms. If there is evidence of infestation, the bitch should be wormed.

A dog may be used at stud from the time he reaches physical maturity, well on into old age. The first time your bitch is bred, it is well to use a stud that has already proven his ability by having sired other litters. The fact that a neighbor's dog is readily available should not influence your choice, for to produce the best puppies, you must select the stud most suitable from a genetic standpoint.

Usually the first service will be successful. However, if it isn't, in most cases an additional service is given free, provided the stud dog is still in the possession of the same owner. If the bitch misses, it may be because her cycle varies widely from normal. Through microscopic examination, a veterinarian can determine exactly when the bitch is entering the estrus phase and thus is likely to conceive.

If infertility is suspected, tests should be run to determine whether the dog or, more commonly, the bitch is hypothyroid. A dog suffering from this condition may evidence other symptoms, including poor coat, darkening of the skin, and weight gain. The bitch's heat cycle also may be erratic.

Some breeders prefer to prove that their bitches are producers before finishing them to championship status. However, it is unusual for Beardie females to be sterile. Having a litter will bring a bitch to external maturity, but her coat may be sacrificed for six months or longer.

Beardies often take their leisure during breeding. Many prefer to court a bit. Owner assistance helps speed the event.

The owner of the stud should give you a stud-service certificate, providing a four-generation pedigree for the sire and showing the date of mating. The litter registration application is completed only after the puppies are whelped, but it, too, must be signed by the owner of the stud as well as the owner of the bitch. Registration forms may be secured by writing The American Kennel Club.

In normal pregnancy there is visible enlargement of the abdomen by the end of the fifth week. By palpation (feeling with the fingers) a veterinarian may be able to distinguish developing puppies as early as three weeks after mating, but it is unwise for a novice to poke and prod and try to detect the presence of unborn puppies.

The gestation period normally lasts nine weeks, although it may vary from sixty-one to sixty-five days. If it goes beyond sixty-five days from the date of mating, a veterinarian should be consulted.

During the first four or five weeks, the bitch should be permitted her normal amount of activity. As she becomes heavier, she can be walked on the leash, but strenuous running and jumping should be avoided. Feed her a well-balanced diet (see the chapter on nutrition), and if she should become constipated, add small amounts of mineral oil to her food.

A whelping box should be set up about two weeks before the puppies are due, and the bitch should start then to use it as her bed so she will be accustomed to it by the time the puppies arrive. Preferably, the box should be square, with each side long enough so that the bitch can stretch out full length and have several inches to spare at either end. The bottom should be padded with an old cotton rug or other material that is easily laundered. Edges of the padding should be tacked to the floor of the box so the puppies will not get caught in it and smother. Once it is obvious labor is about to begin, the padding should be covered with several layers of spread-out newspapers. Then, as papers become soiled, the top layer can be pulled off, leaving the area clean.

It is important to trim the hair around the genitals and nipples. This not only facilitates whelping and aids cleanliness, but prevents the hair from causing damage to the nipples by winding around them while the pups are nursing.

Within twenty-four hours prior to whelping the bitch's normal temperature of 101.5 degrees drops two or three degrees. The bitch should not be left alone once birth becomes imminent. Although Beardies are normally natural whelpers, they often have large litters. Because of the sheer bulk in these instances, they are unable to assist in the birth of the first whelps.

Forty-eight to seventy-two hours before the litter is to be whelped, a definite change in the shape of the abdomen will be noted. Instead of looking barrel-shaped, the abdomen will sag pendulously. Breasts usually redden and become enlarged, and milk may be present a day or two before the puppies are whelped. As the time becomes imminent, the bitch will probably scratch and root at her bedding in an effort to make a nest, and will refuse food and ask to be let out every few minutes.

The bitch's abdomen and flanks will contract sharply when labor actually starts, and for a few minutes she will attempt to expel a puppy, then rest for a while and try again. Someone should stay with the bitch the entire time whelping is taking place, and if she appears to be having unusual difficulties, a veterinarian should be called.

Puppies are usually born head first, though some may be born rear feet first and no difficulty encountered. Each puppy is enclosed in a separate membranous sac that the bitch will remove with her teeth. She will sever the umbilical cord, which will be attached to the soft, spongy afterbirth that is expelled right after the puppy emerges. Usually the bitch eats the afterbirth, so it is necessary to watch and make sure one is expelled for each puppy whelped. If afterbirth is retained, the bitch may develop metritis, become dangerously ill, or even die.

The dam will lick and nuzzle each newborn puppy until it is warm and dry and ready to nurse. If puppies arrive so close together that she can't take care of them, you can help her by rubbing the puppies dry with a soft cloth. If several have been whelped but the bitch continues to be in labor, all but one should be removed and placed in a small box lined with clean towels and warmed to about seventy degrees. The bitch will be calmer if one puppy is left with her at all times.

Whelping sometimes continues as long as twenty-four hours for a very large litter, but a litter of two or three puppies may be whelped in an hour. When the bitch settles down, curls around the puppies and nuzzles them to her, it usually indicates that all have been whelped.

The bitch should be taken away for a few minutes while you clean the box and arrange clean padding. If her coat is soiled, sponge it clean and dry it before she returns to the puppies. Once she is back in the box, offer her a bowl of warm beef broth and a pan of cool water, placing both where she will not have to get up in order to reach them. As soon as she indicates interest in food, give her a generous bowl of chopped meat to which cod-liver oil and dicalcium phosphate have been added.

If there is an imbalance of calcium metabolism during the period the puppies are nursing, eclampsia may develop. Symptoms are violent trembling and rigidity of muscles. Veterinary assistance must be secured immediately, for death may result in a very short time. Treatment consists of calcium gluconate administered intravenously by a veterinarian, after which symptoms subside in a miraculously short time.

Beardies are excellent mothers, completely relaxed. They often regurgitate to wean their puppies, which is the way dogs weaned litters in the wild. Of course, this is not necessary today, with the breeder assisting her by feeding the pups. If the dam persists in the practice, she should not be permitted to stay with the pups, or her food should be continued in the same amounts as when she was nursing.

For weak or very small puppies, supplemental feeding is often recommended. Any one of three different methods may be used: Tube-feeding (with a catheter attached to a syringe); using an eyedropper (this method requires great care in order to avoid getting formula in the lungs); or using a tiny bottle (the "pet nurser" available at most stores).

These are good and easily prepared formulas:

Almost like Mom's
Mix:
1 can evaporated milk, 15 oz.
2 egg yolks
1 carton plain yogurt, uncultured, 8 oz.
For bottle feeding, add 6 oz. boiled water

Supplement or Supper
1 can evaporated milk
2 cans water
2 packages unflavored gelatin
2 beaten egg yolks
1 tablespoon cream
1 tablespoon honey

Mix, first dissolving gelatin in cold water, heating and blending, then adding to other ingredients. Reduce honey if stools become loose.

A veterinarian can tell you which method of administering the formula is most practical in your particular case. It is important to remember that equipment must be kept scrupulously clean. It can be sterilized by boiling, or it may be soaked in a Clorox solution, then washed carefully and dried between feedings.

All puppies are born blind. Their eyes open when they are ten to fourteen days old. At first the eyes have a bluish cast and appear weak, and the puppies must be protected from strong light until at least ten days after the eyes open.

To ensure proper emotional development, young dogs should be shielded from loud noises and rough handling. Being lifted by the front legs is painful and may result in permanent injury to the shoulders. So when lifting a puppy, always place one hand under the chest with the forefinger between the front legs, and place the other hand under the pup's bottom.

Flannelized rubber sheeting or kitchen carpeting is an ideal surface for the bottom of the bed for the new puppies. It is inexpensive and washable, and will provide a surface that will give the puppies traction so that they will not slip either while nursing or when learning to walk.

The puppies' nails grow rapidly and become so long and sharp that they scratch the bitch's breasts. Since the nails are soft, they can be trimmed with ordinary scissors or your own nail clippers.

At about four weeks of age, formula should be provided. The amount fed each day should be increased over a period of two weeks, when the puppies can be weaned completely. Formula can be prepared at home in accordance with instructions from a veterinarian. The formula should be warmed to lukewarm, and poured into a shallow pan placed on the floor of the box. After its mouth has been dipped into the mixture a few times, a puppy will start to lap formula. All puppies can be allowed to eat from the same pan, but be sure the small ones get their share. If they are pushed aside, feed them separately. Permit the puppies to nurse part of the time, but gradually increase the number of meals of formula. By the time the puppies are five weeks old, the dam should be allowed with them only at night. When they are about six weeks old, they should be weaned completely. Three meals a day are usually sufficient from this time until the puppies are about three months old, when feedings are reduced to two a day. About the time the dog reaches one year of age, feedings may be reduced to one each day. (For further information on this subject, see the chapter on nutrition.)

Once they are weaned, puppies should be given temporary distemper and parvovirus injections in accordance with your veterinarian's advice. At six weeks, stool specimens should be checked for worms, for almost without exception, puppies become infested. Specimens should be checked again at eight weeks, and as often thereafter as your veterinarian recommends.

Sometimes owners decide as a matter of convenience to have a bitch spayed or a male castrated. While this is recommended when a dog has a serious inheritable defect or when abnormalities of reproductive organs develop, in sound, normal purebred dogs, spaying a bitch or castrating a male may prove a definite disadvantage. The operations automatically bar dogs from competing in conformation shows as well as preclude use for breeding. The operations are seldom dangerous, but they should not be performed without serious consideration of these facts.

If the animal is to be a companion only, however, neutering is recommended in order to prevent unwanted pregnancies on the part of the female, amorous attempts on the part of the male, and reproductive organ cancer for both.

The future of the Bearded Collie lies with the breeders. It is important to remember the words of Joyce Collis (Beagold): "We never breed just for show potential; we know that from every litter there will be a majority of puppies that will go into pet homes, and hopefully will live to a ripe old age."

"The Shepherd's Dog," by W. Barraud. 1854. Reproduction of etching owned by the author.

"The Shepherd's Dog," by P. Reinagle. Circa 1803. From The British Museum.

History of the Bearded Collie

Many herding breeds evolved from the ancient Puli, Komondor, and Kuvasz kept and bred for herding purposes by the Sumer people about 5000 B.C. Tales have been passed down that the Beardie is an ancestor of the Old English Sheepdog or a descendant of the Border Collie. A theory also exists that it is an offspring of a cross between the Shetland Sheepdog and the Scottish Deerhound.

Researchers and experts of canine history have concluded that the Beardie resembles several European sheepdogs, including the Polish Lowland Sheepdog, Bergamascho, Portuguese Sheepdog, and the Gos d'Atura (Catalan).

Beardie owners are accustomed to hearing people exclaim, "He looks just like an Old English Sheepdog with a tail!" or "She must be an undocked OES!" It is unfortunate that some Beardies have lost their tails because of mistaken identification. Although the Sheepdog is better known, actually the Beardie is believed to be a predecessor of the OES, and possibly the Kerry Blue Terrier and the Border Collie.

Likely, the shepherds of Scotland were not particular about breeding purebreds and maintaining breed type. Dogs often were crossbred to retain herding ability. Bearded Collies, Old English Sheepdogs, Border Collies, and other working dogs were interbred to produce the best workers.

Wolves disappeared from Great Britain as the result of a tariff of three hundred wolves imposed by Prince Edward during the Middle Ages for the express purpose of eliminating the predator from the islands. As the need for large, tough mastiff-type flock guarders faded, they were replaced by gentle, intelligent herding dogs.

About 1514, a Polish ship captain traded three Polish Lowland Shepherds (Owczarek Nizinny) for a pair of valued Scottish sheep. This proved to be a good deal for modern Beardie lovers, for these dogs, two bitches and a male, were surely influential in our breed when crossed with the local herding and flock guarding dogs.

Bearded Collies appear in artwork as early as the 1700s. In 1771 Gainsborough painted a portrait of the third Duke Henry with a Beardie type. Reynolds followed in 1772 with a portrait of the peer's wife "Elizabeth, Duches (sic) of Buccleigh," and her daughter Lady Mary Scott, in the company of their two dogs.

Several breeds of herding dogs bearing various names and resembling the Beardie were found in Scotland, Wales, and England. These are the Mountain Scotch Collie, Old Welsh Grey Sheepdog, Highland Collie, Loch Collie, and the Hairy Moued Collie. All of these names formerly were used for the Beardie.

Because "collie" is included in the breed name, people are surprised that the Beardie doesn't look much like the Rough Collie. The explanation lies in the derivation of the word. "Collie" was a term bestowed upon many herding dogs in Scotland, for the Welsh word "coelio" means trustful and faithful. Both "colley" and "coaley" indicated the black-faced sheep in Scotland.

"The Drove Roads of Scotland," by A. R. B. Haldane, tells of drovers turning their dogs loose to find their own way home after long treks. The owners would then return home by sea or stay at their destination for a time. Although Beardies do not have the reputation of typical drovers—which frequently are thought of as sneaky, misbred dogs, swapped and bred publicly in the common marketplace—they do have the intelligence and stamina necessary for this chore. According to information gathered by Major James G. Logan, they likely were used for droving, as well as the herding chores for which the breed was developed.

Two types of Beardies evolved. The larger, Border type had a long slate-colored coat with straight, harsh hair, and the Highland type carried a shorter, wavy coat, usually brown. The Highland Collie had a reputation of being a quick dog with unusually good sense.

As with all breeds, a dog that looks quite different from today's Beardie appears in early pictures. The dogs were shaggy, rough-coated, with less hair, and were leggier in appearance.

"The Dogs of Scotland," 1891, by D. J. Thomson Gray, contains the earliest description of the Bearded Collie. Gray's description also appeared in articles by the 1880s. "A big, rough-coated, clumsy-looking dog, with rather large head, sleepy look and a peculiar action when running," is at odds with today's Beardie, particularly as pertaining to clumsiness and the sleepy look!

In 1897, the Scottish Kennel Club's president, Mr. H. Parmure Gordon, desired his breed, the Bearded Collie, to be judged by a shepherd at the first recorded appearance of the breed in the show ring. This was circumvented by asking Mr. Gordon to do the honors himself. Naturally, he acquiesced.

It is known that one Highlander moved his sheep and his herding dogs, Bearded Collies, to Dartmoor, Devon, England, in 1918. This family bred the dogs until 1928 when they moved to Hampshire. They recorded their belief that Beardies should be gray or reddish brown, with white markings, since dogs that were primarily all white spooked the sheep and were not visible in the snow.

Beardies were popular herding and show dogs in Scotland during this time, being shown extensively at Peebleshire. When World War I began, shows ended abruptly, but the breed survived as working dogs. The coat was ideal protection from the misty, rainy, cold climate. These dogs were adept on the rough, rocky ground. The demand was for a dog that was sturdy, quick, and intelligent.

J. Russell Greig founded the Bearded Collie Society in Edinburgh, Scotland, in 1912. The Society floundered during the war. Mrs. Cameron Millar attempted a revival in the thirties, but was unsuccessful, and her stock seems to have disappeared from pedigrees.

In 1944 Mrs. G. O. Willison, Bothkennar Grange, England, wanted a working Shetland Sheepdog and reserved one from a breeder. When none was available, a Beardie was substituted, and Mrs. Willison succumbed to the breed charm. With that one little bitch, the modern Beardie breed was born. The brown bitch Jeannie became the matriarch of Mrs. Willison's Bothkennar Kennels, and of all Beardiedom.

Because of the scarcity of the breed, Jeannie was bred to a Beardie-type male, who was thought to have a Border Collie dam. In this first litter, Jeannie had ten puppies, with one being of Border Collie type. All of the puppies were placed and the elderly sire died before the breeding could be repeated. A planned breeding of Jeannie and her only son was thwarted when he died of distemper.

After tracing Jeannie's bloodlines, Mrs. Willison registered her with the British Kennel Club and progressed with her search to find a Beardie male. After many disappointments, she finally discovered the gray dog who became known as Bailie of Bothkennar.

The Beardies seen in the ring today are descended from Bailie and Jeannie. Additional working stock and unregistered dogs were used in breeding programs by Mrs. Willison and other fanciers, but the lines either faded out or were interbred with the Bothkennar stock, for it seems to be impossible to find a pedigree which does not include Bothkennar.

Bailie was believed to be the first Beardie shown at Crufts, England's most prestigious dog show. From the first litter of Jeannie and Bailie, Mrs. Willison retained a female, Buskie, and three males, Bogle, Bruce, and Bravado. Two other females were sold as pets.

Another bitch, Bess, and a male, Britt (who became the first Beardie to win a Championship Certificate), were acquired from working stock about the same time other fanciers were discovering the breed. With careful breeding and selection of stock, several matings were achieved, and Beardies came to international attention.

In 1959 Beardies were able to win Championship Certificates (C.C.'s), and Ch. Beauty Queen of Bothkennar became the first Beardie to earn three C.C.'s and thus become titled. Before that developed, however, her uncle Bannoch of Bothkennar won a Best of Breed at the Crufts show. The first Group winner in the British Isles was Ch. Andrake Persephone. The popular and admired Ch. Edenborough Blue Bracken, R.O.M., "Percy," was the first English Best-in-Show Beardie and is prominent in American pedigrees. Percy earned a total of thirty-nine C.C.'s among numerous other wins! Charncroft Crusader captured a Best in Show at a Scottish Kennel Club Show.

The study of pedigrees is fascinating, and never more so than when a breed can be traced back to its roots, as can the Bearded Collie. Besides Jeannie and Bailie, several other working Beardies were registered and bred in the 1950s.

In addition to Jeannie's sire, Baffler, and her dam, Mist, and Bailie's sire, Dandy, there were many other working dogs that contributed to modern Beardies. Bess of Bothkennar, a working dog, and Britt (mentioned earlier) were a part of the Bothkennar breeding program. The sire and dam of Bess are listed as Bobby and Bett. Britt, who won two C.C.'s in England, was sired by Jock out of Mootie.

Mrs. Willison also used Jennifer of Multan, Newtown Blackie, and Mirk (the sire of Ch. Bobby of Bothkennar) in her lines. Mister, Craig, Fly, Ranger, Symphony, and Brasensoe Bonnie all eventually were bred to Bothkennar stock, begetting the Beardies of the present.

On pages 125 through 128 are two modern pedigrees and two earlier pedigrees, tracing the foundation upon which the breed is built. Further information can be obtained through the *Bearded Collies of Great Britain Partial Studbook*, compiled by Gail Miller, and available from the Bearded Collie Club of America.

British Beardies have achieved success in obedience and agility tests. They have been utilized outside the show ring as Guide dogs, as Search and Rescue Dogs, and for aiding mentally disturbed patients.

Although several working dogs were employed in the re-creation of the breed, today all of these dogs have been bred to the Bothkennar lines, or their strains have died out. It would be a difficult, if not impossible, task to uncover a pedigree that does not trace back to Jeannie and her one surviving litter of registered dogs sired by Bailie.

Suzanne Moorhouse (Willowmead) acquired Barberry from the second breeding of Ridgeway Rob to Bra'Tawny of Bothkennar. Mary Partridge (Wishanger) bought Barley from the same litter. When Mrs. Willison broke up her kennel in 1963, the Osbornes (Osmart) took Bravo and Blue Bonnie. Thus Bothkennar dogs became the future of these and other English kennels, which in turn produced the breed as it exists today in England, North America, and the rest of the world.

Other English dogs that have had a great influence on the breed in North America are Ridgeway Rob, Ch.

Wishanger Barley of Bothkennar, Ch. Wishanger Cairnbhan, Ch. Bravo of Bothkennar, Ch. Willowmead Barberry of Bothkennar, Ch. Willowmead My Honey, Ch. Osmart Bonnie Blue Braid, Ch. Blue Bonnie of Bothkennar, and Ch. Edenborough Blue Bracken.

It is not surprising that Beardies came to the United States in the 1950s, just ten short years after Mrs. Willison brought the breed to the eye of the dog-loving public. Everyone who sees a Beardie soon succumbs to his charm, and it is not amazing that the breed's appeal traveled swiftly to America.

The first Beardied Collies imported to America were two from a litter sired by Ridgeway Rob x Bra-Tawny of Bothkennar. After arriving in 1957, they were pets on a farm in Connecticut, but were not shown and likely were not bred.

Shortly thereafter, the first serious fanciers imported breeding and show stock to begin building the breed in earnest on this side of the Atlantic. The first litter registered in America (1967) belonged to Larry and Maxine Levy (Heathglen), and was by Ksg Cannamoor Cardoonagh x BSgKSg Cannamoor Glen Canach. The Levys had shown the dogs in Europe and had attained championships there.

In 1969, a newspaper story reported that two men on snowmobiles had rescued a dog stranded during a snowstorm in western Massachusetts. The dog's owner later stated that the dog was fourteen years old and had been gone for two weeks, but seemed no worse for its experience. He made the erroneous statement that it was a rare breed, and probably was the only Bearded Collie in the United States.

The dog was one of a pair of Beardies the owner's brother had imported in 1968 for breeding purposes. Shortly after, the man was transferred back to England, and because of the lengthy quarantine period required for dogs entering England, he gave the bitch to his sister in Connecticut and the dog to his brother.

In 1970, breeding activity increased, with the Levys breeding a litter, and D. Ian and Moira Morrison (Cauldbrae) soon following suit.

Thomas and Barbara Davies (Dunwich) bred their first litter the following year, followed by Richard and Linda Nootbaar (Rich-Lin) in 1972, and Anna Dolan (Glen Eire) in 1973. The year 1974 brought litters from several other breeders: Virginia Parsons (Braemoor); Freedo and Barbara Rieseberg (Silverleaf); Robert and Henrietta Lachman (Cricket); and J. Richard and Barbara Schneider (Ha'Penny).

The Bearded Collie Club of America (BCCA) was founded on July 19, 1969. Larry Levy served as the first President for the charter membership of five, which increased to forty-five in the first year. The Registrar, D. Ian Morrison, registered two hundred dogs in the first three years. At the end of 1970, five breeders had bred twelve litters, and thirty-two U.S.-bred Beardies and nineteen imports had been registered. Registrations for the following three years were: 1971, 7 breeders, 10 litters, 63 U.S.-bred dogs, and 41 imports; 1972, 17 breeders, 19 litters, 108 U.S.-bred dogs, and 63 imports; 1973, 29 breeders, 23 litters, 194 U.S.-bred dogs, and 84 imports. In 1974, the number of litters rose to 40.

The British Standard was accepted as the original Standard of the BCCA, and was the accepted description of Bearded Collies until it was amended in 1978. Co-authors of the current Standard are Moira Morrison and Dr. Tom Davies. On January 8, 1974, after two previous rejections by the AKC because of insufficient membership in the club, the breed was accepted for eligibility to compete in the Miscellaneous Class.

Because of the dedication of the early members, Beardies were admitted to the AKC Stud Book in June of 1976, and AKC registration was begun in October of that year. On February 1, 1977, Beardies were admitted to the Working Group and began competing for championship points. During that first year, seventy Bearded Collies completed their championships. At the end of 1977, the Stud Book closed registration of the foundation stock. In January 1983, the Bearded Collie became one of the breeds in the newly formed Herding Group.

A lovely Beardie who was to become Ch. Brambledale Blue Bonnet, C.D., R.O.M., was imported in 1972 by J. Richard Schneider. Accompanying Bonnet were Brambledale Black Diamond, Charncroft Caprice, and Brambledale Beth, who all finished their championships. Beth and Caprice (the latter the dam of Ch. Mistiburn Merrymaid and Ch. Mistiburn Merrymaker, winner of the 1980 BCCA Specialty), went to Jane Turner, who trained them for commercials. Although the commercials did not live up to expectations, the dogs certainly did.

Bonnet became the breed's first United States champion and Companion Dog titleholder. She was co-owned by Mr. Schneider and Henrietta and Robert Lachman through her first two litters. Then the Lachmans became sole owners.

Both American and English judges agree that the breed has come a long way, although there is still room for improvement. It has been noted that movement is better in America, yet many Britishers feel that there is still too much difference in type and that Americans lean toward exaggerations in angles and coats.

During the years the breed was being established, those who owned Bearded Collies worked diligently to set up the Parent Club, approve a Standard, build membership, and exhibit their dogs in the effort to attain both AKC and public recognition. The current breed fanciers can repay their dedication by maintaining the breed as a natural dog, and striving for, but not changing, the ideal.

A solid structure is built with a firm foundation, and knowledge of the breed's roots makes a breeding kennel sound. As G. Olive Willison remarked at a new owner's apology for questions: "Oh, no—never, never stop checking on the smallest bits. You can't know where you're going if you don't know where you've been."

CLUBS

The Bearded Collie Club of America (BCCA) is a member of The American Kennel Club, and represents the various specialty breed clubs. The address of the current BCCA secretary may be obtained from The American Kennel Club, 51 Madison Avenue, New York, New York 10010. Several of the following clubs are nearing AKC-sanctioned show status and the BCC of southeastern Michigan attained that goal in 1986. The clubs serve members and the fancy by hosting matches, educational programs, and training classes, and encouraging the companionship of Beardie lovers. The BCCA will supply addresses of the clubs' secretaries.

- Atlanta BCC (Georgia)
- BCC of Central Florida
- BCC of Greater Cincinnati (Ohio)
- BCC of Greater New York
- BCC of the Golden West (California)
- BCC of Southeastern Michigan
- Chicagoland BCC (Illinois)
- Delaware Valley BCC (Pennsylvania)
- Dixie BCC (Florida)
- Garden State BCC (New Jersey)
- Great Plains BCC (Nebraska)
- Independence BCC (Pennsylvania)
- Minuteman BCC (Massachusetts)
- National Capital BCC (Virginia)
- Northwest BCC (Washington)
- Rocky Mountain BCC (Colorado)
- Sacramento Valley BC Fanciers (California)

Blue merle Beardie in "The Shepherd's Fire," by Pirie. Credit R.S.A. Diploma Collection.

Scraper drawing of Westernisles Loch Eport. Owner, Major James G. Logan.

RESCUING BEARDIES

In 1985, the BCCA initiated a rescue program under the national coordination of Paul Glatzer. With the cooperation of several regional coordinators, the committee—along with two hundred volunteers—has already rescued and placed a number of abandoned, abused, neglected, and needy Bearded Collies. As a result of their efforts, flyers describing and picturing our breed have been sent to shelters, pounds, and veterinarians.

BCCA member Billy Smart accompanies the displaced Beardies to new homes when air shipping is necessary. Members have been generous in donating their time and funds to the cause.

Although the cause is a worthy one, all those who care about Bearded Collies voice the hope that the time will come when the committee can be disbanded—because there are no Beardies that need rescuing. Until that time, anyone finding a Beardie in need of a home can contact the BCCA through the national secretary (whose name and address are available through the AKC) or (if the need is not urgent) by writing P.O. Box 1120, Smithtown, Long Island, New York 11787.

Henry, Duke of Buccleigh, with his dog. By Gainsborough, 1771. From The British Museum.

Elizabeth, Dutchess of Buccleigh, and Lady Mary Scott, with dogs. By Reynolds, 1772. From The British Museum.

Ch. Arcadia's Family Tradition with Jim Shannon.

Influential American Kennels and Breeders

Although the breed has barely finished its first decade of show competition in the United States, several kennels have been dominant in showing and active in breeding. Their breeding programs undoubtedly have had a great influence on the breed as it is today. Among them the following kennels have bred some three hundred champions.

ARCADIA. Jim and Diann Shannon, Loganville, Georgia. Lines based on Rich-Lin and Edenborough. Arcadia has bred more than one hundred champions, including six dogs that have won Best in Show in three different countries, and several Group winners. Ch. Arcadia's Wind Song and Ch. Arcadia's Sugar Plum won BIS in Japan; Ch. Arcadia's Salty Jok O'Emshire, R.O.M., in Canada; and Ch. Arcadia's Country Music, Ch. Arcadia's Benson and Hedges, and Ch. Arcadia's Cotton Eyed Joe, R.O.M., in the United States.

Arcadia's first Beardie was Rich-Lins Rising Son, who died tragically before the breed was recognized by the AKC. Two puppies were retained from his first two litters. The first was Ch. Rich-Lins Molly of Arcadia, R.O.M., who was a daughter of Edenborough Full O'Life, "Shag" (a litter sister to Blue Bracken). The second was Ch. Rich-Lins Whiskers of Arcadia, R.O.M., who was out of Ch. Hootnanny of Bengray, "Nanny" (a daughter of Ch. Wishanger Cairnbhan). Whiskers was bred to Molly, producing five champions from a single litter.

Arcadia imported Edenborough Happy Go Lucky (Ch. Edenborough Blue Bracken, R.O.M., x Davealex Dawn Reign, R.O.M.), who has earned both his championship and Register of Merit titles. The first Lucky x Molly litter of eight puppies *all* finished their championships before sixteen months of age. With the exception of Ch. Edenborough Quick Silver, R.O.M., a blue, the Shannon's foundation stock was black (slate). However, Arcadia is producing blues, blacks, fawns, browns, and tri-colors. Jim Shannon is a breeder/judge.

CAULDBRAE. Moira Morrison, Pawling, New York. This is one of the earliest Beardie kennels in the United States, which, incidentally, also has owned Nizinny. Cauldbrae has bred nearly forty Beardie champions, and produces all colors. The gene pool is from several British kennels, especially Brambledale (through purchase of such well-known dogs as Brambledale Blackfriar; Bona Dea, R.O.M.; and Black Rod, R.O.M.), as well as lines from Tambora (Johnathen Brown of Tambora) and Davealex (including Larky McRory and Rhinestone Cowboy). Breeding and showing actively, Cauldbrae was instrumental in establishing the breed in the United States.

GAYMARDON. Donnell and Gail J. Miller and daughter Gail Elizabeth, Arnold, Missouri. Gaymardon utilized stock from Wishanger, Davealex, and Edenborough lines in their breeding program, producing from only limited breeding a notable record of nearly fifty percent champions and multiple Group winners.

Gaymardon's foundation stock was Ch. Gaymardon's Chesapeake Mist, R.O.M.; her litter brother Ch. Gaymardon's Yorktown Yankee, R.O.M., "Chip"; and Ch. Monyash Tempest Tossed (daughter of Bracken Boy). The first litter was whelped in 1976, by Chip x Tempest Tossed. Blacks and browns are bred. Gail J. is past-President of the Bearded Collie Club of America and remains active in the club. Gail Elizabeth has handled Gaymardon progeny to national BOB and Group wins and is now handling professionally.

GLEN EIRE. Anne and Matt Dolan, Schoharie, New York. The Dolans are building their kennel through the lovely producers Ch. Luath's Bonnie Blue Bairn, R.O.M., and Ch. Glen Eire's Molly Brown, R.O.M. Their lines are based on Osmart and Willowmead stock, with line breedings to Blue Braid.

Glen Eire acquired the great producer Ch. Willowmead's Something Super, R.O.M., who unfortunately was lost to the breed at a young age. They bred a top-producing sire, Ch. Glen Eire's Willy Wonderful, R.O.M. Anne Dolan has been an admirer of Beardies since she owned her first, Jock, when she received him as a present for her ninth birthday. He was a product of working stock. The Dolans have produced some thirty champions of all colors, but mainly blacks and browns.

HA'PENNY. J. Richard Schneider, New York City. Ha'Penny imported some of the first Beardies to be shown, including the top-winning Ch. Brambledale Blue Bonnet, C.D., R.O.M. Breedings have focused mainly on Brambledale lines, with some Edenborough lines being used. Ha'Penny sold "Bonnet" to Henrietta and Robert Lachman's Cricket Kennels, continuing co-ownership through the first two litters.

Ha'Penny has imported or produced top Beardies, including Bonnet, Ch. Ha'Penny Blue Blossom, R.O.M.; American and Canadian Ch. Chauntelle's Limelight, R.O.M.; Ch. Ha'Penny's Moon Shadow, R.O.M.; and Ch. Ha'Penny's Hoyden at Edmar, R.O.M. Progeny from this kennel have many BIS wins, Group placements, and nearly fifty championships. Ha'Penny Beardies have appeared in commercials, demonstrating the beauty and bounce of the breed.

JANDE. De Arle and Jan Masters, Lapeer, Michigan. Rising to prominence in the last few years through selective breeding and importing from Australia, England, and Wales, Jande has twenty champions, many Group winners, and a National Specialty winner to its credit.

Jande imported their top-producing brown Australian, Canadian, and American Ch. Bloody Mary, R.O.M., in 1978. Her first breeding was to Ch. Edenborough Happy Go Lucky, R.O.M., and produced six champions. The Masters have made breedings to Willowmead, Edenborough, and Brambledale stock, producing all colors.

LOCHENGAR. Jim and LaRae Conro, Thorp, Wisconsin. Lochengar was founded on Rich-Lin and Edenborough lines. The Conros' first Beardie was Rich-Lins Honey Bear, R.O.M., with American and Canadian Ch. Rich-Lins Mister Magoo, R.O.M., following shortly after. Their stock is linebred to Blue Bracken, Bonnie Blue Braid, and Cairnbahn.

The Conros have produced several multiple Group winners, despite limited breeding practices, but have been showing actively since the breed was recognized. They consistently have had dogs among the Top Ten Beardies. Lochengar breeds all colors.

PARCANA. Richard and Jo Parker, Longmont, Colorado. This kennel was founded on Ch. Parcana Silverleaf Vandyke, R.O.M., and the lovely Blue Bracken daughter, Ch. Edenborough Parcana, R.O.M., who was BOB at the 1978 BCCA match. Additional lines include Osmart. The Parkers produce all colors. Parcana promotes dogs with working ability as well as championship quality, as evidenced by their many Herding Certified dogs. Jo Parker is another breeder/judge.

RICH-LIN. Richard and Linda Nootbaar, Round Lake Beach, Illinois. Founded in 1970 with Edenborough and Broadholme lines, Rich-Lin's foundation stock included Edenborough Full O'Life, R.O.M., a producer of producers; Edenborough Loch Ness; Ch. Jaseton Princess Argonetta, R.O.M. (a Blue Bracken daughter and the Number One Miscellaneous Class dog in 1972); and Ch. Edenborough Adventure, R.O.M. (half-brother to Blue Bracken).

Rich-Lin can boast some thirty champions, several Group winners, top producers, and the first American-bred Best-in-Show Beardie, Ch. Rich-Lin's Outlaw. The Nootbaars bred the all-time top dam of all breeds, Ch. Rich-Lin's Molly of Arcadia, R.O.M. They received *Dog World's* Outstanding Service Award for contributions to the breed and to their club, and for their effort in achieving breed recognition. Rich-Lin breeds blacks and blues.

SILVERLEAF. Founded by Freedo and the late Barbara Rieseberg, Lafayette, Colorado. Importing from Willowmead and others, Silverleaf's foundation bitch was Ch. Shepherd's Help From Shiel, R.O.M. Silverleaf breeds herding and obedience dogs as well as conformation winners, and imported top-winning and producing American and Canadian Ch. Shiel's Mogador Silverleaf, C.D., R.O.M. After Barbara's death, Betty joined Freedo in marriage and in carrying on the Silverleaf tradition; Silverleaf has produced almost seventy champions to date, and breeds blacks, blues, and browns.

UNICORN. Pam Gaffney and Jennifer Jacoby, Elk Grove, California. Willowmead and Silverleaf lines are the basis for Unicorn breeding. While looking for a dog that could do justice in both obedience and conformation rings, Pam and Jennifer succumbed to the "magic" of Beardies. Their foundation bitches are the lovely Ch. Wild Silk of Willowmead, R.O.M. ("Hobbit"), and Ch. Wyndcliff's Unicorn Sterling, R.O.M., both of whom have been outstanding producers for the kennel. Ch. Unicorn's the Mighty Quinn has been one of Unicorn's top winners.

Thomas and Barbara Davies (**DUNWICH**), Robert and Henrietta Lachman (**CRICKET**), D. Ian Morrison (**CAULDBRAE**), and Larry and Maxine Levy (**HEATHGLEN**), have personally given much to the breed through their dedication in contributing time and energy to help achieve recognition and acceptance of the Bearded Collie.

The breed owes many thanks to the Beardie owners who, because of their love of the breed, served as guiding forces during the formative years of the breed and of the BCCA. Without their diligence and persistence, Beardies would not have been officially registered and brought to the public eye in such a short time.

Ch. Rich-Lin's Whiskers of Arcadia, R.O.M. Owners, Jim and Diann Shannon.

American and Canadian Ch. Gaelyn Copper Artisan, R.O.M.X., and Ch. Artisan Burnish'D Silverleaf, R.O.M.X. Owners, Harry and Ann Witte.

American and Canadian Ch. Jande's Just Dudley, American and Canadian Ch. Jande's Oxford Knight In Blue, Ch. Jande's Lucky Tri, and Ch. Jande's Lucky Mary.

Ch. Wishanger Marsh Pimpernel, C.D.; Ch. Bedlam's Go Get 'Em Garth; Ch. Raggmopp Gaelin Image; and Ch. Raggmopp Intrepid Spirit.

Canadian Kennels and Dogs

Bailie James Dalgliesh, a chief figure in Beardies in Scotland at the turn of the century, exported two dogs to Canada in 1913. These were Ellwyn Ken and Ellwyn Eagle.

The first modern Beardie to enter Canada was Brachy of Bothkennar, imported by Muriel Radner in 1963. Although Brachy was never shown or bred, Muriel Radner served as Vice President of the Bearded Collie Club of Canada (BCCC) when it was founded.

In 1968, Carol Gold (Raggmopp Kennels) imported Ch. Wishanger Marsh Pimpernel, C.D., R.O.M., "Gael" (who became the first Canadian champion). Owner and dog aroused interest in the breed by appearing anywhere and everywhere—at fun matches, on television shows, in school programs, and with drill teams. Although a few pet quality dogs were imported, the show people were slow to react because of the difficulty "new" breeds have in being recognized.

A true dog lover, especially a devoted Bearded Collie enthusiast, can't be kept down, and Carol Gold's persistence brought the breed to the attention of Alice Bixler Clark (Bedlam Kennels) and Barbara Blake (Colbara Kennels). They were instrumental in forming the BCCC. Gael and Raggmopp Kennels laid claim to producing the first Beardie litter whelped in Canada. The nine puppies sired by Osmart Brown Barnaby (Yager Aplomb at Osmart x Ch. Osmart Bonnie Black Pearl) culminated in the breed's being recognized by the Canadian Kennel Club in 1970. A brown bitch from this litter, Raggmopp First Impression, became the first North American-bred champion and also is an American and Canadian C.D.

Kennels most actively influencing the breed in Canada include:

ALGOBRAE. Lindy and Jeanette Waite, Sault Ste. Marie, Ontario. Based on Edenborough lines in 1977, particularly English, Canadian, American and Bermudian Ch. Edenborough Grey Shadow, R.O.M., Algobrae produced Canadian and American Ch. Algobrae Sterling Silver, R.O.M., a top winner and top producer.

BEDLAM. Alice Bixler Clark, Maple, Ontario. Based on Raggmopp (First Impression, alias "Bounce"), Bothkennar, and Osmart lines, Bedlam has bred eighteen Canadian champions, one American, and one American and Canadian. This kennel is the breeder of Bedlam's Go Get'em Garth, American and Canadian C.D., who took Winners Dog and Best Canadian-Bred Dog over the Specials at the 1978 Canadian Specialty when only six months and two days old! Bedlam also bred the first Best Brace in Show.

CLASSICAL. Bea and Kevin Sawka, Queensville, Ontario. The Sawkas are owners of Ch. Algobrae Sterling Silver, R.O.M., Ch. Benbecula Classical Jazz, and Ch. Pottersdale Paris, R.O.M. Both of the latter two were BOS in a United States National Specialty. The kennel is breeding some lovely youngsters.

COLBARA. Colin and Barbara Blake, Waterdown, Ontario. One of the pioneers in Canada, Colbara imported stock from Brambledale, owned the noted winner International Ch. Willowferry's Victor, R.O.M., and bred the first C.D.X. winner, Colbara Black Molly.

RAGGMOPP. Carol Gold, Toronto, Ontario. Based on Wishanger lines, Raggmopp has produced impressive statistics despite averaging less than one litter bred per year. Included are two Specialty BIS, a Specialty BOS, and several other winners. One of these, Ch. Raggmopp Bellarmine, C.D.X., won Reserve BIS in New Delhi, India.

SHAGGYLANE. Barbara Niddrie, Calgary, Alberta. Shaggylane's lines go back to Wishanger and Osmart, through Yager, Cannamoor, Raggmopp, and Wichnor. Shaggylane has been breeding since the early 1970s, and is the home of five champion males, three of which hold both Canadian and American championships and have made several Group wins. Canadian and American Ch. Shaggylane Beaming Teak, R.O.M., has captured wins in both Canada and the United States.

The following are Canada's top Bearded Collies:

American and Canadian Ch. Algobrae Sterling Silver, R.O.M. (International Ch. Edenborough Grey Shadow x Monyash Whirlpool). Owners, Bea and Kevin Sawka. "Tyler" took a BIS at only sixteen months of age. He was Number One BCCC Beardie for 1979, 1981, and 1983, and made multiple wins at the BCCC and other Specialties. He is the sire of some twenty Canadian and American champions. He has wonderful expression and a lovely coat. (Black.)

Ch. Banacek Fawn Fabric, R.O.M. (Ch. Osmart Bonnie Blue Braid x Banacek Black Bobbin). Owner, Carol Gold. "Rodney" is the sire of several winners in both Canada and the United States. (Fawn.)

Canadian and American Ch. Benbecula's Classical Jazz. (Ch. Algobrae Sterling Silver x Algobrae Chelsea Blue). Owners, Bea and Kevin Sawka. "Jasmine" was a champion at eight months, has multiple BOS wins, was BOS at the 1983 BCCA Specialty, and was the Number One BCCC bitch in 1981. Like her name, she is classy and jazzy, a lovely bitch with presence, good structure, and style. (Black.)

Ch. Brambledale Boz, R.O.M. (Braelyn Broadholme Crofter x Brambledale Barberry). Owners, Colin and Barbara Blake. Stud Dog Winner at the 1983 BCCA, Boz is the sire of top winners in both conformation and obedience. He is a happy dog whose tail never stops wagging. (Black.)

English, American, Canadian, and Bermudian Ch. Edenborough Grey Shadow, R.O.M. (Ch. Edenborough Blue Bracken x Broadholme Christina). Owners, Lindy and Jeanette Waite. This Beardie, tops in both obedience and conformation, has a Specialty BIS and four all-breed wins. He is the sire of two BIS winners, Canadian and American Ch. Algobrae Sterling Silver and Ch. Tudor Lodge Koala at Crisch. (Black.)

English, American, and Canadian Ch. Edenborough Kara Kara of Josanda (litter sister to Grey Shadow). Owner, Taylor. "Judy" won BOB at the first BCCA National Specialty and was Number One BCCC Beardie in 1978; she is the dam of an American BIS bitch. (Black.)

American and Canadian Ch. Macmont Mackintosh (Swinford Sky Rocket At Macmont x Charncroft Charisma). Owner, Jean Jagersma. A three-time BIS Specialty winner, Mackintosh was winner of 1986 BCCA Veteran Dogs, at age nine. (Black.)

Ch. Misty Shadow of Willowmead, R.O.M. (1971-1986) (English Ch. Wishanger Cairnbahn x English Ch. Broadholme Cindy Sue of Willowmead). Owner, Jean

Canadian and American Ch. Algobrae Sterling Silver. Owners, Bea and Kevin Sawka.

Canadian and American Ch. Banacek Fawn Fabric. Owner, Carol Gold.

Jagersma. First to win a Group First, and first BIS winner, Misty Shadow is the sire of many winners. He has a beautiful coat and exemplary movement and temperament. (Black.)

Ch. Pottersdale Paris, R.O.M. (Pepperland Lyric John at Potterdale x Blumberg Hadriana at Potterdale). Owner, Sawka and Albarano. A happy boy who captured everyone's heart as a baby in 1983, "Parader" came back the following year to win BOS at the BCCA National Specialty, as a newly finished champion. (Brown.)

Canadian and American Ch. Shaggylane Beaming Teak, R.O.M. (Ch. Raggmopp First Chance x Yager Gigue). Owner, Niddrie. This top winner in Canada is a multiple BIS winner both in Canada and the United States. Teak has an amazing record of thirteen BIS wins, thirty-five Group First wins, and seventy-one Group placements in Canada and the United States. He is also the only Beardie to take all-breed BIS wins in both countries. (Brown.)

Canadian, Bermudian, and American Ch. Willowferry Victor, R.O.M. (1970-1982) (Wishanger Cairnbahn x Filabey Finella). Owner, Blake. "Hamish" scored more than one hundred seventy BOB wins and is the sire of some twenty-five champions. He has a gorgeous head and expression. (Black.)

Ch. Wishanger Marsh Pimpernel, C.D., R.O.M. (Wishanger River Number x Wishanger Creeping Tansy). Owner, Carol Gold. The first Canadian Bearded Collie champion and companion dog title winner, "Gael" has National Specialty BIS wins and several Group wins. She rounded off her accomplishments by ranking in the Top Three for the breed in Canada, and by showing her producing ability as a multiple top Beardie Brood Bitch. (Blue.)

Three of Canada's earliest Beardies. Left, Ch. Wishanger Marsh Pimpernel, C.D.; on chair, Osmart Brown Barnaby; right, Hermione of Stonehall.

Canadian and American Ch. Benbecula's Classical Jazz. Owners, Bea and Kevin Sawka.

American and Canadian Ch. Shaggylane Beaming Teak. Owner, Barbara Niddrie.

Ch. Potterdale Paris (Canadian). Owners, Bea and Kevin Sawka.

73

Ch., O.T.Ch. Windcache A Briery Bess doing her thing. Owner, Barbara Prescott.

Show and Obedience Competition

Centuries ago, it was common practice to hold agricultural fairs in conjunction with spring and fall religious festivals, and to these gatherings, cattle, dogs, and other livestock were brought for exchange. As time went on, it became customary to provide entertainment, too. Dogs often participated in such sporting events as bull baiting, bear baiting, and ratting. Then the dog that exhibited the greatest skill in the arena was also the one that brought the highest price when time came for barter or sale. Today, these fairs seem a far cry from our highly organized bench shows and field trials. But they were the forerunners of modern dog shows and played an important role in shaping the development of purebred dogs.

The first organized dog show was held at Newcastle, England, in 1859. Later that same year, a show was held at Birmingham. At both shows dogs were divided into four classes and only Pointers and Setters were entered. In 1860, the first dog show in Germany was held at Apoldo, where nearly one hundred dogs were exhibited and entries were divided into six groups. Interest expanded rapidly, and by the time the Paris Exhibition was held in 1878, the dog show was a fixture of international importance.

In the United States, the first organized bench show was held in 1874 in conjunction with the meeting of the Illinois State Sportsmen's Association in Chicago, and all entries were dogs of sporting breeds. Although the show was a rather casual affair, interest spread quickly. Before the end of the year, shows were held in Oswego, New York; Mineola, New York; and Memphis, Tennessee. And the latter combined a bench show with the first organized field trial ever held in the United States. In January 1875, an all-breed show (the first in the United States) was held at Detroit, Michigan. From then on, interest increased rapidly, though rules were not always uniform, for there was no organization through which to coordinate activities until September 1884 when The American Kennel Club was founded. Now the largest dog registering organization in the world, the AKC is an association of several hundred member clubs—all breed, specialty, field trial, and obedience groups—each represented by a delegate to the AKC.

The several thousand shows and trials held annually in the United States do much to stimulate interest in breeding to produce better looking, sounder, purebred dogs. For breeders, shows provide a means of measuring the merits of their work as compared with accomplishments of other breeders. For hundreds of thousands of dog fanciers, they provide an absorbing hobby.

Bench Shows

At bench (or conformation) shows, dogs are rated comparatively on their physical qualities (or conformation) in accordance with breed Standards which have been approved by The American Kennel Club. Characteristics such as size, coat, color, placement of eye or ear, general soundness, etc., are the basis for selecting the best dog in a class. Only purebred dogs are eligible to compete and if the show is one where points toward a championship are to be awarded, a dog must be at least six months old.

Bench shows are of various types. An all-breed show has classes for all of the breeds recognized by The American Kennel Club as well as a Miscellaneous Class for breeds not recognized, such as the Greater Swiss Mountain Dog, the Spinoni Italiani, etc. A sanctioned match is an informal meeting where dogs compete but not for championship points. A specialty show is confined to a single breed. Other shows may restrict entries to champions of record, to American-bred dogs, etc. Competition for Junior Showmanship or for Best Brace, Best Team, or Best Local Dog may be included. Also, obedience competition is held in conjunction with many bench shows.

The term "bench show" is somewhat confusing in that shows of this type may be either "benched" or "unbenched." At the former, each dog is assigned an individual numbered stall where he must remain throughout the show except for times when he is being judged, groomed, or exercised. At unbenched shows, no stalls are provided and dogs are kept in their owners' cars, on leash, or in crates when not being judged.

A show where a dog is judged for conformation actually constitutes an elimination contest. To begin with, the dogs of a single breed compete with others of their breed in one of the regular classes: Puppy, Novice, Bred by Exhibitor, American-Bred, or Open, and finally, Winners, where the top dogs of the preceding five classes meet. The next step for Beardies is the judging for Best of Breed. Here the Winners Dog and Winners Bitch compete with any champions that are entered, together with any undefeated dogs that have competed in additional non-regular classes. The dog named Best of Breed then goes on to compete with the other Best of Breed winners in his Group. (The Bearded Collie is a member of the Herding Group.) The dogs that win in Group competition then compete for the final and highest honor, Best in Show.

Championship points are awarded the Winners Dog

and Winners Bitch. The number of points awarded varies, depending upon such factors as the number of dogs competing, the Schedule of Points established by the Board of Directors of the AKC, and whether the dog goes on to win Best of Breed, the Group, and Best in Show.

In order to become a champion, a dog must win fifteen points, including points from at least two major wins—that is, at least two shows where three or more points are awarded. The major wins must be under two different judges, and one or more of the remaining points must be won under a third judge. The most points ever awarded at a show is five and the least is one, so, in order to become a champion, a dog must be exhibited and win in at least three shows, and usually he is shown many times before he wins his championship.

Pure-Bred Dogs—American Kennel Gazette Events Calendar and other dog publications contain lists of forthcoming shows, together with names and addresses of sponsoring organizations to which you may write for entry forms and information relative to fees, closing dates, etc. Before entering your dog in a show for the first time, you should familiarize yourself with the regulations and rules governing competition. You may secure such information from The American Kennel Club or from a local dog club specializing in your breed. It is essential that you also familiarize yourself with the AKC approved Standard for your breed so you will be fully aware of characteristics worthy of merit as well as those considered faulty, or possibly even serious enough to disqualify the dog from competition. For instance, monorchidism (failure of one testicle to descend) and cryptorchidism (failure of both testicles to descend) are disqualifying faults in all breeds.

If possible, you should first attend a show as a spectator and observe judging procedures from ringside. It will also be helpful to join a local breed club and to participate in sanctioned matches before entering an all-breed show.

The dog should be equipped with a narrow show leash and a show collar—never an ornamented or spiked collar. For benched shows, either a bench crate or a metal-link bench chain to fasten the dog to the bench will be needed. For unbenched shows, the dog's crate should be taken along so that he may be confined in comfort when he is not appearing in the ring. A dog should never be left in a car with all the windows closed. In hot weather the temperature will become unbearable in a very short time. Heat exhaustion may result from even a short period of confinement, and death may ensue.

Food and water dishes will be needed, as well as a supply of the food and water to which the dog is accustomed. Brushes and combs are also necessary, so that you may give the dog's coat a final grooming after you arrive at the show.

Familiarize yourself with the schedule of classes ahead of time, for the dog must be fed and exercised and permitted to relieve himself, and any last-minute grooming completed before his class is called. Both you and the dog should be ready to enter the ring unhurriedly. A good deal of skill in conditioning, training, and handling is required if a dog is to be presented properly. And it is essential that the handler be composed, for a jittery handler will transmit nervousness to the dog.

Once the class is assembled in the ring, the judge will ask that the dogs be paraded in line, moving counter-clockwise in a circle. If you have trained your dog well, you will have no difficulty controlling him in the ring, where he must change pace quickly and gracefully and walk and trot elegantly and proudly with head erect. The show dog must also stand quietly for inspection, posing like a statue for several minutes while the judge observes his structure in detail, examines teeth, feet, coat, etc. When the judge calls your dog forward for individual inspection, do not attempt to converse, but answer any questions the judge may ask.

In examining the class, the judge measures each dog against the ideal described in the Standard, then measures the dogs against each other in a comparative sense, and selects for first place the dog that comes closest to conforming to the Standard for its breed. If your dog isn't among the winners, don't grumble. If he places first, don't brag loudly. For a bad loser is disgusting, but a poor winner is insufferable.

Obedience Competition

For hundreds of years, dogs have been used in England and Germany in connection with police and guard work, and their working potential has been evaluated through tests devised to show agility, strength, and courage. Organized training has also been popular with English and German breeders for many years, although it was practiced primarily for the purpose of training large breeds in aggressive tactics.

There was little interest in obedience training in the United States until 1933 when Mrs. Whitehouse Walker returned from England and enthusiastically introduced the sport. Two years later, Mrs. Walker persuaded The American Kennel Club to approve organized obedience activities and to assume jurisdiction over obedience rules. Since then, interest has increased at a phenomenal rate, for obedience competition is not only a sport the average spectator can follow readily, but also a sport for which the average owner can train his own dog. Obedience competition is suitable for all breeds. Furthermore, there is no limit to the number of dogs that may win in competition, for each dog is scored individually on the basis of a point rating system.

The dog is judged on his response to certain commands, and if he gains a high enough score in three successive trials under different judges, he wins an obedience title. Titles awarded are "C.D."—Companion Dog; "C.D.X."

—Companion Dog Excellent; and "U.D."—Utility Dog. A fourth title, the "T.D." or Tracking Dog title, may be won at any time and tests for it are held apart from dog shows. The qualifying score is a minimum of 170 points out of a possible total of 200, with no score in any one exercise less than 50 percent of the points allotted.

Since the C.D., C.D.X., and U.D. titles are progressive, earlier titles (with the exception of the Tracking title) are dropped as a dog acquires the next higher title. If an obedience (or conformation) title is gained in another country in addition to the United States, that fact is signified by the name of the country followed by the title.

Effective July 1, 1977, the AKC approved the awarding of an additional title, Obedience Trial Champion (O.T.Ch.). To be eligible for this title, a dog must have earned the Utility Dog title and then must earn one hundred championship points in competition, placing First three times under different judges.

In late 1979, the Board of Directors of The American Kennel Club approved the test for the Tracking Dog Excellent (T.D.X) title. Eligibility for this title is limited to dogs that have already earned the Tracking Dog title.

Trials for obedience trained dogs, held at most of the larger bench shows and obedience training clubs, are to be found in almost all communities today. Information concerning forthcoming trials and lists of obedience training clubs are included regularly in *Pure-Bred Dogs— American Kennel Gazette Events Calendar* and other dog publications. Pamphlets containing rules and regulations governing obedience competition are available upon request from The American Kennel Club, 51 Madison Avenue, New York, New York 10010. Rules are revised occasionally, so if you are interested in participating in obedience competition, you should be sure your copy of the regulations is current.

All dogs must comply with the same rules, although in broad jump, high jump, and bar jump exercises, the jumps are adjusted to the size of the breed. Classes at obedience trials are divided into Novice (A and B), Open (A and B), and Utility (which may be divided into A and B, at the option of the sponsoring club and with the approval of The American Kennel Club).

The Novice class is for dogs that have not won the title Companion Dog. In Novice A, no person who has previously handled, owned, or co-owned a dog that has won a C.D. title in the obedience ring at a licensed or member trial, and no person who has regularly trained such a dog, may enter or handle a dog. The handler must be the dog's owner or a member of the owner's family. In Novice B, dogs may be handled by the owner or any other person.

The Open A class is for dogs that have won the C.D. title but have not won the C.D.X. title. Obedience judges and licensed handlers may not enter or handle dogs in this class. Each dog must be handled by the owner or by a member of his immediate family. The Open B class is for dogs that have won the C.D. or C.D.X A dog may continue to compete in this class after it has won the U.D. Dogs in this class may be handled by the owner or any other person.

The Utility class is for dogs that have won the title C.D.X. Dogs that have won the U.D. may continue to compete in this class, and dogs may be handled by the owner or any other person. Provided the AKC approves, a club may choose to divide the Utility class into Utility A and Utility B. When this is done, the Utility A class is for dogs that have won the title C.D.X. and have not won the title U.D. Obedience judges and licensed handlers may not enter or handle dogs in this class. All other dogs that are eligible for the Utility class but not eligible for Utility A may be entered in Utility B.

Novice competition includes such exercises as heeling on and off lead, the stand for examination, coming on recall, and the long sit and the long down.

In Open competition, the dog must perform such exercises as heeling free, the drop on recall, and the retrieve on the flat and over the high jump. Also, he must execute the broad jump. The dog must complete the long sit and long down with the owner out of sight.

In the Utility class, competition includes scent discrimination, the directed retrieve, the signal exercise, directed jumping, and the group examination.

Tracking is always done out-of-doors, of course, and, for obvious reasons, cannot be held at a dog show. The dog must follow a scent trail that is about a quarter mile in length. He is also required to find a scent object (glove, wallet, or other article) left by a stranger who has walked the course to lay down the scent. The dog is required to follow the trail a half to two hours after the scent is laid.

Obedience training should be made appealing. Change the pattern of training—for dogs become bored if the routine is always the same. Show the dog that you are enjoying yourself, and make the reward more enticing than temptations.

If you use harsh methods when training your Beardie, he simply will quit. You will become two unyielding beings working against one another, rather than handler and Beardie cooperating with each other as a team. Bearded Collies should be and normally are happy workers.

A Beardie is an intelligent but sensitive dog. He does not respond well to force or to rough handling. The best results are obtained by training with a firm but gentle tone. Training a Beardie requires persistence and patience. As is true with any dog, the owner must maintain the upper hand. A Beardie cannot be allowed to believe he is the boss, or he will gain control of your entire life.

An ideal way to train a dog for obedience competition is

American and Canadian Ch. Beagold's Black Tiffany, C.D.X., Sch. A.D., T.T., R.O.M. Owners, Roy and Joan Blumire.

Ch. Arcadia's Bentley O'Walkoway, C.D.X. Owner, Carli Bates.

to join an obedience class or a training club. In organized class work, beginners' classes cover pretty much the same exercises as those described in the chapter on manners. However, through class work you will develop greater precision than is possible in training your dog by yourself. Amateur handlers often cause the dog to be penalized, for if the handler fails to abide by the rules, it is the dog that suffers the penalty. A common infraction of the rules is using more than one signal or command where regulations stipulate only one may be used. Classwork will help eliminate such errors, which the owner may make unconsciously if he is working alone. Working with a class also will acquaint both dog and handler with ring procedure so that obedience trials will not present unforeseen problems.

Thirty or forty owners and dogs often comprise a class, and exercises are performed in unison, with individual instruction provided if it is required. The procedure followed in training—in fact, even wording of various commands—may vary from instructor to instructor. Equipment used will vary somewhat, also, but usually will include a training collar and leash, a long line, a dumbbell, and a jumping stick. The latter may be a short length of heavy doweling or a broom handle and both it and the dumbbell are usually painted white for increased visibility.

Some training classes do not allow a bitch in season to participate, so before enrolling a female dog, you should determine whether she may be expected to come into season before the classes are scheduled to end. If you think she will, it is better to wait and enroll her in a later course, rather than start the course and then miss classes for several weeks.

In addition to the time devoted to actual work in class, the dog must have regular, daily training sessions for practice at home. Before each class or home training session, the dog should be exercised so he will not be highly excited when the session starts, and he must be given an opportunity to relieve himself before the session begins. (Should he have an accident during the class, it is your responsibility to clean up after him.) The dog should be fed several hours before time for the class to begin or else after the class is over—never just before going to class.

If you decide to enter your dog in obedience competition, it is well to enter a small, informal show the first time. Dogs are usually called in the order in which their names appear in the catalog, so as soon as you arrive at the show, acquaint yourself with the schedule. If your dog is not the first to be judged, spend some time at ringside, observing the routine so you will know what to expect when your dog's turn comes.

In addition to collar, leash, and other equipment, you should take your dog's food and water pans and a supply of the food and water to which he is accustomed. You should also take his brushes and combs in order to give him a last-minute brushing before you enter the ring. It is important that the dog look his best even though he isn't to be judged on his appearance.

Before entering the ring, exercise your dog, give him a drink of water, and permit him to relieve himself. Once your dog enters the ring, give him your full attention and give voice commands distinctly so he will hear and understand, for there will be many distractions at ringside.

American and Canadian Ch. Cannamoor Honey Rose, American and Canadian C.D., T.D.X. Owner, Virginia Parsons.

Katie Keller and "Murphy."

Junior Handlers and Junior Showmanship

The future of dog showing, like the future of the world, lies in the hands of our youth. Young people, as well as their older counterparts, start by training a dog to behave in everyday situations. Juniors may compete in regular competition in obedience and conformation, and The American Kennel Club has established classes in Junior Showmanship.

Junior handling classes are offered at most all-breed and Specialty shows, including the BCCA National Specialty. In these classes, juniors are judged on their ability as a handler. Finesse and professionalism are the items that count, not the quality of the dog. Of course, it helps if the dog is well-trained, but championship or even good show quality is not necessary.

Class divisions are Novice Junior, Open Junior, Novice Senior, and Open Senior. The winners of each class may compete for Best Junior. After three First Place wins in Novice classes, the handler progresses to Open competition. Thus, Novice Junior is for boys and girls ten to thirteen years of age on the day of the show, who have not placed First three times in a Novice class at a licensed show. Open Junior is for boys and girls ten to thirteen years of age who previously have placed First three times.

The Senior classes are for handlers thirteen to seventeen years of age on the day of the show, with other requirements the same as for the Junior classes.

The dog must be owned or co-owned by the junior handler or by the handler's father, mother, brother, sister, uncle, aunt, grandparent, or corresponding step- or half-relatives. The dog must be eligible for regular competition in AKC-licensed shows.

Beardies are attractive, flashy dogs for junior competition. However, Beardies love to play and behave like clowns during applause. Serious competitors need practice to gain control, since a well-behaved dog is a must in the ring.

It also is important for the dog to be well groomed. Nails should be trimmed, ears and teeth clean, coat shining and brushed. The dog should be in good weight.

The judge may ask questions of the junior handler, such as "What kind of bite is preferred?" or "What color is disqualifying?" or "Where is the stifle?" The handler should be knowledgeable of the breed Standard and of general conformation.

The judge may ask the handler to gait the dog on an "L" shaped or a triangular course. All exhibitors should listen closely to the judge's instructions, but the junior handler must pay particular attention and follow requests precisely. This is because the junior is judged on prowess as a handler, whereas judging in other rings is based on the dog itself and on its performance.

The judge sometimes seeks to ascertain whether the handler is confident of the manner in which the dog should be shown. For instance, a judge might move the dog's leg into an incorrect position to see if the junior will correct it. Another maneuver is for the judge to move behind the handler. Since a handler should never block the judge's view of the dog, the junior should move to the other side of the dog.

The handler should keep the dog showing to best advantage at all times, but should not overhandle to the point of making the dog nervous, or seeming "fussbudgety." He should have an eye on the judge and an eye on the dog at all times, and this takes lots of practice.

Some juniors are reared "with a dog leash in one hand and a baby rattle in the other," so competition can be stiff, especially for those not from a dog-oriented family. But the competition provides juniors with opportunities to learn about dogs in general and about their own breed in particular. They enjoy a camaraderie with their dog and with other juniors. Junior competition prepares participants for a future which may include breeding, professional handling, and/or judging. Even if a future in dogs is not the outcome, junior showmanship provides opportunities for learning responsibility and good sportsmanship, and acquiring self-confidence—which help in establishing a good foundation for a future in any field.

The following are some of the junior handlers who have made a name for themselves in Bearded Collies either in the conformation ring or in junior handling competition.

Kirsten Haarsager started out with Saint Bernards at the age of seven, and has also shown Sussex, Clumber, and Springer Spaniels. When she was fourteen she trained and showed Ch. Arcadia's Mint Julep, age fifteen months, to her title. With "Julie," Kirsten was never out of the placings as a junior. Now she is training her dog in obedience and is handling for her parents.

Kathleen Keller is an active junior whose favorite memory is the day she went Best Junior, at age eleven, from the Novice Junior class at an all-breed show. Her competition was twenty-one other juniors, most of whom were older and more experienced. Her dog on that day was a high-spirited eight-month-old puppy, Charisma's Basic Black, "Murphy." Kathleen's sister, **Meaghan** also shows Beardies.

Gail Elizabeth Miller set an impressive record by qualifying for the Westminster Kennel Club show four times and placing second in 1984. She has handled Beardies to some one hundred BOB wins and obedience titles. Gail has finished ten dogs to their championships, and steered two dogs to BOB at the National Specialty show. Ch. Gaymardon's Chesapeake Mist, owned by her parents, won at the 1982 BCCA show, and Ch. Jande's Lucky Tri, C.D., owned by Bruce and Janet Buehrig and Donnell Miller, went BOB at the 1983 Specialty. At twelve, Gail handled Ch. Gaymardon's Baron of Bramel to the W.D. title at the BCCA Specialty. Gail also has won several Group placements with her own dog, Number One American-Bred, 1982, Ch. Gaymardon's Bouncing Bogart, "John." She was the top junior showman by a wide margin, and showed it through her professionalism in both junior showmanship and conformation competition. She now has graduated to professional handling and has recently guided a client's dog to a BIS!

Kirsten Haarsager and "Julie."

A Beardie and her master. Photo by Chris Walkowicz.

Beth Schaeffer started in junior handling at age eleven by taking her seven-month-old puppy, Crisch Panda of Briery Knob, to R.W.B. at the 1983 BCCA Specialty. Beth is showing in both the conformation ring and junior showmanship, along with her sister, **Michelle.**

Elise VanFleet has been building up an impressive list of wins, both at the Specialty and at all-breed shows, with Ch. Artisan Copper Breagan.

Janelle Webb began showing when she was eleven, with Ch. Parcana's Holly of Mereworth, racking up several wins in the junior ring.

Herding Trials

The Bearded Collie Club of America instituted herding-instinct tests and herding-championship tests in 1893. The working committee—Mari (Shaffer) Taggert, Jo Parker, and Sue Holm—created the program, making Bearded Collies the first AKC-registered breed to offer testing and titles of achievement in herding. Several Beardies already have earned the herding instinct certificate, and Rogue's Hollow Tweed, H.Ch., owned by Mari Taggert and Sue Holm, has become the first Herding Champion despite a rocky beginning. After eight homes in his first two years of life, along with neglect and abuse, he survived—and thrived after he finally landed on Mari Taggert's doorstep. Tweed exemplifies the charm, intelligence, and hardiness of the breed.

Beardies are still working as herding dogs in other countries, and even in America we can boast some working Beardies. The herding instinct is being preserved by competitions.

British records show that Bearded Collies were used to gather and circle the flock. The working Beardies are categorized as either "huntaway" or "strong-eyed," with each type having its advocates. The Scottish shepherds prefer the huntaway dog, which ferrets out sheep from the rocks and hills. Showing its eagerness by using noise and agility to drive the sheep from its hiding places, the dog twists its body in fleet turns and maneuvers. It must be a powerful dog, able to take on a disagreeable ram or disgruntled ewe. Shepherds chose Beardies because they are strong, dependable, and good-natured.

This type of herding dog must be especially independent, because it may be out of sight of its master for hours at a time. The continual barking not only moves the sheep but also keeps the shepherd in touch with his dog and flock. Some shepherds, however, prefer that the dog bark only on command.

The very thing that can be irritating to owners—noise—is indicative of herding instinct. The huntaway dog must use noise to gather the sheep and to mark its own location, and must have speed to outrun the sheep, and bone for the demands of working the hill country.

The strong-eyed dog uses its hypnotic stare to control the sheep, and this type is preferred by the English shepherds. These dogs work on command of the shepherd. Of course, strong-eyed dogs also need sturdy bone.

The first Bearded Collies had to be spry and strong, to hold up to the hill country, which was so demanding of working stock. The coat protected them from inclement weather. Even the hair between the pads of the feet served as protection, shielding the feet from sharp-edged rocks.

Hill herding was not the only task required of Beardies, and dogs varied in size according to their jobs. The dogs working in the lowlands were the smallest, with the highland dogs needing more size for gathering and driving the flock to market. The Smithfield (or market) dogs were the largest. Difference in size was taken into account when the British Standard was written, listing the height requirement as being twenty to twenty-four inches.

Tales abound of working Beardies leaping from point to point, sometimes a distance of seven to eight feet! A Highland shepherd attests to his Beardie bringing out his sheep, which mingled with others during the day. At his master's sharp whistles, the dog cut out his own sheep, bringing them home. In six years, he had never brought the wrong sheep home. As the shepherd says, "The Beardie—aye—he's a topper!"

Beardie puppies often show herding instinct by barking, chasing, gripping (nipping), driving, and eyeing. These natural urges should be channeled and developed constructively.

TRAINING

Care must be taken when introducing your Beardie to stock. Wait until the puppy is physically able to avoid injury to himself and is mentally capable of following instructions. Some dogs are ready to begin their training at six months.

Obviously, not everyone who wishes to compete is able to keep herds of cattle or flocks of sheep, so most American trainers use ducks. Three to five ducks are not expensive, and they have the added benefit of being easier to transport and confine, as well as being cheaper to feed.

Trainers recommend teaching the Beardie a few basic commands, finding an open space in which to work, and clipping the wings of the ducks before beginning training. The dog should be trained to "down," preferably at a distance. Teaching the dog to respond to whistle commands is beneficial, because the shrill sound carries farther than does the human voice.

Although hand or vocal commands can be used, it still is wise to teach the dog whistle commands. If the trainer is unable to whistle properly through pursed lips, a shepherd's whistle or two-tone whistle will do.

The dog is trained with a pole about ten feet long, preferably a reed or bamboo pole which is flexible. The dog is taught to bring the ducks in toward the trainer, who backs up, using the commands "walk on" or "steady on." No mouthing is permitted, and the dog is kept at a distance by snapping the pole on the ground and using vocal reprimands. Nipping is allowed for larger livestock, but discouraged when the dog is working with ducks.

The dog is taught to circle to his right when given the command "away to me," and to his left when given the command "go by." This makes the dog proficient in keeping the flock gathered. The distance should be increased until the dog is able to work the flock when as far as two hundred yards from the trainer.

Once the dog is competent in gathering the flock, training requiring more finesse can be introduced, such as flushing from tight areas, halting on a sit or down when entering or leaving a gate, and driving away from the trainer.

According to the parent club regulations, dogs must be six months old and be registered with the AKC or a foreign kennel club, or have Individual Listing Privilege (ILP) in order to compete for the H.C. (Herding Certificate). Neutered dogs and those possessing breed Standard faults are eligible.

To earn the certificate, the dog must "show sustained interest," either by circling or driving. He must be reliable off leash. The dog must not be so aggressive toward the livestock as to threaten their health or safety, and must not be fearful or disinterested. The dog is rated on style, approach, aggressiveness, temperament, "bark," "eye," and "wearing" (tiring).

To earn the herding championship title, a dog must have been awarded fifteen points in herding competition. Owners may have their dogs participate in and earn points from any number of classes in a trial. Points must be won against competition and under at least two different judges. Dogs receiving High in Trial win points for the total number of dogs defeated.

Point schedules and information on competition and hosting certificate and championship trials may be obtained from the Bearded Collie Club of America.

Beardies demonstrating herding expertise.

HERDING CERTIFIED BEARDIES

The following Beardies have received the Herding Certificate. The name of the individual(s) who owned the dog at the time the certificate was awarded follows the name of the dog.

Ch. Aellen's Castle in the Sky, Prescott
Aellen's Cinnamon Rose, Pinder
Ch. Aellen's Dawn of Blue Fantasia, Rutherford
Aellen's Queen of Willister, Kennamer
Ch. Arcadia's Bentley O'Walkoway, C.D.X., Bates
Arcadia Cheyenne, Norman
Ch. Arcadia's Perrier, Haarsager
Arcadia's Rajin Cajun, Holm
Arcadia-Wildwood Blue Bangle, DeFore
Ba-lin's Free Wheelin Willie, Tranquillo
Barney's Bursting Charisma, Gibson
Ch. Beaconview Ebony at Colbara, C.D., Keller
Ch. Bearanson Blue Stocking, Billman
Bearanson Bristol Cream, Gunn
Bi Mi Dorka's Branach Brudich, Dixon
Birchwood Farms Higgins, Kanas
Ch. Black Knight of Thimbleberry, Karnes
Bon Di's Aldebaran of Alamos, Cooper
Ch. Bosques Pampas Patty, C.D., McDonald
Callander Geordie Odhe, Tompkins
Ch. Charisma's Basic Black, Brown and Keller
Charisma's Erin of Beaconview, Lovett
Ch. Charisma's Wee Trousers, Snow
Ch. Classical Achates On Parade, Lewis
Ch. Crisch Debut At Candelaria, Spicer
Daybreak Bearded Dreamer, Lothian
Ch. Daybreak Blue at Lonetree, Edner and Raker
Ch. Daybreak Rising Sun, C.D., Prescott
Ch. Daybreak Storm at Candalaria, C.D., Spicer
Edenborough Black Knight, Smith
Edmar's Darling Chelsea, Peterson
Emshire's Nativity, Brown and Emke
Emshire's Shamanda, Kanas
Foxlane's Chatter Box, Gunn
Foxlane's Tam O'Shanter, Conrad
Ch. Gaymardon's Challenger, Karnes
Ch. Gaymardon's Chesapeake Mist, Miller
Ch. Gaymardon's Crack O'Dawn, Miller
Ch. Gaymardon's Yorktown Yankee, Miller
Ch. Glen Eire's Bedazlin Beethoven, C.D.X., Robinson
Ch. Glen Eire Laird At Lonetree, Edner
Harmony's One Night Stand, Stevens
Haute Ecole Tally-Ho O'the Picts, Radtke and Cline
Ch. Highlander Lorna Doone, Tilson
Ch. Hue N Cry O'the Picts, O'Bryan and Radtke
Ch. Jande Alexander's Ragtime Band, Robinson
Kweo's Bit O'Blue Heaven, DeWitt
Lancer's Eeco of Cin-dee, Sarandos
La Primavera of Lonetree, Edner
LeVontz's Flicker of Fame, Sarandos
Llwynogen's Arcadia Fair Isle, McLeod
Llwynogen's Arcadia Fenwick, Stapler
Lochengar's Going My Way, Leeper and Conro
Lochengar's Going Places, Thompson
Ch. Lonetree's Midnight Blue Nodak, Nolan
Loneview Blk Bobby McArry, Foxworthy
Ch. Longview Blu Chas ClanArry, Jeris
Lord Barclay of Lonetree, Aron
Loud N Clear O'the Picts, Maunder and Cline
Love's Misseur Beaucaire, Ramboud
McNaughtons Marshall Dillon, Lenberg
Mistymorn Jorji of Willowisp, Banfield
Monet's Sunrise at Lonetree, Harris
Paisley Cr Dasher At Oak Meadows, Mickelson
Ch. Parcana Heart Throb, Parker
Ch. Parcana Kylie, Parker
Parcana Pay the Piper, Haarsager
Ch. Parcana's Penosa Chelsea, Beck and Parker
Ch. Parcana Portrait, R.O.M., Parker
Ch. Parcana Reginald, Beck
Ch. Parcana Silverleaf Vandyke, R.O.M., Parker
Parchment Farm's Annie Laurie, Tilson
Ch. Parchment Farm's Mr. Kite, C.D., Tilson
Ch. Raisin's Pepsi Challenge, Reese
Regal Manor's Enchantress, Carroll and Henry
H.Ch. Rogue's Hollow Tweed, Holm and Taggert
Shanna-Dawn's Moussorgski, Ouillette
Shanna-Dawn's Sea Chanty, McCarthy
Ch. Shepherd's Help From Shiel, C.D., Rieseberg
Ch. Shiel's Mogador Silverleaf, C.D., R.O.M., Rieseberg
Shields First Edition, Shields
Shiloh Tales of Romsey Abbey, Barnicoat
Ch. Silverleaf Mirror Image O'Kent, Rieseberg
Ch. Silverleaf Romp'n Tawny, C.D.X., Debusschere
Sir Baxter of Silverleaf, Clements
Surfsong's Amber Thistledown, Fournier
Thimbleberry Bright Contessa, Tranquilo
Thimbleberry Bright Knight, Meyers
Thimbleberry Corvette Time, Melin
Thimbleberry Pantera Time, Sarandos
Thimbleberry Porsche Time, Meyers
Tiburon Cool Breeze at Holm, Haarsager
Tiburon Sancerre of Arcadia, Haarsager
Twilight Mist at Lonetree, Edner
Ch. Unicorn's Colleen of Elf, Nolan
Valdan's Blueboy of Lonetree, Story
Ch. Wenloch's Winston of Arcadia, Russell and Price
Wee Woolie Webster, Krohner
Ch./O.T.Ch. Windcache A Briery Bess, Prescott
Ch. Wyndcliffe Foolery O'The Picts, Cline

Ch. Arcadia's Bita Amber and Ch. Arcadia's Cotton-Eyed Joe. Owners, Arcadia.

Winners

Our breed is still very young when it comes to records. Yet, there already are Beardies that have had an influence on the breed. Certainly, special mention belongs to those Beardies who have proven themselves to produce outstanding quality and who have represented the breed with a Best in Show (BIS).

As the years come and go, listings of top winners change. But winners and producers of winners always have great appeal. Thus, while a complete list of these dogs is still within reasonable numbers, we are including Beardies that have won multiple Group placings, have won at the prestigious shows, and have captured the titles of Register of Merit (R.O.M.), Champion (Ch.), Obedience Trial Champion (O.T.Ch.), or Utility Dog (U.D.) during this first decade following AKC recognition of the breed.

BIS WINNERS

Ch. Arcadia's Benson and Hedges (D) (Ch. Ha'Penny Blueprint of Arcadia, R.O.M., x Ch. Arcadia's Midnight Munday, R.O.M.), Bannon and Shannon. Superior side movement. Multiple BIS. Combining the bloodlines of two top kennels. (Black tri.)

Ch. Arcadia's Cotton-Eyed Joe, R.O.M. (D) (Ch. Arcadia's Bluegrass Music, R.O.M., x Ch. Rich-Lin's Molly of Arcadia, R.O.M.X.), Shannon. Exciting young dog, with good bone and movement. Loves to show, born to be in the ring. (Brown.)

Ch. Arcadia's Country Music (B) (Ch. Edenborough Happy Go Lucky, R.O.M.X, x Ch. Edenborough Quick Silver, R.O.M.X.), Brask. "Loretta" is a lovely girl, with sweet face. Dark blue; superb movement. (Blue.)

Can. Am. Ch. Bendale Special Lady, C.D.X., R.O.M. (B) (Eng. Ch. Edenborough Blue Bracken, R.O.M., x Eng. Ch. Willowmead Summer Wine), Ritter. Elegant bitch with striking movement and appearance, correct size. BOB BCCA and BCCC nationals. A picture of beauty in the breed and obedience rings. Owner handled, multiple wins. (Blue.)

Ch. Brambledale Blue Bonnet, C.D., R.O.M. (B) OFA: BC-17 (Eng. Ch. Brambledale Balthazar, R.O.M., x Brambledale Briar Rose), Lachman. First C.D., first champion, first BIS; BCCA BOB '81; Westminster BOB '78 and '79; Number One Dam '80; Number One Bitch '77-'78; over one hundred BOBs. Imported '72, a gorgeous bitch, called the First Lady of Beardies, with everything—brains, beauty, soundness, and producing ability. (Blue.)

Ch. Briery Knob Winter Harvest (D) (Ch. Willowmead Mid-Winter Boy, R.O.M., x Ch. Silverleaf Autumn Harvest), Rudd. Sound dog, correct size, lovely coat and side movement. Good head. (Brown.)

Eng./Am. Ch. Chauntelle's Limelight, R.O.M.X. (D) OFA: BC-185 (Ch. Edenborough Blue Bracken, R.O.M., x Sheldawyn Amber Tint), Davies and Schneider. English import; Number One male '81; multiple BIS, many Group wins, over one hundred BOBs; imported '80. Flashy and exciting, a showman, proving to be a producer of winners as well; proper size. (Brown.)

Ch. Copper Clarence of Beagold (D) (Beagold Beardsley Lad x Yager Flounce), Larizza. Lovely red coloring. Over one hundred BOBs, with many Group placings, multiple BIS. (Brown.)

Ch. Crisch Midnight Bracken (D) (Ch. Chauntelle Limelight, R.O.M.X, x Ch. Tudor Lodge Koala at Crisch, R.O.M.), Hyman and Schaefer. A fleet, exciting mover; multiple BIS out of two BIS/R.O.M.s. (Black.)

Am./Can./Eng./Ber. Ch. Edenborough Grey Shadow, R.O.M. (D) (Ch. Edenborough Blue Bracken, R.O.M., x Broadholme Christina, R.O.M.), Waite. Canadian dog. International champion, multiple BIS winner. Producer of winners. (Black.)

World/Int./de las Americas/Mex./Am./Can. Ch. Gaelyn Copper Artisan, R.O.M.X. (D) (Ch. Silverleaf Gifted Artisan x Ch. Artisan Silverleaf O'Parcana), Witte. "Cooper" has a BIS in Mexico, as well as many BOB and Group placings, lovely copper brown. First litter of five finished. Not content with all this, now breaking into advertising. (Brown.)

Ch. Geliland Black Bawbee at Chaniam (D) (Eng. Ch. Potterdale Philosopher x Osmart Black Paspolu), Bailey. Very dark dog who finished as a puppy. Imported to round out the breeding force at Chaniam and to top off a show career. Many Group placings. (Black.)

Ch. Ha'Penny Blu Max At Braemar (D) (Ch. Chauntelle's Limelight, R.O.M, x Ch. Daw Anka Snowboots of Ha'Penny), Thomas and Schneider. Good moving, handsome, sound dog. (Blue)

Ch. Ha'Penny Daw Anka Velvet Touch R.O.M.X.(b) (sister to Blu Max), Herzig. Schneider and Greitzer. Pretty, feminine, beautiful expression. Lovely movement. (Fawn)

Ch. Ha'Penny Hoyden at Edmar (B) (Ch. Chauntelle's Limelight, R.O.M.X., x Ch. Ha'Penny Blue Blossom, R.O.M.X.), Moe. Three Group placings as a puppy including a Group First for a major! Nice head, good bone, happy girl. Plush and pretty. Multiple BIS and Group placings, won Group placing at AKC Centennial show. (Black.)

Ch. Ha'Penny Moon Shadow R.O.M. (D) (brother to Hoyden), Greitzer and Schneider. BOW BCCA '81 as puppy. Stayed dark, happy dog, lots of attitude. Nice side movement. Countless BOB's, multiple BIS and Group wins at Westminster. Flashy and exciting. (Black.)

Ch. Rich-Lin's Outlaw (D) OFA: BC-270 (Ch. Rich-Lin's Bandit of Matt-Kev x Ch. Rich-Lin's Talk Of The Town, R.O.M.), Bruzan. Many BOB and Group wins, BIS. Dark dog with minimal markings and proper harsh coat. Well-balanced, sound movement, clean in front and rear, ideal size. Linebred on Rich-Lin's foundation stock. (Black.)

Ch. Shaggylane's Beaming Teak, R.O.M. (D) (Can. Ch. Raggmopp First Chance x Can. Ch. Yager Gigue), Niddrie. Multiple BIS winner, Group winner, Canadian dog, but outstanding winner in U.S. as well, over one hundred BOBs, gorgeous coat and red-brown color, fluid mover. (Brown.)

Am./Can. Ch. Shiels Mogador's Silverleaf, C.D., R.O.M. (D) (Eng. Ch. Sunbrees Magic Moments Of Willowmead x Misty of Mogador), Rieseberg. "Kent" is also a good-working herd dog, with his H.C. Sire of many champions and Group winner. Number One Sire '77. (Black.)

Ch. Tudor Lodge Koala at Crisch, R.O.M. (B) (Ch. Edenborough Grey Shadow, R.O.M., x Ch. Beagold's Black Tiffany, U.D., R.O.M.), Schaeffer. "Marci" is a classic, elegant, non-fading bitch, finishing at nine months. (Black.)
BIS Brace
Ch. Arcadia's Cotton-Eyed Joe, R.O.M. (listed above) and Ch. Arcadia's Bita Amber O'Hemloch (B) (Ch. Ha'Penny Blueprint of Arcadia, R.O.M.X, x Ch. Arcadia's Lucky's Happy Holiday), Shannon. Superbly moving, coated, and animated Beardies. (Browns.)

ALL-TIME TOP SIRE AND DAM

Ch. Edenborough Happy Go Lucky, R.O.M.X. (D) (Eng. Ch. Edenborough Blue Bracken, R.O.M., x Davealex Dawn Reign, R.O.M.), Shannon. Group placings, sire of many Group placers and five BIS get in four countries, and forty-six champions to date. Number One Sire '79-'82, imported '77. Sire of Distinction per Kennel Review. He also has seven sons and two grandsons that have achieved the R.O.M. Producing his excellent bone, head, and coat; enjoyed the ring every minute. (Black.)
Ch. Rich-Lin's Molly of Arcadia, R.O.M.X. (B) (Rich-Lin's Rising Son x Edenborough Full O'Life, R.O.M.), Shannon. Number One Dam '78-'79, Number One Dam All Breeds '79, NOW NUMBER ONE ALL-TIME ALL-BREED DAM, established a standing record by producing nine champions in one year; dam of Canadian and United States BIS winners, thirty-three champions to date. A true Beardie, rarely holding her tail still long enough to take a good picture; has produced champions in every litter by three different studs; a producer of producers, carrying a tradition through four generations to date. Everyone should own such a bitch! (Black tri.)

GROUP PLACEMENT WINNERS

Ch. Arcadias Anisette (B) (sister to Country Music), Hollinsworth. Lovely mover, clean. (Black.)
Ch. Arcadia's Bentley O'Walkoway, C.D.X. (D) (Ch. Walkoway's Sherlock Holmes x Ch. Edenborough Quick Silver, R.O.M.X.), Bates. Championship, Group win, C.D. leg, and HSD Novice B, all in same day. HIT BCCA National, '84 and '85. A registered therapy dog as well! (Black.)
Ch. Arcadia's Bluegrass Music, R.O.M. (D) (brother to Country Music), Lowe. BOS '82 BCCA. Gorgeous coat and head, and producing them. Clean, honest dog. (Blue.)
Ch. Arcadia's Charleston Charlie (D) (Ch. Ha'Penny Blueprint of Arcadia, R.O.M., x Ch. Arcadia's Pepsi Cola), Shannon and Whitley. Won multiple placings as youngster, until he discovered the glories of the swimming pool. Super head and side movement, a real clown. (Brown.)
Ch. Arcadia's Daiquiri Of Tays (B) (Ch. Edenborough Happy Go Lucky, R.O.M.X, x Ch. Rich-Lin's Molly of Arcadia, R.O.M.X.), Shannon. One of the "100% litter." Gorgeous head and coat. Now in Japan. (Black.)
Ch. Arcadia's Foxfire Of Rooban (B) (Ch. Arcadia's Bluegrass Music, R.O.M., x Ch. Rich-Lin's Molly of Arcadia, R.O.M.X.), Bannon and Shannon. Group wins from the classes; elegant; lovely mover and coat. (Blue.)
Ch. Arcadia's Nashville Kat (B) (Ch. Arcadia's Mr. Pibb, R.O.M., x Ch. Arcadia's Virginia Slim, R.O.M.), Shannon. Elegant, nice moving gal. Good bone. Group wins from the classes. (Black.)
Ch. Arcadia's Perrier (D) (younger brother to Bluegrass Music), Haarsager. Best in sweeps '82 BCCA. Very much like his brother, deep chested and good bone. (Blue.)
Ch. Arcadia's Salty Jok O'Emshire, R.O.M. (D) (litter brother to Daiquiri), Emke and Shannon. Only American Beardie to take BIS in Canada. Stayed dark, excellent mover. (Black.)
Arcadia's Savannah Rhythm (B) (sister to Nashville Kat), Blank. Super head, lovely coat and movement. Group placing at seven months. (Black.)
Ch. Arcadia's Silver Nitrate (D) (Ch. Gaymardon's Baron of Bramel x Ch. Edenborough Quick Silver, R.O.M.X.), Croft. Good rear and front, gorgeous head, placed in Group as puppy. (Blue.)
Ch. Arcadia's Summer Sensation (D) (brother to Cotton-Eyed Joe), Shannon, Stepankow, and Coxwell. Group winner from the classes, a "real sweet guy." (Black.)
Ch. Arcadia's Wildwood Periwinkle (D) (Ch. Ha'Penny Blueprint of Arcadia, R.O.M., x Ch. Arcadia's Honky Tonk Angel, R.O.M.), Stepankow and Shannon. Stylish side movement, good coat, and dark eye. (Blue.)
Ch. Arcadia's Whiskey on Ice (D) (Ch. Arcadia's Cotton-Eyed Joe, R.O.M., x Ch. Arcadia's Virginia Slim, R.O.M.), Beauchat. Multiple winner from the classes. Striking dog, with good stride. (Black.)
Ch. Artisan The Sorcerer (D) (Ch. Silverleaf Gifted Artisan x Ch. Artisan Burnish'D Silverleaf, R.O.M.X.), Witte. "Merlin" is like his namesake—gentle, enchanting, and wise. (Black.)
Ch. Artisan Copper Breagan (D) (Dh. Gaelyn Copper Artisan, R.O.M.X, x Ch. Artisan Burnish'D Silverleaf, R.O.M.X), Van Fleet and Witte. "Gabby" has wins in both breed and junior showmanship for his junior handler. (Brown.)
Ch. Bektaras Big Daddy (D) (Blaze A Trail At Deanfield x Penhallow's Proper Madam Of Bektara), Kaye and Mahigian. Dark, large-boned dog, minimal markings. (Black.)
Ch. Bon Di Parcana The Patriot, R.O.M. (D) (Ch. Banacek Fawn Fabric x Ch. Edenborough Parcana, R.O.M.), Moe and McKenna. Many Group wins. "Riot" has a beautiful head, good side movement and bone. (Black.)
Ch. Bosques Pampas Patty, C.D., H.C. (B) (Ch. Heathglen's Jolly Oliver x Ch. Pepperland Liberty Belle), McDonald and Lazar. "Gaelic" is a sweet girl and has shown her ability in breed, obedience, and herding. (Black.)
Ch. Brambledale's Bard (1973-1985) (D) (brother to Blue Bonnet), Mahigian. Medium size, one of the earliest show-men for the breed. (Blue.)
Ch. Brambledale Blackfriar, R.O.M. (D) (Brambledale Balthazar, R.O.M., x Brambledale Bretta), Morrison and Mahigian. Very dark dog with minimal markings. Won Veterans '83 BCCA; holding his age well as a Beardie should. Very masculine. (Black.)
Ch. Cauldbrae's Courie Doon (B) (Ch. Cauldbrae's Brigadoon, R.O.M., x Ch. Cauldbrae's Cecelia), Morrison. BCCA WB '83. Good head and movement. (Black.)
Ch. Cauldbrae's Fionn MacCummhail (D) (Ch. Davealex Rhinestone Cowboy, R.O.M., x Davealex Loch Harbour, R.O.M.), Truax and Pagnetti. An early winner for Cauldbrae. (Black.)
Ch. Cauldbraes Mo Carid (D) (Johnathen Brown Of Tambora, R.O.M., x Brambledale Dona Dea), Goldworm. Large boned, dark dog. (Black.)
Ch. Chordahyers Bonnie Jon (D) (Bengray Crofter x

Karistan Topkopi Chordahyer), Cloman and Kurtzner. Nice coat, flashy dog. (Black.)

Am./Can. Ch. Clans Sterling Silver (D) OFA: CO-429 (Can. Ch. Raggmopp The Boy x Ch. Banacek Bewitched, R.O.M.), Billman. Personality plus; "Houdini" reincarnated. (Black.)

Ch. Crickets Wm McWillie (D) (Ch. Glen Eire Willie Wonderful, R.O.M., x Ch. Brambledale Blue Bonnet, R.O.M.), Lachman. Group winner out of top parentage. (Black.)

Ch. Crisch Debut At Candelaria, H.C. (D) (Ch. Chauntelle Limelight, R.O.M.X., x Ch. Tudor Lodge Koala at Crisch, R.O.M.), Spicer. Typey, nice clean movement. (Black.)

Ch. Crisch Deju Vu at Brynwood (B) (sister of Debut), Brunner and Summerfelt. Nice moving girl. (Black.)

Ch. Crisch Painted Waggin (D) (Ch. Crisch Midnight Bracken x Ch. Crisch Panda of Briery Knob), Schaefer and Hyman. Happy dog, placing as a youngster. (Black.)

Ch. Criterion Weiser O'Mellowitt (D) OFA: BC-175 (Ch. Criterion Silverleaf Rascal, R.O.M., x Criterion Silverleaf Rachel), Witt. Typey, good head and movement. (Brown.)

Ch. Davealex Larky McRory At Lincheal (D) (Marilanz Amber Gleam x Eng. Ch. Cala Sona Westernisles Loch Aber), Morrison. BOS Westminster '78, many Group placings, Reserve CC in England, first of breed to place in Group; part of an exceptionally well-bred litter, very dark with little markings, good head; started American career at age seven. (Black.)

Ch. Davealex Rhinestone Cowboy, R.O.M. (D) OFA: BC-100 (Davealex Iownhim x Willowhurst Dream Awhile), Morrison. Nice moving male with drive. Good skull, ribbing, and angles. (Blue.)

Ch. Di-Gem's Mountain Mist O'Arcadia (D) (Ch. Ha'Penny Blueprint of Arcadia, R.O.M., x Ch. Arcadia's Black Velvet, R.O.M.), Fort. Looks a lot like his grandsire Lucky; excellent head and coat. (Black.)

Ch. Edenborough Happy Go Lucky, R.O.M.X. (D) (Eng. Ch. Edenborough Blue Bracken, R.O.M., x Davealex Dawn Reign, R.O.M.), Shannon. Happy showman, top sire. Good coat and bone. Correct size. (Black.)

Ch. Emshire Patrick O'Toole (D) (Ch. Arcadias Salty Jok O'Emshire, R.O.M., x Ch. Edenborough Wee Bit O'Luck, R.O.M.), Emke. Good moving dog. (Blue.)

Ch. Flanigan At Beagold (D) (Eng. Ch. Davealex Royle Brigadier x Kimrand Morning Star), Taulman. Medium-sized, pretty dog. (Brown.)

Ch. Gaymardon's Baron Of Bramel (D) (Ch. Edenborough Brackenson x Ch. Gaymardon Chesapeake Mist, H.C., R.O.M.X.), Webb. BCCA WD '79 from Puppy class, sire of Group winner and champions from one litter. (Brown.)

Ch. Gaymardon Bouncing Bogart, R.O.M. (D) (Ch. Brisles Mouffy Mister, R.O.M., x Ch. Gaymardon Chesapeake Mist), Miller. Many Group wins, sire of several champions; beautifully trained and handled, happy dog. (Black.)

Ch. Gaymardon Checkmate (D) (Ch. Gaymardon Bouncing Bogart, R.O.M., x Ch. Gaymardon Crack O'Dawn, R.O.M.), Harney. Finished undefeated; typical Beardie sweetness. (Black.)

Ch. Gaymardon's Chesapeake Mist, R.O.M.X. (B) OFA: BC-149 (Eng. Ch. Davealex Royle Baron x Ch. Barnleigh Damaris, R.O.M.), Miller. Westminster BOB '81; BCCA BOB '82 at the age of 8½ from Veterans; top bitch '82; Number One Dam '82; ten champions and multiple Group winners; a notable winner and producer. (Black.)

Ch. Gaymardon's Haughty Hollie (B) (Ch. Brisles Mouffy Mister, R.O.M., x Ch. Gaymardon Chesapeake Mist, H.C., R.O.M.X.), Davis. Very harsh coat; lovely movement. (Brown.)

Ch. Gaymardon T Is For Toby (D) (brother to Hollie), Katz. Super head; lovely mover; gentle boy. (Black.)

Ch. Gaymardon's Tartan Tona (B) (Ch. Jande's Lucky Tri, C.D., x Ch. Gaymardon's Crack O'Dawn, R.O.M.X.), Miller. Finished at one year. Group placing from classes. (Black.)

Ch. Gaymardon's Yorktown Yankee, R.O.M. (D) OFA: BC-150 (litter brother to Chesapeake Mist), Miller. "Chip" has multiple Group wins; gorgeous head and expression. (Brown.)

Ch. Geminis Rondo (D) (Ch. Edenborough Adventure, R.O.M., x Wayfarin's Butterscotch), Elliott. Good bone; presented himself well. (Black.)

Ch. Glen Eire's Harvest Moon (D) (Ch. Glen Eire Willie Wonderful, R.O.M., x Ch. Glen Eire Good Gracious), Riehle. Large-boned, flashy dog. (Brown.)

Ch. Glen Eire's Willie Wonderful, R.O.M. (D) OFA: BC-140 (Ch. Misty Shadow of Willowmead, R.O.M., x Ch. Luath Bonnie Blue Bairn, R.O.M.), Dean and Dolan. Westminster BOS '80; BCCA BOS '79; top American-Bred sire; pretty dog. (Black.)

Ch. Greysteel Atomic Joshua (D) (Ch. Shiel's Mogador's Silverleaf, C.D., R.O.M.X., x Ch. Warbonnet Silverleaf Breta, R.O.M.), Tullis. Flashy, dark dog. (Black.)

Ch. Ha'Penny Black Lightning (B) (sister to Hoyden), Schneider, Greitzer, and Green. Pretty girl; nice movement; flashy. Lots of animation. (Black.)

Ch. Ha'Penny Black Orpheus (D) (brother to Hoyden), Howard and Schneider. Group placing as youngster. (Black.)

Ch. Ha'Penny Blue Blossom, R.O.M.X. (B) (Ch. Brambledale Boz x Ch. Brambledale Blue Bonnet), Schneider. Number One bitch '79-'80; over one hundred BOB wins; dam of champions and Group winners; a top winning bitch from Ha'Penny's first litter, making a lovely beginning for a top kennel. (Blue.)

Ch. Ha'Penny Blueprint Of Arcadia, R.O.M. (D) (Ch. Chauntelle's Limelight, R.O.M.X., x Ch. Ha'Penny Blue Blossom, R.O.M.), Shannon. Lovely side movement; beautiful head; good bone; producing Group winners as well as winning. (Blue tri.)

Ch. Ha'Penny Blu Max At Braemar (D) (Ch. Chauntelle's

Ch. Brambledale Blue Bonnet, C.D., R.O.M. Owners, Henrietta and Robert Lachman.

Limelight, R.O.M., x Ch. Daw-Anka Snowboots of Ha'Penny), Thomas and Schneider. Good moving, handsome sound dog. (Blue.)

Ch. Ha'Penny Daw Anka O'Sandcastle (B) (Ch. Diotima's American Dream x Ch. Ha'Penny Lucy Locket, R.O.M.), Ayotte and Schneider. Sweet, pretty girl, with correct size and lovely side movement. (Brown.)

Ch. Ha'Penny Daw Anka Velvet Touch (B) (sister to Blu Max), Ayers and Moore. Pretty, feminine, sweet expression. Nice movement. (Fawn.)

Ch. Ha'Penny Havoc (D) (brother to Hoyden), Greitzer and Schneider. Good bone, proper size. Multiple wins as youngster. (Blue.)

Ch. Heathglens Jolly Oliver (D) (Ch. Willowferry Victor, R.O.M., x Ch. Charncroft Country Rose), Lazar. One of the first Beardies introducing the breed to the country. (Black.)

Ch. Jande's Just Dudley, R.O.M. (D) (Ch. Edenborough Happy Go Lucky, R.O.M.X., x Ch. Beardie Bloody Mary, R.O.M.X.), Masters. Several Group wins, beautiful head, bone and coat, producing winners, one of a multi-champion litter. (Black.)

Ch. Jande Lucky Tri, C.D. (D) (litter brother to Dudley), Buehrig and Miller. Lovely well-structured and well-muscled dog. Beautiful coat; BCCA BOB '83. (Black tri.)

Ch. Jande's Oxford Knight In Blue (D) (litter brother to above two dogs), McPhail. Several group wins, loved to show; beautiful, substantial bone and luxurious coat; flashy, exciting mover. Siring champions from first litter. (Blue.)

Ch. Jande's Pocono Hershey (D) (Ch. Tamevalley Highland Ballad, R.O.M., x Ch. Beardie Bloody Mary, R.O.M.X.), Masters. Beautiful head, thick coat. Many wins as youngster. (Brown.)

Ch. Knightsbridge Dudley (D) (Ch. Chauntelle Limelight, R.O.M.X., x Ch. Cauldbrae's Tangle O'the Isles, R.O.M.), Leadbetter. Nice side movement. (Black.)

Ch. Lochengar Great Expectations (D) OFA: BC-209-T (Am./Can Ch. Rich-Lins Mister Magoo, R.O.M., x Rich-Lins Honey Bear, R.O.M.), Conro. "Fletcher" is a sweet Beardie with typical breed temperament and expression. (Blue.)

Ch. Lochengar Kyloe Having It All (B) (Ch. Lochengar Great Expectations x Ch. Excellent Outfit Queen), Rankinen and Conro. "Hilary" is a dark, flashy Beardie with a remarkable puppy career. BOS Sweeps at '85 national. (Black.)

Am./Can. Ch. Lochengar Kernel Pikering, Can. C.D. (D) (Ch. Rich-Lins Mister Magoo, R.O.M., x Ch. Excellent Outfit Queen, R.O.M.), Newland. "Pickers" is a sire of Group winners. Exuberant, loves everybody. (Black.)

Ch. Lochengar Never Surrender (B) (Ch. Lochengar's Kernel Pikering x Lochengar's Old Curiosity Shop, R.O.M.), Conro. "Jenny" has built up quite a record, despite limited showing; lots of substance, style, and expression. (Black.)

Ch. Lochengar Our Finest Hour (D) (litter brother to above), Conro. "Winston" is a double Magoo grandson; Group placing at only eight months. (Black.)

Ch. Lochengars Our Mutual Friend (D) (Ch. Rich-Lins Mister Magoo, R.O.M., x Rich-Lins Honey Bear, R.O.M.), Pechmann. "Ashley" has good movement, coming and going. Like his sire, beautiful expression. (Black.)

Ch. Melita Grand Menhir Brise (D) (Ch. Rich-Lin's Shamrock O'Rosamba x Ch. Bonnie Brighton By The Sea), Richland and Siri. Finished at nine months. Good bone. (Black.)

Ch. Miller's Silverleaf Blu Kilty (D) OFA: BC-232

Ch. Arcadia's Bluegrass Music, R.O.M. Owners, Dave and Marilyn Lowe.

Ch. Arcadia's Salty Jok O'Emshire. Owners, Emke and Shannon.

(Am./Can. Ch. Osmart Silverleaf Goldmine, R.O.M., x Ch. Silverleaf Scottish Heather, R.O.M.), Miller. Large-boned; nice head; dark coloring. (Blue.)

Ch. Mistiburn's Merrymaid (B) OFA: BC-170 (Ch. Willowmead Something Super, R.O.M., x Ch. Charncroft Caprice, R.O.M.), Albarano. "Cozy" exhibits beautiful movement; lovely bitch, nice head and coat. (Black.)

Ch. Mistiburn's Merrymaker (D) OFA: BC-170 (litter brother to Merrymaid), Turner. "Dundee" was Westminster BOS '79, BOB '82; BCCA BOB '80. Very masculine dog. These littermates captured many wins for their owners and breeders. (Black.)

Ch. O'Kelidon's Meadow Master (D) (Ch. Cauldbrae's Royle Windsor x Ch. Shenedene Miss Crispen, R.O.M.), McHugh. Good bone. (Brown.)

Ch. O'Kelidons Merry Glen-Mog (D) (litter brother to above), Beorup. Straightforward mover. (Black.)

Ch. Osmart Smokey Silver Starter at Chaniam (D) OFA: BC-240 (Eng. Ch. Osmart Bonnie Blue Braid, R.O.M., x Eng. Ch. Queen Arwin Of Kenstaff, R.O.M.), Bailey. A car accident cut his show career short and retired him to a life of herding and producing champions. (Blue.)

Am./Can. Ch. Padworth Miss Muffet (B) OFA: BC-97 (Calderlin Leal x Sallen Queenie), Lewis. English import. (Brown.)

Ch. Parcana Jake McTavish (D) (Ch. Parcana Silverleaf Vandyke, R.O.M., x Ch. Osmart Smoky Blue Parcana, R.O.M.), Parker. Handsome, flashy dog. (Black.)

Ch. Parcana's Penosa Chelsea, H.C. (B) (sister to Jake), Beck and Parker. Lovely dark bitch, with gorgeous head. (Black.)

Ch. Parchment Farm's Rob Roy (D) (Ch. Brambledale Bard x Tambora's Black Rose Marie), Rodenbarger. Good dark color and pigment. (Black.)

Ch. Pennypackers Aengus (D) (Ch. Glen Eire Willie Wonderful, R.O.M., x Ch. Cricket Tick Bird Of Brunswig), Heilbrunn. Very dark slate; medium-sized dog; well presented. (Black.)

Ch. Raisin's Chinatown (D) (Ch. Umilik Shaggylane's Brandy x Ch. Raisin's Certainly Cindy, R.O.M.), Rubenstein. Lots of coat. (Brown.)

Ch. Rich-Lin's Justin Case (D) (Ch. Rich-Lin's Feelin' Free x Ch. Rich-Lin's Talk Of The Town, R.O.M.), Einbinder and Nootbaar. Exuberant dog; good coat; good head. (Black.)

Am./Can. Ch. Rich-Lin's Mister Magoo, R.O.M. (D) OFA: BC-73 (Ch. Rich-Lin's Pride of Jason, R.O.M., x Ch. Rich-Lins Royal Shag, R.O.M.), Conro. Top five every year shown; multiple Group winner; sired Group winners. Flashy, a real showman, loved the ring and showed it. (Black.)

Ch. Rich-Lin's R.C. (D) (litter brother to Justin Case), Franc. Winner Sweeps '80 BCCA. Beautiful dog; gorgeous movement; very masculine. (Black.)

Ch. Rich-Lin's Whiskers Of Arcadia, R.O.M. (D) (Rich-Lins Rising Son x Ch. Hootnany Of Bengray), Shannon. Several Group placings, Number One American-Bred Beardie '77; extreme shoulder and outstanding movement, putting them on his progeny. Judges said the best side-moving Beardie they ever saw. Unfortunately used too little before breeding accident rendered him sterile. (Black tri.)

Ch. Savage Wind at Wildwood (D) (Ch. Arcadia's Cotton-Eyed Joe, R.O.M., x Ch. Sunnylane Song Sung Blue, C.D., R.O.M.), Jones. "Shad" is a sound, plush sweetheart. Good mover, with Group placings as a puppy. (Blue.)

Ch. Scotdale's Teak O'Walkoway (D) (Ch. Arcadia's Paprika, R.O.M., x Ch. Walkoway's Victoria Holt, R.O.M.), Ross and Shaw. Dark, harsh coat, with super shoulder and side movement. Placed from classes. (Black.)

Ch. Silverleaf English Leather, C.D., R.O.M. (D) (Ch. Shiel's Mogador's Silverleaf, R.O.M.X., x Hyfield Hyteeny, R.O.M.), Rieseberg. Sire of several champions; multiple Group winner; good medium size. (Brown.)

Ch. Silverleaf Lord Blu-Bottom (D) (Ch. Shiel's Mogador's Silverleaf, C.D., R.O.M.X., x Parcana Possibility, R.O.M.X., Grue. "Smudgie" is a Canadian resident, but has won in the United States as well. Produced by top producing parents. (Blue.)

Ch. Silverleaf Romp'N Tawny, C.D.X., H.C. (D) OFA: BC-262-T (Am./Can. Ch. Osmart Silverleaf Goldmine, R.O.M., x Am./Can. Ch. Thaydom Silverleaf Cinnamon, R.O.M.), De Busschere. Good movement and proper coat, beautiful head and expression, lovely color. (Brown.)

Am./Can. Ch. Silverleaf Sesame Stick, C.D. (D) (Ch. Shiel's Mogador's Silverleaf, C.D., R.O.M.X., x Am./Can. Ch. Thaydom Silverleaf Cinnamon, R.O.M.), Osloond. Balanced dog, good bone, good head; dark chocolate. (Brown.)

Ch. Sno-Berry Black Lad (D) (Cauldbrae's Tunes Of Glory x Camshron Babs), Jozwiak. Dark, good-sized dog. (Black.)

Ch. Stonybrooks Fantasia (B) (Ch. Copper Clarence at Beagold, R.O.M., x Stonybrook's Wind Chime), Frame and Larizza. Nice mover. (Brown.)

Ch. Swinford Cheyenne (D) (Eng. Ch. Pepperland Lyric John At Pottersdale x Swinford Skylark), Murphy. Proper coat and loving temperament. (Black.)

Tekla Magic Myrrhlen (D) (Ch. Willowmead Midnight Black x Glen Eire's Winter Magic), Brown. Group placing from the classes. (Black tri.)

Ch. Unicorn The Mighty Quinn (D) (Ch. Spring Magic of Willowmead, C.D., R.O.M., x Ch. Wild Silk Of Willowmead, R.O.M.), Gaffney. "Quincy" is a beautiful, typey dog, good bone. Exceptional head, expression, and movement. (Black.)

Ch. Unicorn Joel Of Timber Ridge (D) (Ch. Aellen's Cocoa Joe x Ch. Unicorn Tabitha Of Timber Ridge), McClaren and Colavecchio. Well-coated dog. (Brown.)

Ch. Unicorn's Kilcharen Ben Scot (D) (Unicorn's Grey Casper x Ch. Wild Silk of Willowmead, R.O.M.), Folendorf. Scotty has a beautiful head; good chest and pigmentation. Typical Beardie temperament plus. (Black.)

Ch. Walkoway's Dartmouth, C.D. (D) (Ch. Arcadia's Paprika, R.O.M., x Ch. Arcadia's Marcy of Rich-Lin, C.D., R.O.M.), Price. Happy dog with lovely side movement; placing from the classes. (Black.)

Ch. Wildwood Bat Mast'Rs'N Arcadia (D) (Ch. Arcadia's Midnight Son x Ch. Arcadia's Honky Tonk Angel, R.O.M.), Stepankow and Shannon. Dark dog; full of animation, driving movement; filled with joy at just being alive. Linebred Molly grandson. (Black tri.)

Mex. Ch. Wildwood's Sunrise (B) (Ch. Edenborough Happy Go Lucky, R.O.M.X., x Ch. Sunnylane Song Sung Blue, C.D., R.O.M.), Diaz and Calderon. BIS in Mexico. Lovely free-flowing movement. Sweet expression. (Black.)

Ch. Willowmead Mid-Winter Boy, R.O.M. (D) (Willowmead Red Ruaridh x Willowmead Winter Memory), Schroeder. Cocoa brown coloring; nice head; producing well. (Brown.)

Ch. Willowmead Summer Magic (D) (Glenwhin Kinlochalie x Willowmead Touch of Magic), Gaffney and Colavecchio. Import with beautiful movement and bone. "Shane" won BOS '85 BCCA and BOB '86. Good, sound Beardie. (Black.)

BCCA NATIONAL SPECIALTY SHOW WINNERS

1979—First Show
BOB, WB (BOW)—Eng./Can. Ch. Edenborough Kara Kara Of Josanda, Taylor
BOS—Ch. Glen Eire's Willie Wonderful, Dolan
WD—Gaymardon's Baron Of Bramel, Webb
RWD—Unicorn's The Mighty Quinn, Gaffney
RWB—Lovenmist Blue Jeans, Holava

1980
BOB—Ch. Mistiburn Merrymaker, Turner
BOS—Ch. Brambledale Blue Bonnet, C.D., Lachman
WD—Cricket's Lookin' Good, Albarano
WB (BOW)—Glen Eire Good Gracious, Dean and Dolan
RWD—Amulree Argo Whauphill, Hooper
RWB—Bannock Brae's Brandywine, Hossack
HSD—Ch. Cauldbrae's Maudi Gras, Nussbaum

1981
BOB—Ch. Brambledale Blue Bonnet, C.D., Lachman
BOS—Ch. Chauntelle's Limelight, Ha'Penny, Goldworm, and Davies
WD—HaPenny's Moonshadow, Greitzer and Schneider
WB (BOW)—Ha'Penny Sweetwater Agility, Garrett
RWD—Walkoway's G. K. Chesterton, Walkowicz and Lamb
RWB—Bannochbrae's Country Bumpkin, Taylor
HSD—Sno-Berry's Black Blazer, Giewartowski

1982
BOB—Ch. Gaymardon's Chesapeake Mist, Miller
BOS—Ch. Arcadia's Bluegrass Music, Lowe and Shannon
WD (BOW)—Wyndcliff Foolery O'The Picts, Cline and O'Bryan
WB—Glen Eire's Hope of Dendarra, Fischer
RWD—Whitshiel's Solitary Man, Kerr
RWB—Callander Hi Fly'n Jenny, Gomez
HSD—Windcache A Blustery Day, U.D., Wilson

1983
BOB—Ch. Jande's Lucky Tri, Buehrig and Miller
BOS—Ch. Benbeccula's Classical Jazz, Sawkes
BOW, WD—Britannia Just Jeffrey, Ritter
WB—Cauldbrae's Courie Doon, Morrison
RWD—Mistiburn's Hey Mickey, Albarano
RWB—Crisch Panda Of Briery Knob, Schaefer
HSD—Raggmopp Leading Lady, Tuck and Gold

1984
BOB—Ch. Littlefalls Rose Ellen, Foster and Hossack
BOS—Am./Can. Ch. Pottersdale Paris, Sawka
WD—Bearanson Blue Peter, Yeakle
BOW, WB—Shiloh's Breezy Blue Angel, Ellington and Lindemoen
RWD—Lovenmist Blackbriar, Winger
RWB—Padworth Black Beauty, Masters
HSD—Ch. Arcadia's Bentley O'Walkoway, C.D., Bates

1985
BOB—Ch. Bendale Special Lady, C.D., Ritter and Stoneybrook
BOS—Ch. Willowmead Summer Magic, Colavecchio and Gaffney
WD—Lord Barclay of Lonetree, Aron
BOW, WB—Harmonys Show Biz, Berry
RWD—Can. Ch. Kinleslyn's L'Angus, Belfit
RWB—Edmar Pandora of Lajosmegyi, Quigley and Turner
HSD—Ch. Arcadia's Bentley O'Walkoway, C.D.X., Bates

1986
BOB—Ch. Willowmead Summer Magic, Colavecchio and Gaffney
BOS, WB—Shadowmist Promise of Spring, Hays
WD—Crisch Midnight Braid, Tuck
RWD—Classical Champagne Charlie, Sawka
RWB—Tudor Lodge Abbey at Crisch, Girty
HSD—Britannia Master Thinker, Weiss and Hartzell

Ch. Unicorn's The Mighty Quinn. Owners, Pam and Pat Gaffney.

Ch. Luath Bonnie Blue Bairn, at six months. Owner, Anne Dolan.

"SELECT" BEARDIES

The 1986 BCCA National Specialty is the first in which worthy dogs were chosen "Select." Best of Breed is awarded Select 1, with BOS being Select 2, followed by as many as eight Select Champions. In 1986, these dogs were:

Ch. Willowmead Summer Magic, Colavecchio and Gaffney
Shadowmist Promise of Spring, Hays
Ch. Regal Manor's Sir Launcelot, Carroll
Ch. Crisch Midnight Bracken, Hyman and Schaefer
Ch. Blueweiries Master Rhett, Dorman
Ch. Ha'Penny Daw Anka O'Sandcastle, Ayotte and Schneider
Ch. Tudor Lodge's Walter Raleigh, Blumire
Ch. Ha'Penny Moon Shadow, Greitzer and Schneider
Ch. Rich-Lin's Carrington Blue, Nootbaar and Panno
Ch. Ha'Penny Blu Max at Braemar, Herzig, Thomas, and Schneider

Brace Class at BCCA Show. Ch. Mistiburn Merrymaid and Ch. Cricket's Elegant Eloise, C.D. Owner, Nona Albarano.

95

INTERNATIONAL KENNEL CLUB
SHOW WINNERS
Two shows per year

1977
BOB—Ch. Brambledale's Blue Bonnet, C.D., Lachman
BOS, WD—Rich-Lin's Mister Magoo, Conro
WB—Camshron Babs, Jozwiak

BOB—Ch. Edenborough Adventure, Nootbaar
BOS, WB—Rich-Lin's Ms. Liberty, Kothman
WD—Rich-Lin's Pride of Jason, Cole and Nootbaar

1978
BOB—Ch. Brambledale's Blue Bonnet, C.D., Lachman
BOS—Ch. Davealex Larky McRory Of Linchael, Morrison
WD—Brambledale Boz, Blake
WB—Edenborough My Fair Lady, Shannon and Staser

BOB—Ch. Rich-Lin's Mister Magoo, Conro
BOS, WB—Sweet Romance Of Willowmead, Jagersma
WD—Smallhavens Fife N Drum, Bankus and Hauff

1979
BOB—Ch. Cauldbraes Mo Cariad, Goldworm
BOS—Ch. Rich-Lin Primrose O'Rosamba, Roark
WD—Sno-Berry Black Wizard, Jozwiak
WB—Rich-Lin's Blue Sugar Bear, Roberts

BOB—Ch. Edenborough Happy Go Lucky, Shannon
BOS—Sno-Berry Chrysanthemum, Schnute
WD—Dovmar Beau Briar, Masters
WB—Jande's Winsome Winnie, Masters

American and Canadian Ch. Rich-Lin's Mr. Magoo, R.O.M. Owners, James and LeRae Conro.

1980
BOB—Ch. Rich-Lin's Mister Magoo, Conro
BOS—Ch. Rich-Lin's Charlie's Blue Angel, Foster
WD—Brambledale Blaise, Jozwiak
WB—Bedlams Echo Ere Raggmopp, Roskin

BOB—Ch. Brambledale's Blackfriar, Morrison and Mahigian
BOS—Ch. Jande's Winsome Winnie, Masters
WD—Pepperland Rolling Stone, Rieseberg and Holdren
WB—Beardie Bloody Mary, Masters

1981
BOB—Ch. Geminis Rondo, Elliott
BOS—Ch. Rich-Lin's Blue Sugar Bear, Nootbaar
WD—Jande's Just Dudley, Masters
WB—Beardie Bloody Mary, Masters

BOB—Ch. Lochengar Kernel Pikering, Newland
BOS—Ch. Bedlams Echo Ere Raggmopp, Roskin
WD—Sno-Berry Tried And True, Jozwiak
WB—Wildwood Repunzel, Proet and Stepankow

1982
BOB—Ch. Rich-Lin's Outlaw, Bruzan
BOS, WB—Rich-Lin's Solitaire Of Dearlove, Einbinder
WD—Tame Valley Highland Ballad, Masters

BOB—Ch. Rich-Lin's Outlaw, Bruzan
BOS, WB—Sno-Berry Black Ruffle, Jozwiak
WD—Bearanson Black Bart, Schnute

1983
BOB, WD—Bearanson Black Bart, Kothe and Schnute
BOS—Ch. Lochengar Never Surrender, Conro
WB—Walkoway's Victoria Holt, Shaw and Walkowicz

BOB—Ch. Wildwood Bat Mast'rs'N Arcadia, Stepankow and Shannon
BOS, BOW—Winterwood Empress Lilly, Bearjar
WD—Amulree Argo Whauphill, Hooper

1984
BOB—Ch. Rich-Lin's Outlaw, Bruzan
BOS, BOW, WB—Dawne's Holly Go Litely, Odom and Foster
WD—Gaymardon's Percy's Price, Nolan and Miller

BOB—Ch. Ha'Penny Hoyden at Edmar, Moe
BOS—Ch. Jande's Just Dudley, Masters
WD, BOW—Dawnes McDuff, Ryan
WB—Jande's Glorious Gloria, Masters

1985
BOB—Ch. Bendale Special Lady, C.D., Ritter and Stonybrook
BOS—Bonnytown's Fifth Avenue, Blieden
WD—Bearanson Bristol Cream, Gunn
WB, BOW—Arcadias Wildwood White Gold, Stepankow and Shannon

BOB—Ch. Ha'Penny Daw Anka Sandcastle, Ayotte and Schneider
BOS—Ch. Arcadia's Cotton-Eyed Joe, Shannon
WB, BOW—Regal Manor's Enchantress, Carroll and Henry

1986
BOB—Ch. Ha'Penny Daw Anka Sandcastle, Ayotte and Schneider
BOS—Ch. Ha'Penny Blu Max at Braemar, Herzig and Schneider
WD, BOW—Gunstock Paint It Black, Gunn
WB—Ha'Penny Daw Anka Sandpebble, Marth

WESTMINSTER KENNEL CLUB SHOW WINNERS

1978
- BOB—Ch. Brambledale Blue Bonnet, C.D., Lachman
- BOS—Ch. Davealex Larky McRory Of Linchael, Morrison
- WD—Brambledale Boz, Blake
- WB—Edenborough My Fair Lady, Shannon and Staser

1979
- BOB—Ch. Brambledale Blue Bonnet, C.D., Lachman
- BOS—Ch. Mistiburn Merrymaker, Turner
- WD—Copper Clarence At Beagold, Reinlieb
- WB—Mistiburn Merrymaid, Turner

1980
- BOB—Ch. Ha'Penny Blue Blossom, Schneider
- BOS—Ch. Glen Eire's Willie Wonderful, Dean and Dolan
- WD—Blue Gatling of Dovmar, Newman
- WB—Jande's Winsome Winnie, Masters

1981
- BOB—Ch. Gaymardon Chesapeake Mist, Miller
- BOS—Ch. Chauntelle's Limelight, Schneider
- WD—Cauldbraes Blue Cuillin, Morrison
- WB—Willowmead Lady In Black, Glatzer

1982
- BOB—Ch. Mistiburn Merrymaker, Turner
- BOS—Ch. Ha'Penny Sweetwater Agility, Garrett
- WD—Kimrand Drummer Boy At Beagold, Reinleib and Carruthers
- WB—Mistiburn Mistletoe, Carson

1983
- BOB—Ch. Chauntelle's Limelight, Schneider, Davis, and Lott
- BOS—Ch. Knights Bridge Delta Dawn, Natwin
- WD—Dovmars New Man About Town, Newman
- WB—Ha'Penny Braebourne Bonnie, Fallon

1984
- BOB—Stonybrooks Fantasia, Frame
- BOS—Ch. Knightsbridge Dudley, Leadbetter
- WD, BOW—Ha'Penny Nickolas Nickelby, Constable
- WB—Violets are Blue at Glen Eire, Glatzer

1985
- BOB—Ch. Ha'Penny Hoyden at Edmar, Moe
- BOS—Ch. Ha'Penny Moon Shadow, Greitzer and Schneider
- WD, BOW—Maccorkindale's Tawny Rogue, Swan
- WB—Chrisch Midnight Summer Sun, Schaefer

1986
- BOB—Ch. Ha'Penny Moon Shadow, Greitzer and Schneider
- BOS—Ch. Bendale Special Lady, C.D.X., Ritter and Folendorf
- WD—Cauldbrae's Challenger, Morrison
- WB, BOW—Ha'Penny Silver Morn Lindsay, Rayano

1987
- BOB—Ch. Ha'Penny Moon Shadow, Greitzer and Schneider
- BOS—Ch. Ha'Penny Black Lightning, Green, Schneider and Greitzer
- WD, BOW—Crisch Midnight Magic, Schaefer
- WB—Mardeck's Misty Miracle, Layng

Ch. Mistiburn Merrymaker
Owner, Jane Turner.

SANTA BARBARA KENNEL CLUB SHOW WINNERS

1977
 BOB—Ch. Shiel's Mogador's Silverleaf, Rieseberg
 BOS, WB—Bengray Bonnie Jean, Cordes and Kayer
 WD—Glenhys Marshal Silverleaf, Howey
1978
 BOB—Ch. Shaggylanes Beaming Teak, Niddrie
 BOS, WB—Honey Buns Of Thimbleberry, Karnes
 WD—Wyndcliff Fleetwood Mac, Greenspan
1979
 BOB—Ch. Ha'Penny Blue Blossom, Schneider
 BOS—Ch. Shaggylanes Beaming Teak, Niddrie
 WD—Chordahyers Ashley, Ayer and Cordes
 WB—Ha'Penny Blue Sascha, Schneider
1980
 BOB—Ch. Arcadia's Blue Crown Royal, Tompkins
 BOS—Ch. Arcadia's Daquiri Of Tays, Watanabe
 WD—Parchment Farms Mr. Kite, Tilson
 WB—Melodys Abbey Of Glen Eire, Schwartz and Keller
1981
 BOB—Ch. Chauntelle's Limelight, Ha'Penny
 BOS—Ch. Arcadia's Daquiri Of Tays, Watanabe
 WD—Arcadia's Bluegrass Music, Lowe
 WB—Arcadia's Emmy Lou Harris, Davis
1982
 BOB—Jande's Just Dudley, Masters
 BOS—Callander Bobbin Hallmark, Tompkins
 WD—Ha'Penny Daw Anka New Harmony, Stevens and Schneider
 WB—Harmony's Golddigger, Miller and Stevens
1983
 BOB—Ch. Arcadia's Perrier, Haarsager
 BOS—Ch. Callander's High Fly'n Jenny, Gomez
 WD—Caros Show Off, Strunge
 WB—Arcadia's Coco Ribe, Shook and Haarsager
1984
 BOB—Ch. Arcadia's Perrier, Haarsager
 BOS—Ch. Ha'Penny Daw Anka Velvet Touch, Ayers and Moore
 WD—Callander Geordie Odhe, Tompkins
 WB, BOW—Melita Candee Dancer, Cullen

1985
 BOB—Ch. Ha'Penny Black Lightning, Green, Schneider, and Greitzer
 BOS—Ch. Unicorn Joel of Timberridge, McClaran
 WD—Willow Winds of Kilcharen, Folendor and Becker
 WB, BOS—Shiloh's Breezy Blue Angel, Ellington and Lindemoen
1986
 BOB—Ch. Ha'Penny Black Lightning, Green
 BOS—Ch. Arcadia's Brushed Bronze, Lowe
 WD, BOW—Time's Rob Roy of Bonnie Brae, Ober
 WB—Traleigh Lady of Destiny, Swarts and McClaren

"Here we are, America!" Photo of the Minuteman statue, Concord, Massachusetts, which appeared in the Centennial Issue of *Pure-bred Dogs/American Kennel Gazette*, July 1976.

Gail Elizabeth Miller and American and Canadian Ch. Briery Knob Winter Harvest.

AKC CENTENNIAL SHOW WINNERS (1984)

 BOB—Ch. Ha'Penny Hoyden at Edmar, Moe
 BOS—Ch. Knightsbridge Dudley, Leadbetter
 WD—Midnight Blue of Dundee, Cowles
 WB, BOW—Padworth Black Beauty, Masters
 RWD—Gladenmead's Mr. Super Bowl, Glatzer
 RWB—Classical's Star Baby, Sawka

Canadian and American Ch. Bedlam's Go Get 'Em Garth. Owner, Alice Bixler.

Ch. Arcadia's Benson and Hedges. Owners, Pat Bannon and Diann Shannon.

American and Canadian Ch. Orora's Faith, C.D.X., T.T. Owners, Roy and Joan Blumire.

Ch. Tudor Lodge's Anne Boleyn, C.D.X., T.T. Owners, Roy and Joan Blumire.

Minuteman Bearded Collie Club entry at Top Dog competition of New England Association of Obedience Clubs, and judges. From left: Ruth Ivers with Ben Jo O'Braemoor, C.D., T.D.; Judy Ryder with Barrister O'Braemoor, C.D.; Becky Parsons with Brisken O'Braemoor, C.D.; and Virginia Parsons with Ch. Branikin O'Braemoor, C.D. T.D.

TOP-ACHIEVING OBEDIENCE DOGS

Obedience Trial Champion
O.T.Ch. Windcache A Briery Bess (B) (Shiel's Sweetgale Kittihawk x Windcache Brillig O'Braemoor), Barbara Prescott. "Bess" was the first Beardie to earn a Utility Dog title, and later became the first Obedience Trial Champion of the breed.

Utility Dog
Windcache A Blustery Day, U.D. (B) (sister of Briery Bess), Barbara Wilson. Second U.D., following her illustrious sister.

Sno'berry's Black Blazer, U.D. (D) (Ch. Sno-berry's Black Lad x Brambledale Bala, R.O.M.), Lynn Giewartowski. The first male to acquire the U.D.

Ch. Glen Eire Bedazlin Beethoven, U.D. (D) (Ch. Glen Eire Willie Wonderful x Glen Eire Skye O'Cauldbrae), Kiann and Kandy Robinson. Affectionately known as the "mouth of the South," because of voicing his exuberance while working.

Am./Can. Ch. Beagold's Black Tiffany, U.D., SCh. A.D., T.T., R.O.M. (B) (Ch. Edenborough Star Turn At Beagold x Beagold's Pennyroyal), Roy and Joan Blumire. One who's just about done it all!

Pandora, U.D. (B) (Unknown x Unknown), Mary Jayne Frantz. A foundling who was found on the Frantz doorstep and made it to the top!

Ch. Tudor Lodge's Anne Boleyn, U.D. (B) (Ch. Edenborough Grey Shadow, R.O.M., x Ch. Beagold's Black Tiffany, U.D.), Blumire. Following in her dam's "paw steps."

Companion Dog Excellent
Windcache Brillig O'Braemoor, C.D.X (B) (Justice of Tambora x Jedriana Nantua), Kay Holmes and Janice Scott. First Beardie to win a C.D.X., dam of the great working O.T.Ch./Ch. Windcache A Briery Bess and Windcache A Blustery Day, U.D. Killed in a car accident before completing her U.D. or championship titles.

Ch. Cauldbrae's Tam O'Shanter, C.D.X. (D) (Ch. Cauldbrae's Brigadoon, R.O.M., x Knick Knack of Tambora), Blumire. Top obedience Beardie for '76.

Ch. Brisles Glen Nadia, C.D.X., Ber. C.D. (B) (Can. Ch. Happy Hooligan of Bengray x Ch. Barnleigh Damaris), Betty Brask. Multiple-titled dog.

Can./Am. Ch. Orora's Faith, C.D.X., T.T. (B) (Eng. Ch. Osmart Bonnie Blue Braid, R.O.M., x Eng. Ch. Mignonette of Willowmead at Orora), McKinney and Blumire. Another all-round worker for Tudor Lodge.

Ch. Arcadia's Bentley O'Walkoway, C.D.X. (D) (Ch. Walkoway's Sherlock Holmes x Ch. Edenborough Quick Silver), Carleton J. Bates. Two times H.I.T. at BCCA, '84 (at fourteen months) and again in '85.

Tracking Dog Excellent
Ch. Cannamoor Honey Rose, Am./Can. C.D., T.D.X. (B) (1972-1985) (Rowdina Rustler x Wishanger Comb Honey), Virginia Parsons. First Tracking Dog Beardie and tied for first Companion Dog with the following dog.

Ch. Brambledale Blue Bonnet (B) (Eng. Ch. Brambledale Balthazar x Brambledale Briar Rose, R.O.M.), Robert and Henrietta Lachman. Tied for title of Companion Dog, and the only Beardie to appear in lists of top winners, top producers, and top obedience dogs.

Tracking Dog
Brigand O'Braemoor, T.D. (D) (Ch. Chauntelle Limelight x Ch. Branikan O'Braemoor, C.D.), Ruth E. Ivers. Continuing the Braemoor tradition.

SHUMAN SYSTEM RECORDS

Records for the breed published in "Front and Finish," and the Shuman System rating, supplied by Robert T. Self, editor, follow:

1977
1. Windcache A Briery Bess, Prescott
2. Ghillie, Smith
3. Cauldbraes Tam O'Shanter, Blumire

1978
1. Windcache A Briery Bess, Prescott
2. Cauldbrae Mount Archer Jamie, Jewett
3. Sealight Torg, Ewon
4. Ch. Spring Magic Of Willowmead, DeBorha

1979
1. Windcache A Briery Bess, U.D., Prescott
2. Windcache A Blustery Day, Wilson and Holmes
3. Pepper Countess Of Kemora, Corigleano
4. Ch. Spring Magic Of Willowmead, DeBorha

1980
1. Ch./O.T.Ch. Windcache A Briery Bess, H.C., Prescott
2. Windcache A Blustery Day, C.D.X., Wilson and Holmes
3. Sno Berry Black Blazer, Giewartowski
4. Gaymardons Bronze Brigadier, Miller

1981
1. Ch./O.T.Ch. Windcache A Briery Bess, H.C., Prescott
2. Windcache A Blustery Day, C.D.X., Wilson and Holmes
3. Sno Berrys Black Blazer, C.D.X., Giewartowski
4. Ch. Silverleaf Rompn Tawny, Debusschere

1982
1. Ch./O.T.Ch. Windcache A Briery Bess, Prescott
2. Windcache A Blustery Day, U.D., Wilson and Holmes
3. Ch. Brisles Glen Nadia, C.D.X., Ber. C.D., Brask
4. Braw Banner Of Three Oakes, C.D.X., Doto
   Windy Hill Mariah, C.D.X., Prescott

1983
1. Ch. Glen Eire's Bedazlin Beethoven, C.D.X., Robinson
2. Windcache A Blustery Day, U.D., Wilson and Holmes
3. Glen Eire's Storm O'Longview, C.D.X., Karen and Laurence Jeris
4. Sno Berry's Black Blazer, C.D.X., Giewartowski

1984
1. Ch. Windy Hill ReRun, C.D.X., Barbara Wilson
2. Pandora, Frantz
3. Ch. Glen Eire Bedazlin Beethoven, U.D., H.C., Robinson
4. Bon Di Aldebaran Of Alamos, C.D.X., J. M. Cooper

1985
1. Pandora, U.D., Frantz
2. Ch. Daybreak Storm At Candelaria, C.D.X., H.C., Price and Prescott
3. Ch. Arcadia's Bentley O'Walkoway, C.D.X., Bates
4. Ch. Chaniam Morga Callin, C.D.X., Gould

Ch. Rich-Lin's R.C. Owner, Sondra Franc.

English Ch. Edenborough Blue Bracken, top winning dog in England. Owner, Shirley Holmes.

TOP OBEDIENCE DOGS

In 1983 Ch. Windcache A Briery Bess attained her title of Obedience Trial Champion and was chosen by the BCCA as the top Beardie obedience dog for the year. At that time, Kandy Robinson developed a system to determine the top dog for each class, with the following results:

1984
Novice—Ch. Arcadia's Bentley O'Walkoway, C.D., Bates
Open—Ch. Windyhill's Rerun, C.D.X., Wilson
Utility—Ch. Glen Eire's Bedazlin Beethoven, U.D., Robinson

1985
Novice—Lennakay B.C. at Gair Paravel, C.D., Ralph
Open—Ch. Arcadia's Bentley O'Walkoway, C.D.X., Bates
Utility—Pandora, U.D., Frantz

English, Canadian, Bermudian, American Ch. Edenborough Grey Shadow. Owners, Jeanette and Lindy Waite.

Ch. Wyndcliff Unicorn Sterling, R.O.M. Owners, Unicorn Hill and Aellen.

Ch. Jande Just Justin. Owner, Kathy Kyle.

Great Producers

No less great are the Beardies who produced the winners of ribbons, titles, and hearts. The top kennels were founded on these truly outstanding Beardies, many of which have produced twice the number necessary to achieve the Register of Merit title!

Can./Am. Ch. Algobrae's Sterling Silver (Int. Ch. Edenborough Grey Shadow, R.O.M., x Monyash Whirlpool), Sawka. Canadian dog by a top sire. (Black.)

Ch. Arcadia's Bluegrass Music (Ch. Edenborough Happy Go Lucky, R.O.M., x Ch. Edenborough Quick Silver, R.O.M.), Lowe. Out of a Top Ten Dam by the Number One Sire; winner of BCCA BOS. (Blue.)

Ch. Arcadia's Honky Tonk Angel (Ch. Edenborough Happy Go Lucky, R.O.M., x Ch. Rich-Lin's Molly of Arcadia, R.O.M.), Shannon and Stepankow. By the Number One Sire and out of the Number One Dam. Finished at ten months. (Brown.)

Ch. Arcadia's Marcy of Rich-Lin, C.D. (Ch. Rich-Lin's Whiskers of Arcadia, R.O.M., x Rich-Lin's Molly of Arcadia, R.O.M.), Walkowicz. Following a family tradition of top producers, passing on her lovely side movement. Marcy loved to "dance," even at inopportune moments. Foundation bitch for Walkoway. (Black.)

Ch. Arcadia's Midnight Munday (litter sister to Marcy), Shannon and Pruitt. Continuing the legacy of producing great movement and temperament. (Black.)

Ch. Arcadia's Virginia Slim (Ch. Ha'Penny Blueprint of Arcadia, R.O.M., x Ch. Arcadia's Midnight Munday, R.O.M.), Shannon. Daughter of two top producers; third generation R.O.M. (Black.)

Ch. Artisan Burnish'D Silverleaf (Ch. Shiel's Mogador's Silverleaf, C.D., R.O.M., x Parcana Possibility, R.O.M.), Witte. Tommi is a dominant producer, as were her sire and dam. (Brown.)

Ch. Barnleigh's Damaris (Marksman Of Sunbree x Cannamoor Corndolly), Warren. Bonnie is the dam of Chesapeake Mist and another top producer, Mouffy Mister, among others. Lovely temperament and expression. (Black.)

Aust./Am. Ch. Beardie Bloody Mary (Ch. Calderlin Leal x Ch. Penreen's Annie Laurie), Masters. Sweet, pretty bitch, dam of several champions and multiple Group winners. (Brown.)

Eng. Ch. Brambledale Balthazar (Eng. Ch. Osmart Bonnie Blue Braid x Brambledale's Heather Mead Moonlight), Evans. Sire of top winner and producer Bonnet, among many others. (Black.)

Ch. Brambledale Blackfriar (Brambledale Balthazar x Brambledale Bretta), Mahigian and Morrison. Group winner. (Black.)

Ch. Brambledale Blue Bonnet, C.D. (Eng. Ch. Brambledale Balthazar, R.O.M., x Brambledale Briar Rose, R.O.M.), Lachman. BIS winner. Lost to the fancy in 1985. (Blue.)

Ch. Brambledale Boz (Braelyn Broadholme Crofter x Brambledale Barberry), Blake. Canadian dog. (Black.)

Am./Can. Ch. Brisles Mouffy Mister (Rich-Lin's Rising Son x Ch. Barnleigh's Damaris, R.O.M.), Stinson. "Teddy" comes from a top sire and dam. (Black.)

Ch. Cauldbrae's Brigadoon (Braelyn Broadholme Crofter x Brambledale Bumble), Morrison. Sired many winners for Cauldbrae. (Black.)

Cauldbrae's Cocoa Puff (Ch. Cauldbrae's Brigadoon, R.O.M., x Cauldbrae's Amazing Grace), Morrison. By a top-producing sire. (Brown.)

Ch. Chauntelle's Limelight (Ch. Edenborough Blue Bracken, R.O.M., x Sheldawyn Amber Tint), Davies and Schneider. Out of an English top producer and winner. BIS winner. (Brown.)

Criterion Silverleaf Rachel (Ch. Silverleaf English Leather, R.O.M., x Ch. Shepherdess Help from Shiel, R.O.M.), Stark. Out of two top producers. (Black.)

Ch. Edenborough Adventure (1972-1983) (Rowdina Grey Fella x Broadholme Christina), Nootbaar. "Moosey" was an exuberant Beardie, barking his thanks for applause. He enjoyed being the focus of attention, showing off by flopping on his back. Won a national match BOB. Was named "Top Mountain Dog" after retirement from breed ring. (Black.)

Eng. Ch. Edenborough Blue Bracken (1970-1983) (Rowdina Grey Fella x Blue Maggie from Osmart), Holmes. Winner of an unbelievable forty-two CC's, and producer of many winners, both United States and England. Only Beardie to win BIS at English championship all-breed show, an entry of nine thousand dogs! (Blue.)

Edenborough Full O'Life (1970-1982) (Rowdina Grey Fella x Blue Maggie from Osmart), Nootbaar. "Shag" was the first Beardie owned by Rich-Lin, and was "full o'love," as well. Sensitive to her owners' moods, celebrating and despairing with them. Shag adored her kennelmates, and would breed only to them. She copied their actions, even to lifting her leg when the males did! Produced four champions, including Royal Shag, R.O.M., and the All-Time Top-Producing Dam, Molly. (Black.)

Ch. Edenborough Happy Go Lucky (Ch. Edenborough Blue Bracken, R.O.M., x Davealex Dawn Reign, R.O.M.), Shannon. Top All-Time Beardie Sire. (Black.)

Ch. Edenborough Parcana (Ch. Edenborough Blue Bracken x Davealex Dawn Reign), Parker. "Nibby" was a foundation bitch for Parcana Kennels. (Brown.)

Ch. Edenborough Quick Silver (Heyescott Jack Tar x Tamboras Penny Black, R.O.M.), Shannon and Walkowicz. "Sally" is both sweet and smart. An angel in the house and an imp in the kennel. Producing beautiful heads, bone, and coat. Was a foundation bitch for both Arcadia and Walkoway Kennels, producing a BIS, BCCA BOS, and many Group placers. (Blue.)

Ch. Edenborough Wee Bit O'Luck (sister to Quick Silver), Emke and Shannon. Typical of the breeding—pretty, with lovely head and coat. (Blue.)

Ch. Excellent Outfit Queen (Edenborough Replica x Withymoor Midnight Magic), Conro. An import that built a foundation for Lochengar. (Black.)

Ch. Gaelyn's Copper Artisan (Ch. Silverleaf Gifted Artisan x Ch. Artisan Silverleaf O'Parcana), Witte. Listed in Group winners. (Brown.)

Ch. Glen Eire Good Gracious (Ch. Willowmead Something Super, R.O.M., x Ch. Glen Eire's Molly Brown, R.O.M.), Dean and Dolan. Good pigment; sweet girl. (Black.)

Ch. Gaymardon's Chesapeake Mist (Eng. Ch. Davealex Royle Baron x Ch. Barnleigh Damaris, R.O.M.), Miller. Listed in Group winners.

Ch. Gaymardon's Crack O'Dawn, H.C. (Ch. Gaymardon Yorktown Yankee, R.O.M., x Monyash Tempest Tossed),

International (English, Norwegian, Swedish, Finnish) Ch. Beagold David Blue (sitting) and son. Breeders, Beagold Kennels, England.

American and Canadian Ch. Classical's Star Baby, H.C. Owners, Nona Albarano and Bea Sawka.

Miller. "Heidi's" sire is a top producer also. Correct harsh coat. (Black.)

Ch. Gaymardon's Yorktown Yankee, H.C. (Ch. Davealex Royle Baron x Ch. Barnleigh Damaris, R.O.M.), Miller. "Chip" is a Group winner out of a top producer.

Ch. Glen Eire Molly Brown, R.O.M. (Ryjo Holtye x Glen Eire Meaghan O'Cauldbrae), Dean and Dolan. A sound, lovely bitch, producing her equal; dam of another top producer—Good Gracious. (Brown.)

Ch. Glen Eire's Willie Wonderful (Ch. Misty Shadow of Willowmead, R.O.M., x Ch. Luath Bonnie Blue Bairn, R.O.M.), Dolan and Dean. The test of a good producer is whether he or she produces winners and other producers, and Willie was yet another example of that. Group winner out of two top producers. (Black.)

Ch. Ha'Penny Blue Blossom (Ch. Brambledale Boz, R.O.M., x Ch. Brambledale Blue Bonnet, R.O.M.), Schneider. Group winner and producer out of two top producers. (Blue.)

Ch. Ha'Penny Blueprint of Arcadia (Ch. Chauntelle's Limelight, R.O.M., x Ch. Brambledale Blue Bonnet, R.O.M.), Harris and Shannon. Group winner out of two top producers. (Blue.)

Ch. Ha'Penny Lucy Locket (sister to Blossom), Schneider. Finished undefeated in class competition. (Black.)

Ch. Jande's Just Dudley (Ch. Edenborough Happy Go Lucky, R.O.M., x Ch. Beardie Bloody Mary, R.O.M.), Masters. Continuing the tradition of top producers. Group winner. (Brown.)

Ch. Jande's Oxford Knight in Blue (litter brother to Dudley), MacPhail. Group winner. (Blue.)

Ch. Jande's Winsome Winnie (Ch. Edenborough Silver Shadow x Ch. Mistiburn Pocahontas), Masters. Dark, lovely girl, exhibiting good movement. (Black.)

Ch. Johnathen Brown Of Tambora (Eng. Ch. Osmart Bonnie Blue Braid, R.O.M., x Eng. Ch. Edelweiss of Tambora), Morrison. Another top producer for one of the top kennels, Cauldbrae. (Brown.)

Ch. Luath Bonnie Blue Bairn, R.O.M. (1974-1982) (Eng. Ch. Osmart Bonnie Blue Ribbon x Luath Nutmeg), Dolan. An all-around bitch: show-ring, producer, obedience, and, above all, companion. (Blue.)

Ch. Misty Shadow of Willowmead (Eng. Ch. Wishanger Cairnbahn x Eng. Ch. Broadholme Cindy Sue of Willowmead), Jagersma. Listed in Canadian dogs. (Black.)

Eng. Ch. Osmart's Bonnie Blue Braid (Ch. Bravo of Bothkennar x Ch. Blue Bonnie of Bothkennar), Osborne. English dog. Loved the ring, asking for the win. When he wasn't immediately given his BOB winner's rosette to wear at the prestigious Crufts show, he did Beardie bounces down the mat until he achieved his way. Sire of many winners, in both England and the United States. (Blue.)

Ch. Osmart Silverleaf Goldmine (Eng. Ch. Osmart Bonnie Blue Braid, R.O.M., x Osmart Silver Kracker), Rieseberg. Sound, friendly dog. (Fawn.)

Ch. Osmart Smoky Blue Parcana (Eng. Ch. Osmart Bonnie Blue Braid, R.O.M., x Eng. Ch. Queen Arwen of Kenstaff), Parker. Another lovely producer for Parcana. (Blue.)

Ch. Parcana Portrait (Ch. Parcana Silverleaf Vandyke, R.O.M., x Ch. Edenborough Parcana, R.O.M.), Parker. Finished with four majors; a top producer out of top producers. (Black.)

Parcana Possibility (Davealex Iownhim x Amber from Davealex), Rieseberg. "Riskie" never finished, due to an injury, but became a top producer. (Blue.)

Ch. Parcana Silverleaf Vandyke, H.C. (Ch. Shiel's Mogador's Silverleaf, C.D., R.O.M., x Shepherd's Help From Shiel, C.D., R.O.M.), Parker. Correct size, good head. Working herding dog. One of the first Beardie showmen. (Black.)

Pepperland Pandamonium (Eng. Ch. Davealex Royle Brigadier x Pepperland's Osmart Bronze Pandora), O'Bryan and Surber. Produced Eng. Ch. Pepperland Lyric John at Pottersdale. (Brown.)

Ch. Rich-Lin's Molly of Arcadia, R.O.M. (Rich-Lin's Rising Son x Edenborough Full O'Life, R.O.M.), Shannon. Top All-Time All-Breed Dam. (Black.)

Ch. Rich-Lin's Mr. Magoo (Ch. Rich-Lin's Pride of Jason, R.O.M., x Ch. Rich-Lin's Royal Shag, R.O.M.), Conro. Out of a top dam. Group winner. (Black.)

Rich-Lin's Rising Son (1974-1976) (Ch. Edenborough Adventure, R.O.M., x Ch. Jaseton Princess Argonetta), Shannon. In his producing span cut short by an accident, he produced two of the Arcadia foundation stock, Whiskers and Molly, as well as another top producer, Mouffy Mister. (Black.)

English Ch. Osmart Bonnie Blue Braid. Owner, Jenny Osborne.

Ch. Rich-Lin's Royal Shag, R.O.M. (Edenborough Loch Ness x Edenborough Full O'Life, R.O.M.), Nootbaar. "Gin-G" is the ideal dam, taking on maternal duties (even nursing) at the age of eleven, by adopting the puppy of another. She is the dam of top producer Mr. Magoo. (Black.)

Ch. Rodoando Culloden at Chaniam (Kimrand Simon x Robdave Wild Affair), Bailey. "Vally" is soaring in the ratings. Top producer 1985. (Black.)

Ch. Shenedene Miss Crispen (Davealex Willy Wumpkins x Davealex Midnight Mood), McHugh. Sweet, sound, and sparkling. Proper coat. (Black.)

Ch. Shepherdess From Shiel (Sunbrees Magic Moment O'Willowmead x Breckdale Beauty Maid), Surber. Stayed black. (Black.)

Ch. Shepherds Help From Shiel, H.C. (Marksman Of Sunbree x Tarskavaig Forget Me Not), Rieseberg. "Shiela" is also non-fading. (Black.)

American and Canadian Ch. Hootnanny of Bengray. Owners, Davis and Keller.

Ch. Shiel's Mogador's Silverleaf, C.D. (Eng. Ch. Sunbree's Magic Moments of Willowmead x Misty of Mogador), Rieseberg. BIS winner. (Black.)

Ch. Silverleaf English Leather (Ch. Shiel's Mogador Silverleaf, C.D., R.O.M., x Hyfield Hyteeny, R.O.M.), Rieseberg. The red-brown "Morgan" is a Group winner as well as a producer. (Brown.)

Tambora's Penny Black, R.O.M. (Ch. Edenborough Blue Bracken, R.O.M., x Ch. Edelweiss Of Tambora), Holmes. Dam of top producer Quick Silver. (Black.)

Ch. Thaydom Silverleaf Cinnamon (sister to English Leather), Berger and Rieseberg. Finished with four majors. (Brown.)

Ch. Tudor Lodge Koala at Crisch (Ch. Edenborough Grey Shadow, R.O.M., x Ch. Beagold's Black Tiffany, C.D.X., R.O.M.), Schaeffer. BIS winner, dam of BIS Ch. Crisch Midnight Bracken. (Black.)

Ch. Wild Silk of Willowmead, R.O.M. (Edenborough Soaring High x Breckdale Pretty Maid), Gaffney. Proper coat, clean front, sweet expression. Foundation bitch of Unicorn Beardies. (Black.)

Ch. Willowmead's Something Super (Rowdina Rustler x Breckdale Pretty Maid), Dolan. Lost too soon to the breed, but became a top producer despite his short breeding career. (Black.)

Ch. Wyndcliff Unicorn Sterling (Shiel's Sweetgale Kittihawk x Shepherdess From Shiel), Colavecchio and Gaffney. BOB BCCA match '76. (Blue.)

Ch. Rich-Lin's Whiskers of Arcadia, R.O.M. Owners, Jim and Diann Shannon.

Glengorm Auld Clootie. Owner, Major James G. Logan, Scotland.

Ch. Excellent Outfit Queen, R.O.M. Owners, Lochengar.

A Polski Owczarek Nizinny (PONS). Kerberac's Nemo, imported from Holland. Owners, Polaris Kennels. The PONS is thought to be one of the ancestors of the Beardie.

Ch. Cricket's Lookin' Good. Owner, Nona Albarano.

Ch. Arcadia's Tennessee Rose. Owner, Marilyn Lowe.

106

REGISTER OF MERIT TITLEHOLDERS

The Register of Merit (R.O.M.) title is bestowed by the BCCA upon dogs and bitches that have produced a specified number of quality progeny. The title is even more important than that of champion, since a champion that does not produce is unable to contribute to the improvement of the breed and to the owner's breeding program.

Diann Shannon was appointed by the BCCA as committee chairman to institute the program. Serving on the R.O.M. committee were Terri Stepankow and Gail Miller.

The R.O.M. tabulation is based on similar programs for other parent clubs, such as the German Shepherd Dog, Great Dane, and Old English Sheepdog Clubs of America, which in turn took precedents from the merit system for purebred cattle. To earn the R.O.M. title, Bearded Collie R.O.M. sires must have at least five champion progeny, and R.O.M. dams need at least three. In late 1986, the BCCA board voted to award the coveted R.O.M.X. to sires that have fifteen or more champions, and to dams producing ten or more champions.

R.O.M.X. SIRES

Ch. Edenborough Happy Go Lucky	46
Ch. Chauntelle's Limelight	42
Am./Can. Ch. Sheil's Mogador's Silverleaf, C.D.	37
Ch. Glen Eire Willie Wonderful	25
Ch. Gaymardon Yorktown Yankee, H.C.	21
Ch. Cauldbraes Brigadoon	18
Ch. Brambledale Boz	16
Ch. Gaelyn Copper Artisan	16
Am./Can. Ch. Algobrae Sterling Silver	15

R.O.M. SIRES

Ch. Brisles Mouffy Mister	13
Ch. Misty Shadow Of Willowmead	12
Ch. Rich-Lins Mister Magoo	12
Ch. Ha'Penny Blueprint of Arcadia	12
Ch. Arcadias Bluegrass Music	12
Ch. Edenborough Adventure	11
Ch. Silverleaf English Leather	11
Johnathen Brown Of Tambora	11
Ch. Parcana Silverleaf Van Dyke, H.C.	11
Brambledale Balthazar	10
Eng. Ch. Edenborough Blue Bracken	10
Eng. Ch. Osmart Bonnie Blue Braid	10
Ch. Osmart Silverleaf Goldmine	10
Ch. Willowmead Something Super	10
Ch. Jande's Just Dudley	10
Ch. Brambledale Blackfriar	10
Ch. Arcadia's Cotton-Eyed Joe	10
Ch. Banacek Fawn Fabric	9
Ch. Davealex Rhinestone Cowboy	9
Ch. Willowmead Mid Winter Boy	9
Ch. Edenborough Grey Shadow	9
Ch. Baffler O'Braemoor, C.D., T.D.	9
Glen Eire Starstruck	9
Ch. Waldo of Carruthers	9
Ch. Glenhys Marshall Silverleaf	8
Ch. Rich-Lins Pride Of Jason	8
Ch. MacMont MacIntosh	8
Ch. Tamevalley Highland Ballad	8
Ch. Arcadia's Paprika	8
Ch. Cauldbrae's Royal Windsor	8
Ch. Bon Di Parcana The Patriot	8
Bagpiper O'Braemoor	7
Ch. Rich-Lin's Whiskers of Arcadia	7
Shiel's Sweetgale Kittihawk	7
Ch. Wyndcliff Michaelangelo	7
Ch. Shaggylane's Beaming Teak	7
Ch. Arcadia's Salty Jok O'Emshire	7
Ch. Copper Clarence at Beagold	7
Willowmead Midnight Blue	7
Ch. Ha'Penny Blu Max at Braemar	7
Ch. Parcana Heart Throb	7
Wyndcliff Foolery O' the Picts	7
Happy Hooligan Of Bengray	6
Ch. Willowferry Victor	6
Ch. Jande's Oxford Knight in Blue	6
Ch. Osmart's Smoky Silver Starter Chan	6
Ch. Brambledale Black Rod	5
Ch. Criterion Silverleaf Rascal	5
Davealex Willie Wumpkins	5
Ch. Glen Eire Laird at Lonetree, H.C.	5
Ch. Heathglen's Jolly Oliver	5
Ch. Spring Magic O'Willowmead, C.D.	5
Ch. Gaymardon Bouncing Bogart	5
Ch. Pepperland Rolling Stone, Am./Can. CD	5
Ch. Arcadia's Mr. Pibb	5
Ch. Jande's Lucky Tri	5
Ch. Jande's Just Justin	5
Ch. Ha'Penny's Havoc	5
Penstone Masterpiece	5
Ch. Potterdale Paris	5
Ch. Unicorn Gandalf the Wizard	5

R.O.M.X. DAMS

Ch. Rich-Lins Molly Of Arcadia	33
Parcana Possibility	18
Ch. Edenborough Quick Silver	18
Ch. Ha'Penny Blue Blossom	16
Ch. Wild Silk Of Willowmead	12
Ch. Rodoando Culloden at Chaniam	11
Ch. Gaymardons Chesapeake Mist, H.C.	10
Ch. Artisan Burnish'D Silverleaf	10
Ch. Beardie Bloody Mary	10

R.O.M. DAMS

Ch. Wyndcliff Unicorn Sterling	9
Ch. Glen Eire Good Gracious	9
Ch. Gaymardon's Crack O'Dawn, CD H.C.	9
Criterion Silverleaf Rachel	8
Ch. Luath Bonnie Blue Bairn	8
Ch. Thaydom Silverleaf Cinnamon	8
Ch. Shepherds Help From Shiel, H.C.	8
Ch. Arcadias Midnight Munday	8
Ch. Ha'Penny Lucy Locket	8
Ch. Arcadias Marcy Of Rich-Lin, C.D.	8
Ch. Brambledale Blue Bonnet	7
Ch. Edenborough Parcana	7
Ch. Shepherdess From Shiel	7
Ch. Parcana Portrait	7

Ch. Jande's Winsome Winnie	7
Ch. Excellent Outfit Queen	7
Ch. Edenborough Wee Bit O'Luck	7
Ch. Tudor Lodge Koala at Crish	7
Ch. Osmart Smoky Blue Parcana	7
Ch. Barnleigh Damaris	6
Cauldbraes Cocoa Puff	6
Pepperland Pandamonium	6
Ch. Rich-Lins Royal Shag	6
Tamboras Penny Black	6
Ch. Shendene's Miss Crispen	6
Ch. Arcadia's Honky Tonk Angel	6
Ch. Arcadia's Virginia Slim	6
Brambledale Briar Rose	5
Ch. Charncroft Caprice	5
Ch. Glen Eire Molly Brown	5
Ch. Jaseton Princess Argonetta	5
Ch. Rich-Lins Talk Of The Town	5
Ch. Silverleaf Scottish Heather	5
Ch. Banacek Bewitched	5
Ch. Pepperland Liberty Belle	5
Briardale Wild Heather	5
Ch. Cauldbrae Loch Ness	5
Ch. Cauldbrae Tangle O'The Isles	5
Ch. Parcana Braemor's Goldigger	5
Ch. Mistiburn Merrymaid	5
Am. Can. Ch. Bendale Special Lady, C.D.X.	5
Ch. Arcadia's Black Velvet	5
Ch. Silverleaf A Cameo of Chelsea	5
Ch. Brambledale Beth	4
Brambledale Bona Dea	4
Broadholm Christina	4
Ch. Deanfield Ocean Mist	4
Davealex Loch Harbour	4
Edenborough Full O'Life	4
Glen Eire Skye O'Cauldbrae	4
Glen Eire Bide-A-Wee Brown	4
Honours Galore From Davealex	4
Graylen Bonnie From Robdave	4
Tamboras Black Rose Marie	4
Ch. Branikan O'Braemoor, C.D., T.D.	4
Beagold Black Tiffany	4
Ch. Scothills Evidently Edith	4
Brambledale Bala	4
Edenborough Showboat	4
Ch. Unicorn Katharine of Aragon, C.D.	4
Ch. Raisin's Certainly Cindy	4
Ch. Silverleaf Licorice Revel	4
Ch. Silverleaf Autumn Harvest	4
Ch. Rich-Lin's Wee Bit O'Blue	4
Ch. Unicorn's Charley's Angel	4
Eng. Ch. Willowmead Perfect Lady	4
Ch. Silverleaf Moody Blue	4
Ch. Sunnylane Song Sung Blue	4
Ch. Jande's Maryjane	4
Ch. Cauldbrae's Black-Eyed Susan	4
Ch. Criterion Darla O'Mellowit	4
Arcadia's Midnight Maggie	4
Thaydom's Silverleaf Cinnamon	3
Breckdale Pretty Maid	3
Blindbluff Love In A Mist	3
Ch. Camshron Babs	3
Cauldbraes Browyn	3
Ch. Cauldbraes Lorna Doon	3
Ch. Davealex Dawn Reign	3
Gwenelog Rambler	3
Glen Eire Bonnie Blue Flag	3
Grayona Jubilee Easter Lily	3
Ch. Hootnanny Of Bengray	3
Hyfield Hyteeny	3
Ch. Kashmir Silverleaf Lynn	3
Ch. Malachi Mariah Of Silverleaf	3
Ch. Mistiburn Pocahontas	3
Ch. Padworth Miss Muffet	3
Eng. Ch. Queen Arwen Of Kenstaff	3
Rich-Lins Honey Bear	3
Ch. Top Secret Of Willowmead	3
Ch. Withymoor Classical Gass	3
Ch. Warbonnet Silverleaf Breta	3
Ch. Cauldbrae's Bridget Blue	3
Ch. Cricket's Pennyroyal	3
Ch. Rich-Lins Charlies Blue Angel	3
Ch. Rosamba Buttercup	3
Willowmead Lady in Black	3
Cauldbrae's Blue Columbine	3
Ch. Glen Eire Ardsley Black Dot	3
Ch. Lady Brooke O'Bannochbrae	3
Ch. Miracle Maid of Lonetree	3
Silverleaf Virginia Reel	3
Ch. Umilik Genii of Dandenong	3
Ch. Timberidge's Unicorn Tabitha	3
Thaydom Greysteel Artisan	3
Padworth Honey	3
Ch. Parcana Holly of Mereworth	3
Ch. O'Kelidon's Megan M'Luv	3
Ch. Jande's Lucky Mary	3
Ch. Ha'Penny Hoyden at Edmar	3
Algobrae Chelsea Blue	3
Ch. Bon Di Chasing Rainbows	3
Am./Can. Ch. Algobrae Liquorice Candy	3
Benbecca's Black Edition	3
Ch. Beaconview Ebony at Colbara	3
Cauldbrae's Corrie Doon	3
Ch. Cauldbrae's Cecilia	3
Ch. Dawne's Gathers No Moss	3

Rich-Lins Honey Bear, R.O.M., winning the Miscellaneous Class at nine months. Owners, James and LeRae Conro, and Eugene and Ronnie Barno.

The First Decade—Champions of Record

Data in the following listing was first published in *Purebred Dogs/American Kennel Gazette*. The dates shown here are the dates of the issues of the magazine in which the information appeared. The name(s) following the dog's name is that of the person(s) who owned the dog at the time the championship was attained.

5/77	Brambledale Blue Bonnet (B), Lachman
6/77	Davealex Larky McRory Of Linchael (D), Morrison
	Rich-Lin's Mister Magoo (D), Conro and Nootbaar
	Shepherdess From Shiel (B), Surber
	Shiel's Mogador's Silverleaf (D), Rieseberg
	Wyndcliff Michaelangelo (D), Surber
7/77	Barnleigh Damaris (B), Warren
	Davealex Rhinestone Cowboy (D), Morrison
	Gaymardon Chesapeake Mist (B), Miller
	Rich-Lin's Whiskers Of Arcadia (D), Shannon
	Seykoe Clan Chieftain At Beagold (D), Reinlieb
8/77	Banacek Bewitched (B), Murphy
	Brisle's Mouffy Mister (D), Stinson
	Glen Eire's That's A Statement (B), Westphal
	Haute Ecole Banner O'Braemoor, C.D. (D), Cline and Holmes
	Jaseton Princess Argonetta (B), Nootbaar
9/77	Brambledale Black Diamond (D), Schneider
	Cauldbrae's Brigadoon (D), Morrison
	Charisma Bonnie Brae Bonny Jo (B), Koplow
	Glen Eire Ton Mhor Tosh (D), Hazera
	Karistan Topkopi Chordahyer (B), Cordes and Ayer
	Rich-Lin's Molly Of Arcadia (B), Shannon
	Rich-Lin's Wee Bit O'Blue (B), Scarff
	St. Andrew's Just Plain Emily (B), Terricone and St. Lifer
10/77	Bonnie Brae's Hunnypot (B), Shimek
	Gaymardon Yorktown Yankee (D), Miller
	Strathourn Highland Lilt (B), Clark
11/77	Charncroft Caprice (B), Turner
	Colbara Blue Spruce (D), Blake and Holava
	Dunwich Thistle Of Balmoral (B), Davies and Hayes
	Flanigan At Beagold (D), Taulman
	Hopelynn Heritage (D), McKee
	Loch 'N Mead B'rer Bear (D), Schaefer
	Parcana Silverleaf Vandyke (D), Parker
	Sirhan Ember Glow (D), Benbow
	Wyndcliff's Stonemark Oliver (D), Gross
12/77	Baffler O'Braemoor (D), Parsons
	Brisle's Thimbleberry Heather (B), Taulman
	Camshron Babs (B), Jozwiak
	Cauldbrae's Mo Caraid (D), Goldworm
	Edenborough Adventure (D), Nootbaar and Kottmeier
	Glenhy's Marshall Silverleaf (D), Howey
	Ha'Penny Blue Hyzenthlay (B), Schneider
	Nel-Von's Macduff O'Silverleaf (D), Huber
	Rich-Lin's Royal Shag (B), Nootbaar
	Shaggylane's Beaming Teak (D), Niddrie
	Silverleaf English Leather (D), Rieseberg
	Silverleaf's Wenlock O'Glenn (D), Wolcott and Rieseberg
1/78	Beagold's Black Tiffany (B), Blumire
	Blindbluff Ben Nevis My Honey (D), Lingswiler
	Cannamoor Honey Rose, C.D., T.D. (B), Parsons
	Chordahyer's Bonnie Jon (D), Cloman and Kurtzner
	Edenborough Blue River (B), Link
	Gaymardon Crack O Dawn (B), Miller
	Glennamoor Cayjen O'Glen Eire (B), Droll
	Little Biddy Aberdeen O'Banff (B), Weise
	Misty Shadow Of Willowmead (D), Jagersma
	Osmart Blue Chips (D), Goldworm
	Rich-Lin's Pride Of Jason (D), Cole and Nootbaar
	Sno-Berry's Chrysanthemum (B), Jozwiak and Schnute
2/78	Brambledale Benedict (D), Chylack
	Buccaneer O'Braemoor (D), Droll
	Charncroft Country Rose (B), Levy
	Edenborough Parcana (B), Parker
	Glen Eire's Molly Brown (B), Dean and Dolan
	Katie's Wiff N Pooh (D), Keyes
	Kittyhawk First Generation (D), De Vore and Rosdail
	Raggmopp Holly Go Lightly (B), Simcoe and Gold
	Spring Magic Of Willowmead, C.D. (D), De Borba
	Thaydom Silverleaf Cinnamon (B), Berger and Rieseberg
3/78	Bengray Bonnie Jean (B), Cordes and Ayer
	Cauldbrae's Lorna Doon (B), Morrison
	Cauldbrae's Rascallion (D), Patrick
	Glen Eire Willie Wonderful (D), Dolan and Dean
	Silverleaf Gifted Artisan (D), Witte and Rieseberg
4/78	Amberwood's Challenge (D), Shannon and Staser
	Cauldbrae's Loch Ness (B), Hazera
	Kashmir Silverleaf Llyn (B), Rieseberg
	Rich-Lin's Blue Streak (D), Baker and Nootbaar
5/78	Andrew Of Thimbleberry (D), Taulman
	Brambledale Belle Blue (B), Mahigian
	Cauldbrae's Bridget Blue (B), Winter
	Edenborough Brackenson (D), Abrams
	Edenborough Grey Shadow (D), Waite
	Glen Eire's Bonnie Blue Flag (B), Edner
	Willowferry Victor (D), Blake
6/78	Criterion Silverleaf Rascal (D), Stark
	Ha'Penny Blue Blossom (B), Schneider
	Kashmir Silverleaf Llyn (B), Rieseberg
	Withymorr Classical Gass (B), Shimek
7/78	Bonnie Brae's Charles Of Olney (D), Orlando
	Brambledale Beth (B), Turner
	Cauldbrae Tam O'Shanter (D), Blumire
	Forister's Black Jack (D), Stark and Forister
	Parcana Heart Throb (D), Parker
	Rich-Lin's Ms. Liberty (B), Kothman
	Silverleaf Scottish Heather (B), Rieseberg
	Sno-Berry's Black Lad (D), Jozwiak
	Wild Silk Of Willowmead (B), Gaffney
	Willowmead Something Super (D), Dolan
8/78	Arcadia's Midnight Raider (D), Bartosch
	Beagold Caprice, C.D. (B), Reinlieb
	Brisle's Kirriemuir (B), Jenkins
	Cauldbrae's Wind Song (B), Plimpton
	Chordahyer's MacKenzie (D), Cordes and Ayer
	Dune Arrakis (D), Barnard
	Gaymardon Challenger (D), Karnes
	Gray Rogue Of Rippleshire (D), Rubens
9/78	Brambledale Bard (D), Mahigian
	Brisle's Glen Nadia (B), Brask
	Glen Eire's Black Callioch (B), Schwartz
	Mistiburn Promise Of Victory (D), Albarano

Ch. Walkoway's G. K. Chesterton. Owners, Charles and Beverly Lamb and Chris Walkowicz.

Ch. Lochengar Great Expectations. Owners, LeRae and Jim Conro.

Bagpiper O'Braemoor, R.O.M. Owner, Virginia Parsons.

Ch. Glen Eire Willie Wonderful, R.O.M. Owner, Anne Dolan.

Parcana Silverleaf Betse Ros, C.D. (B), Rieseberg
Rich-Lin's Feelin' Free (D), Nootbaar
Top Secret Of Willowmead (B), Droll
Willowmead Perfect Promise (B), Morrison
10/78 Blindbluff Talisman (D), Cummings
Cricket Tick Bird Of Brunswig (B), Farrer
Excellent Outfit Queen (B), Conro
Silverleaf Sesame Stick (D), Osloond
11/78 Cauldbrae Marcresta O'Bria (B), Hueholt
Cauldbrae's KC Jones (B), Kaye and Broughton
Rich-Lin's Mischief Maker (D), Smith and Finucane
Rich-Lin's Primrose O'Rosamba (B), Roark
Rich-Lin's Talk Of The Town (B), Nootbaar
Sperryville's Ladybug (B), Warren
Winterwood Alexander (D), Watson and Winter
12/78 Arcadia's Midnight Son (D), Shannon
Bobbie Brie (D), Sutter
Cauldbrae's Butterscotch (B), Davies and Morrison
Edenborough My Fair Lady (B), Bryan and Shannon
Glullari Butterscotch (B), McKee
Wyndcliff Unicorn Sterling (B), Colavecchio and Gaffney
1/79 Arcadia's Midnight Munday (B), Shannon and Pruitt
Bramblewick Dax MacDuff, C.D. (D), Lantelme
Edenborough Happy Go Lucky (D), Shannon
Glennamoor Beachbumm Braid (D), Droll and Schoen
Mistiburn Merrymaker (D), Turner
2/79 Cauldbrae Lass Of Marlie (B), Traux
Criterion Weiser O Mellowitt (D), Witt
Glen Eire's Red Button (D), Thomas
Luvnstuf Of Kelabarossa (D), Nystrom
Mistiburn Pocahontas (B), Masters
Rich-Lin's Forever Spring (B), Shutan and Nootbaar
Unicorn's Gandalf The Wizard (D), Gaffney
3/79 Artisan Silverleaf O'Parcana (B), Rieseberg and Witte
Criterion's Ebony Frost (B), Stark
Edenborough Quick Silver (B), Shannon
Osmart Silverleaf Goldmine (D), Rieseberg
Osmart Smoky Blue Parcana (B), Parker
Smallhaven's Fife 'N Drum (D), Bonkus and Hauff
4/79 Bon Di Parcana The Patriot (D), Davis
Brambledale Boz (D), Blake
Cauldbrae's Tangle O'The Isles (B), Morrison
O'Kelidon's Caledonia (B), McHugh
Parcana's Holly Of Mereworth (B), Webb
Sassye Of Millar, Baldwin
The Rocky Mountain Bandit (D), Stark
Thistle (B), Lachman
5/79 Bogyi O'Braemoor (D), An and Khaw
Cauldbrae's Glenfiddich Rory (D), McKenney
Cauldbrae's Sweet Donniboy (D), Sweet
Criterion's First Harvest (D), Lewis
Kiln's Barrister O'Braemoor (D), Ryder
Mistiburn Merrymaid (B), Turner
Padworth Miss Muffet (B), Lewis
Parcana Portrait (B), Parker
6/79 Agape's Malachi Cinder (B), Kertz
Edenborough Wee Bit O'Luck (B), Emke and Shannon
Forister's Mandy (B), Forister
Glen Eire's Bide-A-Wee Brown (B), Dolan and Dean
Gypsy Lass of Silverleaf (B), McNeill
Orora's Faith (B), Blumire
Silverleaf Oliver Twist (D), Ray
7/79 Copper Clarence At Beagold (D), Reinlieb
Criterion Silverleaf Spirit (B), Stark and Rieseberg
Edenborough Silver Shadow (D), Waite
Ha'Penny Macn Dufftown (D), Pritchard and Schneider
Honey Buns Of Thimbleberry (B), Karnes
Kaycees Spring Storm (D), Anderson
Rich-Lin's Black Max (D), Foster
Rich-Lin's Kristal Blue (B), Foster
Silverleaf Liberty O'Tresta (B), Price and Rieseberg
Sperryville's Royal Flush (D), Sperry
Thomas's Day Zee Of Silverleaf (B), Thomas
Waldo Of Caruthers (D), Witt
8/79 Arcadia's Daquiri Of Tays (B), Shannon
Believable Belle (B), Mitchell
Brambledale Blackfriar (D), Morrison and Mahigian
Heathglen's Jolly Oliver (D), Lazar
Sno'Berry's Black Wizard (D), Jozwiak and Roberts
Wyndcliff Fleetwood Mac (D), Greenspan
Wyndcliff Ruby Hollyhock (B), Tompkins
9/79 Albemarle's Cinnamon Koffy (B), Hazera and Ines
Arcadia's Jonny Walker (D), Green and Shannon
Arcadia's Southern Comfort (D), Houston
Cauldbrae's Tawny Pippit (B), Morrison and Chylack
Glen Eire Chimney Sweep (D), Weise
Salmar Blu Mac O'Fleetwood (D), Swain
Winterwood Argyll (D), Kaul
Wyndcliff Stonemark Megan (B), Gross
10/79 Arcadia's Marcy of Rich-Lin (B), Walkowicz
Arcadia's Martini (B), Trinco
Arcadias Salty Jok O'Emshire (D), Emke and Shannon
Bo Bruin O'Braemoor (D), Parsons
Cauldbrae Black Tam (D), Norton
Chordahyer's Ashley (D), Ayer and Cordes
Glennamoor's Bartholemew (D), Sullo
Ha'Penny Blue Sasha (B), Schneider
Lochengar's Our Mutual Friend (D), Pechmann
Luath Bonnie Blue Bairn (B), Dolan
Monyash Tempest Tossed (B), Miller
11/79 Blindbluff Sugar Cookie (B), Sperry
Brambledale Belldorlyn (B), Haas
Criterion's Darla O Mellowitt (B), Witt
Deanfield Ocean Mist (B), Morrison and Gallagher
Unicorn's The Mighty Quinn (D), Gaffney
12/79 Arcadia's Black Velvet (B), Lemons and Shannon
Cauldbrae's Cecelia (B), Morrison
Ha'Penny Lucy Locket (B), Schneider
Rich-Lin's Bandit Of Matt-Kev (D), Burke
Rich-Lin's Blue Sugar Bear (B), Nootbaar
Sunnylane Song Sung Blue (B), Stepankow
Thimbleberry's Laura Belle (B), Taulman and Whitman
Warbonnet Silverleaf Breta (B), Osloond
1/80 Arcadia's Blue Crown Royal (D), Tompkins
Bonnie's Misty Morn, C.D. (B), Banfield
Gaymardon's Baron Of Bramel (D), Webb
Silverleaf Eli (D), Hagen
Sir Dana Of Silverleaf (D), Frasier
Thimbleberry's Mobile Buddy (D), Taulman and Whitman
2/80 Arcadia's Jack Daniels (D), Rosenbloom
Bear Hills Wisp O Willow (B), Loprinzo
Criterion Cachet's Spanky (D), Robertson
Davealex O-Kelidons Gus (D), McHugh
Greysteel Annie Leithall (B), Hall
Hootnanny Of Bengray (B), Davis and Kellar
3/80 Bunwell Springfields (D), Dolan

Clan's Sterling Silver (D), Billman
Daw-Anka Snowboots Of Ha'Penny (B), Jameson
Dovmar Beau Briar (D), Masters
Lochengar's Miss Havisham (B), Conro
MacMont Mackintosh (D), Jagersma
Scothill's Evidently Edith (B), Guihen
Tudor Lodge Koala At Crisch (B), Schaefer
Tudor Lodge's Anne Boleyn (B), Blumire

4/80 Bedlam's Go Get'Em Garth (D), Bixler-Clark
Brambledale Black Rod (D), Morrison
Cauldbrae Cordon Bleu (B), Furth
Cauldbrae's Angus Of Cahoon (D), Patrick and Bing
Edenborough Heaven Scent (B), Shannon
Edenborough Kara Kara Of Josanda (B), Taylor
Greysteel Betcha Be Becca (B), Moore
Parcana British Sterling (D), Cronin
Parcana Promice Of A Rainbow (B), Davis
Three Oaks The Entertainer (D), Moffatt and Lewis

5/80 Silverleaf Shannon (B), Badhorse
St. Lawrence Shaggy (D), Stahel
Windy Hill Rerun (D), Wilson

6/80 Arcadia's Sugar Plum (B), Watanabe
Chani Of Dune (B), Howard
Damalee Mcduff Of Silverleaf (D), Rea
Emily's Casey Of Silverleaf (D), Swanson
Glen Eire's Forty-Love (D), Marshall
Rich-Lin's Charlies Blue Angel (B), Foster
Poppin Fresh (B), Elledge

7/80 Arcadia's Hot Toddy (D), Dockstader
Bloomfield Laird Mongo (D), Clark and Liebold
Chordahyer's Abbey Rose (B), Fischer
Criterion's Mellowitt Muffin (B), Witt and Stark
Jande's Amy Of Bramel (B), Webb
Jande's Winsome Winnie (B), Masters
Melita Grand Menhir Brise (D), Richland and Siri
Wyndcliff Salmars Rumours (B), Swain

8/80 Arcadia's Honky-Tonk Angel (B), Shannon
Bonnie's Brighton By The Sea (B), Richland and Siri
Cauldbrae's Royle Windsor (D), Winter
Da-Cor's Criterion Boozer (D), Wyatt
Glen Eire Tam O'Shanter (B), Weise
Hickory Hill's High Pocket's, C.D. (D), Howard
Melita Rugby Goaltender (D), Richland
Silverleaf Indian Summer (B), Lang
Three Oaks Mr. Higgins (D), Lewis and Cookman
Unicorn's Theodore Bare (D), Feliciano

9/80 Bedlam's Echo Ere Raggmopp (B), Roskin
Brambledale Blaise (D), Jozwiak
Cauldbrae's Maudi Gras (B), Nussbaum
Cauldbrae's Paisley Promise, C.D. (B), Fowler
Cauldbrae's Robin Of Arrochar (B), Robertson
Eastryd Amber Sam (D), Solomon
Glennamoor Braidshadow Blue (D), Glatzer
Miracle Maid Of Lonetree (B), Riegelhuth
Rich-Lin's R C (D), Franc
Shepherd's Help From Shiel, C.D. (B), Rieseberg
Thaydom Sugar Frosting (B), Strunge
Three Oaks Status Symbol (D), Lewis
Whipshel's Longfellow (D), Kilduff
Wych-Elm's Starry Skies (B), Special

10/80 Arcadia's Chantilly Lace (B), Pagel
Cauldbrae's Chanter (D), Sweet
Cauldbrae's Kweo Rag-A-Muffin (D), Kaye and Morrison
Cricket's Elegant Eloise (B), Kirshner

Gemini's Rondo (D), Elliott
Glen Eire Three Times Lucky, C.D. (B), Steger and Corey
Greysteel's Atomic Joshua (D), Tullis
Sheepscot Valley Bagpiper (D), Plimpton
Silverleaf Licorice Revel (B), Wretlind
Silverleaf Romp'N Tawny (D), De Busschere
Silverleaf's Virginia Reel (B), Thomas
Willowmead Midnight Black (D), Dolan
Wyndcliff Leonardo Da Vinci (D), Cline and Radtke

11/80 Arcadia's Hot Buttered Rum (D), Besteman
Bramel's Master Toby (D), Alter
Colbara Black Legacy (D), Blake
Higgit Gamoth Of Padworth (B), Lewis
My Sweet Angel Of Fetter (B), Fetter and Sweet
Parcana Silverleaf Shadows (B), Parker
Raggmopp Trillium Amber (B), Roskin and Gold
Rich-Lin's Justin Case (D), Nootbaar

12/80 Cricket's Lookin Good (D), Albarano
Criterion's Clementine (B), Stark
Criterion's Diamond Bessie (B), Walton
Edenborough Crown Prince (D), Kennedy
Glen Eire Good Gracious (B), Dean and Dolan
Lochengar Great Expectations (D), Conro
Miller's Silverleaf Blu Kilty (D), Miller
Parchment Farm's Mr. Kite (D), Tilson
Whipshel's Shilo, C.D. (D), Kilduff

1/81 Cricket's Pennyroyal (B), Lachman
Emshires Wee Myth O'Karrie (B), Foster
Gaelyn Copper Artisan (D), Witte
Parchment Farm's Black Watch (D), Mahigian
Pepperland Liberty Belle (B), Lazar
Raggmopp Hilarity (B), Dixon
Unicorn's Enchanted Elf, C.D. (B), Frisbey
O.T.Ch. Windcache A Briery Bess, U.D. (B), Prescott

2/81 Algobrae Sterling Silver (D), Sawka
Arcadia's Leroy Brown, C.D. (D), Podell and Shannon
Bendale Special Lady (B), Ritter
Cricket's Commotion (D), Lachman
Cricket's Wm Mcwillie (D), Lachman
Glen Eire's Starstruck (D), Dolan and Dean
Knightsbridge Able Jack (D), Reinlieb

3/81 Arcadia Ambergris O'Westwind (B), Yeske and Briney
Arcadia's Mister Sand Man (D), Shannon, Hammond, and Yeske
Brambledale Belladora (B), Mahigian
Cauldbrae's Black Eyed Susan (B), Kaye
Glen Eire's Phebe (B), Stradley
Ha'Penny Frost Flower (B), Greitzer and Schneider
Osmart Smokey's Silver Shadow (B), Reinlieb
Osmart Smokey's Silver Starter Chan (D), Bailey
Rodoando Culloden At Chaniam (B), Bailey
Unicorn Katherine Of Aragon, C.D. (B), Collavecchio
Unicorn's Bound For Glory (B), Feliciano
Unicorn's The Critic (D), Cushing
Wyndcliff Renoir O'The Picts (D), Radtke

4/81 Arcadia's Silver Nitrate (D), Croft
Arcadia's Sugar Cookie (B), Christianson and Shannon
Black Knight Of Thimbleberry (D), Karnes
Chauntelle Limelight (D), Schneider
Gaymardon Bouncing Bogart (D), Davis and Miller
Thimbleberry's Sassy Suches (B), Davis
Thimbleberry's Vagabond (D), Taulman and Whitman
Windmere Bruffle O'Braemoor (D), McIntire and Parsons

Ch. Arcadia's Cotton-Eyed Joe. Owners, Shannon and Stepankow.

Ch. Brambledale Black Diamond. Owners, J. Richard Schneider and Charles Phillips.

Ch. Walkoway's Victoria Holt. Owner, Karen Shaw.

Winterwood Dandi-Lion (D), Van Heel
5/81 Arcadia's Blue Bayou (B), Yeske and Shannon
Rheannon's Aurora Borealis (B), Matusik
6/81 Bon Di Chasing Rainbows (B), Nadeau and Jewett
Bramel's Abby Rose Of Bevlee (B), Stockfelt and Webb
Branikan O'Braemoor (B), Parsons
Clan's Birchwood Blue Genes (B), Kanas and Murphy
Glen Eire Bedazlin Beethoven (D), Robinson
Hyatt's Aislin Ann Of Glen Eire (B), Schroeder
Kweo's Misty Towmond (B), Kaye
Parcana Reginald (D), Beck and Parker
Silverleaf's True Harmony, C.D. (B), Stevens
Willowmead Style In Black (D), Glatzer
7/81 Aellen's Wizard Of Oz (D), Collavecchio
Blue Gatling Of Dovmar (D), Newman
Cauldbrae's Sweet Smoky Mt Boy (D), Sweet
Forister's Blue Dorothea (B), Forister
Gaymardon T Is For Toby (D), Katz
Piper's Super Cricket, C.D. (B), Bussmann and Dinan
Raisin's Orangeblos'Om Spec'Al (B), Guihen
8/81 Banacek Fawn Fabric (D), Gold
Cauldbrae's Cameron (D), Aitken and Morrison
Cauldbrae's Fionn Maccumhail (D), Truax and Pagnetti
Edenborough Great Attraction (D), Koplow
Glennamoor Brigade Bye Braid (D), Soloff
Lochengar Our Finest Hour (D), Conro
Rich-Lin's Blue April Fool (D), Hoffman
Sulayman's Silverleaf Sage (B), Hull
Sweet Wingate Wild Idea (B), Folley
Swinford Cheyenne (D), Murphy
9/81 Arcadia's Carbon Copy (D), Lowe
Arcadia's Patrick O'Riley (D), Special
Bairn's Last Chance O Glen Eire (D), Murdock and Dolan
Briardale's Wild Heather (B), Lang
Cauldbrae's Midnight Blue (B), Thompson and Hamilton
Cauldbrae's Piper Wumpkins (B), Winter
Culloden's Faithful Flora (B), Ware and Scarff
Lochengar Kernel Pikering (D), Newland
Rich-Lin's Raz'N Cain At Bosque (B), Franc
Shenedene Miss Crispen (B), McHugh
Silverleaf Sweet Relish (B), Rieseberg
10/81 Arcadia Rothchild O'Sulayman (D), Hull
Beardie Bloody Mary (B), Masters
Braer Honey O Donbarien (B), Marshall
Briardale's Sweet Honesty, C.D.X., T.D. (B), McGovern
Cauldbrae's Highland Heather (B), Pollitzer
Culloden's Gallant Mcgruder (D), Johnson and Scarff
Culloden's Lady Of Lochaish (B), Johnson and Scarff
Glen Eire Extra Special, C.D. (B), Ostra
Greysteel Daisimae Kingsroe (B), Parke and Osloond
Jande's Just Dudley (D), Masters
Jande's Oxford Knight In Blue (D), MacPhail
Leannakay's Princess Andrea (B), Stinson
Ragmuppett Diamond Meadows At Chani (B), Bailey
Raisin's Certainly Cindy (B), Guihen
Tudor Lodge Kiss Me Kate (B), Beierle
Unicorn Charley's Angel, C.D. (B), Ellington
11/81 Arcadia's Emmy Lou Harris (B), Davis
Gaymardon's Love Of Rich-Lin (B), Nootbaar
Glen Eire Murphy O'stonehaven (D), Carson
Lochengar's Piglet (B), Dorman

Teasel O'Tay Donbarien (B), Murphy
12/81 Beaconview Ebony At Colbara, C.D. (B), Keller
Bellbreed's Black Hampus (D), Long
Glen Eire Ardsley Black Dot (B), Doland and Fountain-Lantelme
Ha'Penny Moon Shadow (D), Greitzer and Schneider
Leannakay's Prince Andy Star (D), Stinson
Umilik Genii Of Dandenong (B), Dixon and Howarth
Wych-Elm's Total Eclipse (B), Houston
1/82 Arcadia's Bluegrass Music (D), Lowe
Edenborough Della Of Arcadia (B), Haarsager and Shannon
Glen Eire Better Than (B), Lachman
Lovenmist Black Bozley (D), Holava
2/82 Aellen's Cocoa Joe (D), Colavecchio
Arcadia's Country Music (B), Brask
Banacek Golden Guinea At Chaniam (B), Bailey
Callander Bobbin Hallmark (B), Tompkins
Mellowitt's Calico Flo (B), Witt
Unicorn Aellen's Frosted Buff (B), Gaffney
Whispered Wish O Donbarien (D), Marshall
Willowmead Mid-Winter Boy (D), Schroeder
3/82 Baybrook Silverleaf Summer (B), Young
Edmar's Dawns Early Light (D), Moe
Glen Eire Laird At Lonetree (D), Edner and Dolan
Parcana Jake Mctavish (D), Parker
Silverleaf's Bonnie Belle (B), Berkler
Timberridge Unicorn Tabitha (B), Hillyard and Gaffney
4/82 Arcadia's Queen O'Diamonds (B), Weaver
Cauldbrae's Blue Cuillin (D), Robertson and Morrison
Chaniam Dubh Buachaille (D), Bailey
Hapenny Lotts Highland Chief (D), Lott
Ha'Penny Smashing Basher (D), Fahey and Schneider
Ha'Penny Sweetwater Agility (B), Garrett
Trillium Anise Of Raggmopp, C.D., T.D. (B), Tuck
5/82 Aellen's Tale Of Eldorado (D), Granick
Chaniam Dubh Ban-Righ, C.D. (B), Shine and Bailey
Geliland Black Bawbee At Chaniam (D), Bailey
Lady Brooke Of Bannochbrae (B), Schnute
Lonetree Midnight Blue Nodak (D), Nolan
Mistiburn's Mistletoe (B), Carson
6/82 Edmar's Amber Dawn, C.D. (B), Reese and Peterson
Mistiburn's Windfiddler (B), Albarano and Turner
My Sweet Jas-O-Mine (B), Sweet
Rich-Lin's Outlaw (D), Bruzan
Walkoway's G. K. Chesterton (D), Lamb and Walkowicz
7/82 Amulree Toby Tyler (D), Morgan
Arcadia's Easy Lovin (B), Mirante and Shannon
Artisan Burnish'D Silverleaf (B), Witte
Cricket's Hubba Bubba (D), Autrey-Quinn
Jande's Lucky-Mary (B), Besteman
Kalamity's Benchmark Duchess (B), Miller
Mellowitt's Scotch Puddin (B), Witt
Raisin's Positively Polly (B), McKenna
Silverleaf Barbara's Girl (B), Rieseberg
8/82 Aellen's Castle In The Sky (B), Prescott
Arcadia's Paprika (D), Koenig
Bi Mi Dorka's First Edition (D), Dixon
Bosque's Tumblin' Tumbleweed (B), Bodour
Cauldbrae's Shandy Lea (B), Norton
Ha'Penny Blu Max At Braemar (D), Thomas and Schneider
Osmart Blueprint Of Braid (B), Rieseberg

9/82 Artisan The Sorcerer (D), Witte
Callander's Captain Jack (D), Tompkins
Gaymardon's Amy At Leannakays (B), Stinson
Gaymardon's Piper On The Hill (B), Phillips
Gladenmead Winsome Will (D), Racz
Glen Eire Windfiddler's Song (B), Albarano
Parcana's Penosa Chelsea (B), Beck and Parker
Sir Ivanhoe O'Braemar (D), Bicchman

10/82 Artisan Sorcery At Greysteel (B), Witte and Osloond
Bosque's Pampas Patty (B), McDonald
Cauldbrae's Bodach Of Arrochar (D), Robertson and Walsh
Dawne's Black Magic (D), Jessen
Kimrand Drummer Boy At Beagold (D), Reinlieb and Carruthers
O'Kelidon's Meadow Master (D), McHugh
Rosamba Buttercup (B), Roark
Scotchmarn Bronze Beowulf (D), Simcoe
Shaggylane Beamin Pride And Joy (D), Niddrie
Sno-Berry's Tried and True (D), Jozwiak
Tamevalley Highland Ballad (D), Masters

11/82 Aellen's Lyrical Lorien (B), Anderson and Collavecchio
Arcadia Augie Dawgi Highland (D), Mirante and Shannon
Arcadia's Perrier (D), Haarsager
Bernbrae's Bairn Lesleigh (B), McGovern
Blu Chip's Barnaby Jones (D), Swain
Calico's Nantucket Bandit (D), Gugenheim
Daybreak Blue At Lonetree (D), Edner and Raker
Gaymardon Bramel Superstar (B), Webb
Glen Eire Hope At Dendarra (B), Fischer
Ha'Penny Blueprint Of Arcadia (D), Shannon
Jande's Lucky Tri, C.D. (D), Buehrig
Ken-Bea's Blue Bell (B), Kennedy
Kything's Braemoor Black Lace (B), Parsons
Malachi Mariah Of Silverleaf (B), Kertz and Clu
Silverleaf A Cameo Of Chelsea (B), Marlow
Unicorn's Kilcharen Ben Scot (D), Folendorf

12/82 Briardale's The Blacksmith (D), Lang
Callander's High Fly'N Jenny (B), Gomez
Cauldbrae's Sixgun O'Bannon (D), Mickelson
Chandelle's Fly Me To Charisma (D), Weaver
Emshire's Patrick O'Toole (D), Emke
Gaymardon's Haughty Hollie (B), Davis
Greysteel Crackerjack (D), Osloond
Halton's Lordy Of Blu Kilty (D), Halton
Ha'Penny Black Bairn (D), De Janosi and Schneider
Lochengar Never Surrender (B), Conro
Lovenmist Blue Jeans (B), Holava
O'Kelidon's Merry-Glen Mog (D), Boerup
Silverleaf Autumn Harvest (B), Rudd
Winterwood Fantazja (B), Wright

1/83 Dawne's Gathers No Moss (B), Foster
Knights Bridge Delta Dawn (B), Natwin
Lovenmist Black Highlander (D), Schultz
Mellowitt's Salt Of The Earth (B), McCool
Penstone Shadow Of Beth (B), Hays
Rocks Anna Of Willowisp, C.D. (B), De Borba

2/83 Artisan Sorcer'R's Apprentice (D), Witte
Attleford Brown Bess (B), Dolan and Schroeder
Bosque's Hot Tamale (B), Lazar
Bosque's Saguaro Sam (D), Durgin
Cauldbrae's Briggin De Kweo (D), Forister
Cauldbrae's Perpetual Motion (B), Heon
Ha'Penny Bo O'Braemoor (B), Peterson and Schneider
Revel's Blueberry Surprise (D), Darling
Rich-Lin's Ms Bridgette (B), Einbinder
Silverleaf Lord Blu-Bottom (D), Grue
Silverleaf Shining On (D), Rieseberg
Sno Berry's Handsome Lad (D), Jozwiak

3/83 Arcadia's Cotton-Eyed Joe (D), Shannon
Arcadia's Mr Pibb (D), Smith and Haarsager
Cauldbraes Calley (B), Thurston
Chaniam Dubh Bannoch (D), Bailey
Dovmar's Creaggorm (B), Stiles and Newman
Gaymardon Bramel's Choice (B), Webb
Gaymardon's Misty Shamrock (B), Hays
Lavontz's Daisy Glow (B), Vontz
O'Kelidon's Megan M'Luv (B), Lazar and Bodour
Silverleaf Touch Of Class (B), Rieseberg
Umilik Shaggylane's Brandy (D)
Wyndcliff Foolery O'The Picts (D), O'Bryan and Cline

4/83 Arcadia's Tennessee Rose (B), Lowe
Chaniam's Tousy Dubh Awnie (B), Kennedy
Charncroft Christabel (B), Brown
Forister's Gold Toffee (B), Forister
Glen Eire Harvest Moon (D), Riehle
Ha'Penny Thistledown Jigs (D), Fallon and Schneider
Hue'N Cry O'The Picts (B), O'Bryan and Radtke
Hy-Jinx' Jokers Wild (D), Jenkins
Jande Just Justin (D), Masters
Littlefall's Blue Bethanne (B), Foster
Longview Blu Chas Clan Arry (D), Jeris
Melita Poppy's A Poppin' (B), Richland
Parcana Braemar's Golddigger (B), Thomas
Pennypacker's Aengus (D), Heilbrunn
Palaneid Adamant Of Joncy's (D), Behardt and Burns
Salmars' Magic Moment Of Time (D), Tranquillo
Walkoway's Sherlock Holmes (D), Panno
Willowmead Special Angel (B), Schroeder

5/83 Blackwatch Mackenzie Blue (D), Peters
Briardale's Summer Fantasy (B), Eichholz
Brigand O'Braemoor, T.D. (D), Ivers
Callander Parcana Starla (B), Vontz
Clan's Lotsa Pizzazz (B), Yankoviz
Crisch Deja Vu At Brynwood (B), Brunner and Sommerfelt
Di-Gem Dasher (D), Russell and Lemons
Dovmar's New Man About Town (D), Newman
Higgins Of Forest Park (D), Culver
Jande Mahogany Rose (B), Kyle
Pepperland Rolling Stone, C.D. (D), Holdren and Rieseberg
Willowmead Midnight Blue (D), Dolan

6/83 Arcadia's Brocade O'Hemloch (B), Bannon and Shannon
Braemar's Blackjack (D), Epstein
Erinleigh's Timeless Classic (D), Bosworth
Stardust's Twinkle, C.D. (B), Clarke

7/83 Arcadia's Mint Julep (B), Haarsager
Artisan Copper V V Loscann (D), Lange and Witte
Brannit O'Braemoor (B), Gosselin and Parsons
Ha'Penny Pepsi Challenger (D), Byne
Jande Rose Bush (B), Masters
Kalamity's Robbie Burns (D), Riegelhuth
Melita Abby (B), Latty
Parcana Cash Mccool (D), McCool
Parcana The Sonsie Tyke (B), Carroll
Penstone Masterpiece (D), Jagersma
Rich-Lin's Solo Of Dunrobin (B), Winnie

8/83
- Shiloh's Ange Beauseant (D), Ellington
- Thaydom Greysteel Artisan (B), Witte
- Walkoway's Victoria Holt (B), Shaw and Walkowicz
- Aellen's Dawn Of Blue Fantasia (B), Byers-Rutherford and Rutherford
- Arcadia's Georgia Peach (B), Shannon
- Arcadia's Summers Easy Tempo (D), Van Wilkes
- Baybrook's Brown Bibelot (B), Ferguson and Young
- Bearanson Black Bart (D), Kothe and Schnute
- Crisch Debut At Candelaria (D), Spicer
- Ha'Penny Dawanka New Harmony (D), Stevens and Schneider
- Lord Of The Unicorn (D), Gaffney
- Oakengate's Gillyflower (B), Steger and Stallings
- Silverleaf Miror Image O'Kent (D), Rieseberg
- Tudor Lodge's Beau Brummel (D), Blumire

9/83
- Aellen's A Different Unicorn (D), Gaffney
- Algobrae Liquorice Candy (B), Campbell
- Arcadia's Pepsi Cola (B), Shannon
- Benbecula's Cream Of The Crop (D), Goldman
- Blu Chip's Child O'The Wynd (B), Hann
- Emshire Casey O'Janken (D), Ballard and Emke
- Glen Eire Moonglow Misthaven (D), Matthews
- Ha'Penny Hoyden At Edmar (B), Moe
- Ha'Penny Lott's Crisch Crunch (D), Lott and Schneider
- Highglade Wanderin' Star At Beagold (D), Larizza
- Jande Maryjane (B), Masters
- Knightsbridge At Beagold (D), Feld
- Silverleaf Golden Girl (B), Pollard
- Wildwood Bat Mast'Rs'N Arcadia (B), Stepankow and Shannon

10/83
- Arcadia's Benson And Hedges (D), Bannon and Shannon
- Arcadia's Virginia Slim (B), Shannon
- Artisan Copper Breagan (D), Van Fleet and Witte
- Briarcliff Spirit Of St Louis (D), Franc
- Britannia Classie Lassie (B), Pollack
- Britannia Just Jeffrey (D), Ritter
- Di-Gem's Whisker Whizo' Arcadia (D), Russell and Price
- Gaymardon Once N Future King (D), Buehrig
- Greysteel Mystic Silverleaf (B), Osloond
- Knightsbridge E Muffin (B), Reinlieb
- Malenbrae's Sweet Rascal (D), Bridenbaker
- Raisin Pepsi Challenge (B), Reese and Hollingsworth
- Revel's Chocolate Sundae (B), Darling
- Revel's Country Bumpkin (D), Wretlind
- Rich-Lin's Rhapsody In Blue (B), Hodges
- Unicorn's Gemini Of Lands End (D), Becker and Scott

11/83
- Bektara's Big Daddy (D), Kaye and Mahigian
- Benbecula's Classical Jazz (B), Sawka
- Cricket's Constant Comment (D), Saunders
- Emshire's Shawn O'Casey (D), Gross
- Gai-Lejend Parcana The Rose (B), Nadeau and Douglas
- Knightsbridge Dudley (D), Leadbetter
- Lochengar Kyloe Kenilworth (D), Rankinen and Conro
- O'Kelidon's My Wysteria, C.D.X. (B), Knapp
- Silverleaf Sweet Promise (B), Murphy
- Sno-Berry's Black Ruffle (B), Jozwiak
- Unicorn's Colleen Of Elf (B), Nolan
- Wildwood Erlyrise Hollyhill (D), Holt and Stepankow

12/83
- Arcadia's Bita Amber O'Hemloch (B), Shannon
- Arcadia's Trapper John (D), Brask and Shannon
- Artisan Sir Winston Copper (D), Witte
- Bi Mi Dorka's Highland Heather (B), Dixon
- Braw Banner Of Three Oakes, C.D.X. (D), Doto
- Brianna From Geliland At Chaniam (B), Bailey
- Britannia Bad Brown Lad (D), Marshall
- Cauldbrae's Courie Doon (B), Morrison
- Cricket's Sun Bonnet (B), Lachman
- Gaymardon Checkmate (D), Harney
- Gaymardon Chocolate Kiss (B), Holmes
- Glen Eire Dendara Reveille (D), Dean and Dolan
- Jande Just Jacob (D), Masters
- Knightsbridge Dudley (D), Leadbetter
- Littlefall's Rose Ellen (B), Foster and Hossack
- Oakengate's Blackberry (D), Steger
- Roses Are Red At Glen Eire (B), Kirtley
- Stonybrook's Fantasia (B), Frame and Larizza
- Unicorn Joel Of Timberridge (D), McClaran and Colavecchio

1/84
- Aaron Of Timber Ridge (D), Hillyard
- Apple's Maid O' Cotton Of Agape (B), Bossio and Kertz
- Artisan Copper Sileen (B), Witte
- Artisan The Magician (D), Witte
- Braemar Sweet Georgia Brown (B), Thomas
- Calico's Good Time Gal (B), Stengel and Walton
- Classical Lasting Impression (B), Pechmann
- Em Shire's Foxi Roxi (B), Emke
- Emshire's Paul Masson Of Tara (D), Meyer
- Gladenmead Carrie Cocoa (B), Glatzer
- Glen Eire Naughty But Nice (B), Dean and Dolan
- Ha'Penny Havoc (D), Schneider
- Jande's Shawn The Fawn (D), Masters
- Lovenmist Black Molasses (B), Aftewicz and Holava
- Parcana Kylie (B), Parker

2/84
- Arcadia's Foxfire Of Rooban (B), Bannon and Shannon
- Arcadia's Wildwood Flower (B), Brown and Tomkinson
- Briardale's Promise To Keep (B), Lang
- Charisma Of Chandelle Farms (B), Weaver and Koplow
- Mistiburn's Mariah (B), Albarano

3/84
- Arcadia's Dr. Pepper (D), Bennett
- Arcadia's Wildwood Periwinkle (D), Stepankow and Shannon
- Bosque's Tic Tac Tony (D), Stanek
- Briardale Catch Me If You Can (B), Rice and Lang
- Briardale's Copper Artisan (D), Land and Witte
- Briardale's Coppersmith (D), Flannigan
- Bryan O'Braemoor, C.D.X. (D), Ryder
- Campbell's Chandelle Laddie, C.D. (D), Campbell-Gracie
- Chaniam Ard Talam Rince (D), Bailey
- Chaniam Sona Muirnin (B), Bailey
- Crish Midnight Bracken (D), Schaefer
- Glen Eire Dedarra Patience, C.D. (B), Robinson
- Ha'Penny Ms Mayhem (B), Kaplan and Schneider
- Paddington Bear Of Willowisp (D), De Borba
- Raisin's Fortunatly Frosty (B), Guihen
- Stonybrook's Hampton T-Dancer (D), Wessberg and Larizza

4/84
- Glen Eire Dendarra Charity (B), Giangregorio and Dolan

5/84
- Arcadia Peppermint Schnapps (B), Simpson and Shannon
- Cricket's Megara Macgillvray (B), Autrey-Quinn and Lachman

Above: Ch. Rich-Lin's Justin Case. Owners, Arnold and Dee Einbinder.

Above: Ch. Raggmopp First Impression, American and Canadian C.D. First North American-bred Beardie to earn the title of champion.

Below: Ch. Arcadia-Walkoway's Carte Blanche. Photo by Rich Johnson.

Below: English Ch. Pepperland Lyric John at Potterdale. Owner, Mike Lewis.

Below: Ch. Mistiburn's Mistletoe. Owners, Ralph and Irene Carson.

Dawne's Blue Robin (B), Lewis
Di-Gem's Mountain Mist Arcadia (D), Fort
Edmar's Sweet Betse (B), Moe
Hapenny Daw-Anka Sunnyside (B), Schneider and Jameson
Ha'Penny Sir Winston (D), Ring
Jande Cara Belle (B), Masters
Lovenmist Blue Britannia (D), Hecker
Unicorn-Aellen Queen of Night (B), White

6/84 Arcadia's Thyme O'Beau Geste (D), Helverson and Shannon
Bosque's Sasson Joshua (D), Sabisch
Braemar's Beautiful Runner (D), Kline
Raisin's Chinatown (D), Rubenstein
Sno-Berry's Tristan (D), Jozwiak
Unicorn's The Dragon Lady (B), Folendorf and Gaffney
Violets Are Blue At Glen Eire (B), Glatzer
Wildwood Whirlwind O'Arcadia (B), Shannon and Stepankow

7/84 Anastasia's Magic O'Mellowitt (B), Witt
Arcadia's Amaretto (B), Hooper and Shannon
Arcadia's Irish Mist (B), Kyle
Blu Chip's Katie (B), Swain
Dawne's Holly Go Litely (B), Odom and Foster
Gaymardon Canterbury Tale (D), Davis
Ha'Penny's Thistledown Kerry (B), Christel and Chapman
Kamarla Smoke Shadow O'Lannra (D), Raines and Davis
Willowmead Summer Magic (D), Gaffney and Colavecchio

8/84 Birkhill's Ebony Dexter (D), Henderson
Braemar Robbie At Briarpatch (D), Campbell-Gracie
Chaniam Morga Cailin (B), Gould
Charisma Mcduff Brigadoon (D), Nily
Glen Eire Going Great Guns (D), Dolan
Glennamoor Amazing Grace (B), Carruthers
Ha'Penny Dashing Dudley (D), Shevlo
Ha'Penny Daw-Anka Velvet Touch (B), Ayers and Moore
Jande Pocono Hershey (D), Masters
Lochengar Winnie The Pooh, C.D. (B), Boettger
Melita Strathdern Vale (D), Richland
Paisley Cr Dasher At Oak Mdws (D), Mickelson
Parcana Paragon Miss (B), Bennett
Winterwood Empress Lilly (B), Bearjar

9/84 Arcadia's Bentley O'Walkoway (D), Bates
Daybreak Storm At Candelaria (B), Spicer
Dewey Hollybush (D), Tanning
Gaymardon Annapolis Braid (D), Johnson
Gaymardon's Percy's Pride (D), Nolan and Miller
Kweo's Lilliputian (B), Kaye
Shiloh's Angel Of Blackfriar, C.D. (D), Ellington
Sir Beauregard Of Aspenleaf (D), Chaknova
Sunryze Cor Tray Beau (D), Stillman

10/84 Arcadia Lucky's Happy Holiday (B), Hamilton
Aspenleaf The Schoolmarm (B), Bowes
Blu Chip's Pound Sterling (D), Swain
Braemar Caitlin At Glenmead (B), Williams and Thomas
Dawne's Sassafras (B), Foster
Gaymardon's Tartan Tona (B), Miller
Ha'Penny Nicholas Nickelby (D), Constabile
Kweo's Rastaban Of Alamos (D), Cooper

Mistymor Megan Of Willowmead (B), Carmejoole
Raisin's Cherry Blossom Time (B), Cummings and Guihen
Tekla Midas Magic (D), Ayotte
Unicorn-Aellen Scarlet Gem (B), Colavecchio-Fowler and Colavecchio

11/84 Arcadia's Ebony 'N Ivory (B), Carroll
Bendale Magician (D), Ritter
Crisch Panda Of Briery Knob (B), Schaefer
Dawne's Glynn Liv'It (D), Glynn
Daybreak's Rising Sun (D), Prescott
Dearlove's Billy The Kidd (D), Einbinder
Gladenmead Silver Sparkle (B), Glatzer
Ha'Penny Black Lightning (B), Schneider, Greitzer, and Green
Ha'Penny Daw-Anka O'Sandcastle (B), Kotrba
Heathglen's Morna Mica (B), Cox
Laird Robby Of Nottingham (D), Cox
Meadows' Just Right (D), McNulty
Potterdale Paris (D), Sawka
St. Lawrence Pride Of Rich-Lin (B), King
Timberock's Voo-Doo Man (D), Hitchcock
Windfiddler's Bobi Mactavish (D), Fees

12/84 Arcadia's Charleston Charlie (D), Whitley and Shannon
Bi Mi Dorka's Highland Mcdugle (D), Dixon
Braemar's Bonnie Bride (B), Mcclung
Briery Knob Winter Harvest (D), Rudd
Calico's Raggedy Andy (D), Morgan
Chelsic Highland Mist (B), Hanson
Dolinbrook's Misty Moonlight (B), Billman
Ha'Penny Brabourne Bonnie (B), Robinson
Jande Charming Charlotte (B), Robinson
Jande Moonlight Sonata (B), Eckhardt
Mistiburn's Hey Mickey (D), Albarano
Savage Winds At Wildwood (B), Jones
Sunshine Of Silverleaf (D), Cullen

1/85 Braemar's Chocolate Chip (D), Line and Thomas
Brisken O'Braemoor, C.D. (B), Parsons
Cauldbrae's Blue Columbine (B), Aitken
Ha'Penny Black Orpheus (D), Howard and Schneider
Jande Alexander Ragtime Band (B), Robinson
Kollybarb's Royle Galahad (D), Finch
Shaggylane's Mr. Bojangles (D), Medock
Walkoway's Insp'ctor Clouseau (D), Ehlers

2/85 Blu Chip's Lady Di (B), White and Swain
Blueweiries Master Rhett (D), Dorman
Everwynd Canadian Spirit (B), Cummings, Guihen, and Schoeberger
Highlander Lorna Doone (B), Tilson
Stumpy Acres Scottish Topaz (B), O'Leary and Blanco
Unicorn Aellen Sun Chariot (D), Folendorf

3/85 Arcadia's Caraway (B), Billman and McKenny
Arcadia Wildwood Marigold, Klomp and Stepankow
Artisan Copper Clown (D), Witte
Bearanson Bluestocking (B), Schnute and Billman
Birchwood Farms Higgins (D), Kanas
Charisma's Basic Black (D), Brown and Keller
Em Shire's Natasha (B), Brown
Glen Eire Just In Time (B), Heon
Ha'Penny Chancellor Higgins (D), Sulewsky
Ha'Penny Moonlight Hunter (D), Green
Kalamity's Lady Of The Unicorn (B), Jacoby and Gaffney
Shorelane Silverleaf Pedro (D), Fronig
Silverleaf's Blue Mist (B), Young

	Unicorn Aellen's Corey (D), Wussow
	Walkoway's Bryn Mawr (B), Walkowicz
4/85	Blu Chip's Queen Elizabeth (B), Swain
	Cauldbrae's Winsongs Haven (B), Johnson
	Chaniam Kyna (B), Fynan
	Clan's High Flyer Goodie (B), Kovach and Murphy
	Fox Lane's Chatter Box (B), Gunn and Billman
	Ha'Penny Blossom Too (B), Fallon and Lott
	Jande Premium Jacob Best (D), Bearjar
	Kweo's The Cullinan (D), Kaye
	Melita Candee Dancer (B), Cullen
	Mistiburn Happy Memories (B), Carson and Turner
	Oakengate's Gold Standard (D), Arnold
	Parcana Blue Willow (B), Parker
	Tekla Argyle Jenny (B), Brown
5/85	Braemoor's Brigadoon (D), Powell
	Chaniam Broch (D), McMahon
	Chaniam Lufar Dana (B), Currier and Bailey
	Charisma's Wee Trousers (B), Snow and Keller
	Glen Eire Just In Time (B), Heon
	Padworth Black Beauty (B), Masters
6/85	Arcadia's Dixieland Delite (B), Bates and Shannon
	Arcadia's Good Day Sunshine (B), Coxwell and Shannon
	Briarpatch Crystal Candy (B), Campbell-Gracie
	Glen Eire Glad Ashley (B), Farrington
	Glen Eire Moonlight Magic (D), Blacke
	Greysteel Black Magic (D), Conroy and Osloond
	Unicorn-Aellen Hobbitstar (B), Gaffney and Jacoby
7/85	Callander Geordie Odhe (D), Tompkins
	Chaniam Liath Seadon (D), Bailey
	Dusty J's Wildspring Britania (B), Folendorf and Feliciano
	Ha'Penny Sophia Sforzando (B), Cooperman
	MacAndrew Nelson Of Wildeve (D), Simons
	MacLaury Laird O'Donbarien, C.D., Cullen
	Willowmead Ring O'Gold (D), Cookman and Lewis
8/85	Arcadia's Dixies Like Heaven (B), Berie
	Arcadia's Wildwood White Gold (B), Stepankow and Shannon
	Bearanson Blue Peter (D), Yeakle
	Cameo Classy Chassis (D), Reeb
	Curious Megan Of Brookwood (B), Clemmer
	Ha'Penny Judith Of Stonybrook (B), Rubenstein and Schneider
9/85	Arcadia's Diamond In The Ruff (B), Coxwell and Helland
	Ballycastle's Blue Bear (D), Doherty
	Braemar Boatswain's Mate (D), Thomas
	Buckingham Ha'Penny Mcdoogal (D), Boland
	Classical's Star Baby (B), Albarano and Sawka
	Crisch Midnight Summer Sun (B), Schaefer
	Five Oak's Scottish Heather (B), O'Leary
	Gai-Lejend Sweet William (D), Widell
	Ha'Penny Precious Tiffany (B), Ayotte
	Lochengar Great Inspiration (B), Clarke and Conro
	Lochengar Kyloe Having It All (B), Rankinen and Conro
	Marjac's Merry Bit O'Sunshine (B), Murphy
	Ms'ississi Rivers End (D), Whitley
	Raisin's Kung Fu (D), Cummings
10/85	Arcadia's Full O'Life, C.D. (B), Alison
	Briarpatch Knight-Rider (D), Williams and Campbell-Gracie
	Buckingham Ha'Penny Bogart (D), Marini
	Chaniam Alden (D), Bailey
	Chaniam Cuyler (D), Bailey
	Crisch Kringle At Parcana (D), Parker
	Dolinbrook's Go For The Gold (B), Conrad and Besteman
	Emshire Ce Ge Sang The Blues (B), Emke
	Jande Glorious Gloria (B), Masters
	Jande Magic Melody (B), Kolditz
	Kamarla's Smoke Signal (D), Davis
	Knightsbridge ExtraSpecial (B), Reinlieb
	Nathan Of Timber Ridge (D), Folendorf
	Oakengates Paisley Patch (B), Steger and Stallings
	Silverleaf's Magic Moments (D), Kolditz
	Sir Dworking Of Arrochar (D), Williamson
	Walkoway's Sarah Lawrence (B), Frey
	Whipshel's Shannon Victoria, C.D. (B), Reese and Aiken
	Wildwood Arcadia Magic Maker (D), Beck and Stepankow
11/85	Amulree Argo Whauphill (D), Hooper
	Arcadia's Brushed Bronze (D), Lowe
	Artisan Gypsy Baron (D), Witte
	Braemar's Marathon For Stuart (B), Kline
	Braemar's Rufus Fitzgerald (D), Sicheistiel and Thomas
	Bramel's Duncan Macgregor (D), Sufall
	Cameo Lucky Lindy (D), Nolan
	Cauldbrae Morag Of Arrochar (B), Robertson and Morrison
	Cauldbrae's Captain Mctavish (D), Hall
	Charisma's Erin Of Beaconview (B), Lovett
	Dawne's Sir Jon Henri Roffey (D), Roffey and Quinn
	Edmar Black Eyed Susan (B), Brask and Moe
	Edmar Pandora Of Lajos Megyi (B), Quigley and Turner
	Ha'Penny Blue Bracken Too (D), Farrington and Schneider
	Ha'Penny Chelsea Mackenelsea (B), Barthelmess and Schneider
	Ha'Penny Maywood Mac Crea (B), Byers-Rutherford and Rutherford
	Harmony's One Night Stand (D), Stevens and Layman
	Harmony's Show Biz (B), Berry
	Kweo's Yorkshire Pudding (B), Kaye
	O'Kelldon's Keepin In Touch (D), Kinnon, McWilliams, and McHugh
	Riley's Life Of Charisma (D), Gibson and Keller
	Rutgers Of Walkoway-Avalon (D), Tuck
	Shiloh's Breezy Blue Angel (D), Ellington and Lindemoen
	Silverleaf Tequila Sunrise (B), Rieseberg
	Tekla Harry P. Bear (D), Brown
	Thaydom Greysteel Frolic (B), Grue
	Unicorn-Aellen Barney Blue (D), Russell
	Windfiddler's Walloch (B), Plum
	Win-Somm Blue Angel Lace (B), Saputo and Brown
12/85	Arcadia's Family Tradition (B), Shannon
	Brae Oaks' Jenny Lynn (B), Daetwyler
	Briardale Windigo Artisan (B), Fijal
	Cameo Graystoke Of Edgewood (D), Ray
	Crisch Painted Waggin (D), Schaefer
	Daw-Anka Ha'Penny Feminity (B), Jameson
	Dawne's Blue Belle (B), Foster
	Gaymardon Second Time Around (B), Waldman
	Ha'Penny Jeremy Blue (D), O'Donnel and Schneider

Haute Ecole Hocus Pocus (D), De Witt
Levontz's Shepherd Citation (D), Vontz
Lochengar Great Acclaim (D), Clarke
Monet's Sunrise at Lone Tree, C.D. (D), Harris
Sandcastle's Astro Smash (D), Kotrba
Tall Trees Morgan O'Derk (D), Wantland and Hueholt
Tudor Lodge Summerdowne Star (B), Greitzer
Winterwood Scottish Mist (B), Kramer and Winter

1/86 Arcadia's Atlanta Blue (B), Fort
Arcadia's Summer Sensation (D), Coxwell, Stepankow, and Shannon
Briery Knob Highland Wind (D), Wernegreen
Britannia Fawn Lady (B), Franc
Chaniam Dougal At Whirling D (D), Weaver
Classical's Achates On Parade (D), Lewis
Greysteel Huggy Bear (D), Freedland
Greysteel Jonadi (B), Freedland
Ha'Penny Daw-Anka Polo (D), Pienkosz and Kennedy-Jameson
Honeysuckle Of Tambora (B), Mahigian, Kaye, and Tilson
Jande Nicholas Nickleby (D), Masters
Jande Victoria Victorious (B), Lewis and Masters
Kweo's Chutney (D), White and Kaye
Lord Barclay Of Lonetree (D), Aron
Lord Bentley Of Danspence (D), Cruger
Loud 'N Clear O'The Picts (B), Manunder and Cline
Megan's Margret Of Brookwood (B), Clemmer
Orora's Thrift (D), Shannon and Coxwell
Sheldawyn Blue Snowdrift (D), Brown and Emke
Silverleaf Moody Blue (B), Thomas
Tudor Lodge's Brittany (B), McKinney and Rodenbarger

2/86 Bearanson Bristol Cream, C.D. (D), Gunn
Benbecula's Crystal D'Arque (B), Perry and Sawka
Bosque's The Bee's Knees (D), Gerber
Britannia Sweet Lady (B), Ritter
Chaniam Happy Hogmanny (D), Bailey
Conifer Rachel At Greykay (B), Wing and Osloond
Edmar Muirfield Spectre (B), Moe and Field
Gaymardon's Could Be Colin (D), Jansberg and Miller
Glen Eire Lady Holly Of Caira (B), Garber and Wiko
Ha'Penny Such Sweet Thunder (B), Herzig and Schneider
Haute Ecole The Great Houdini (D), Dixon
Jande Marcella Marvelous (B), Masters
Parcana A Cameo Of Portia (B), Marburger and Marlow
Regal Manor's Sir Launcelot (D), Carrol
Sirhan Whiskers Galore (D), Hottois
Stormy Night At Wildwood (B), Sinor, Stepankow, and Shannon
Tudor Lodge's Walter Raleigh (D), Blumire
Unicorn-Alashaw Star Jasmine (D), White and Gaffney
Willowmead Red Ruairidh (D), Shroeder and Moorhouse
Windfiddler's W. W. Willoughby (D), Fees

3/86 Arcadia's Annisette (B), Hollandsworth
Bonnytown's Fifth Avenue (D), Blieden
Braemar's Marathon For Stuart (B), Kline
Cathi's Clown At Oak Meadows (D), Mickelson and Cline
Crisch Midnight Crystal Mist (B), Herzig
Culloden's Dame Of Dunvegan (B), Whitley
Dolinbrook's Pair O Dice (D), Besteman

Erinleigh's Main Chance (D), Wood
For Pete's Sake O The Picts (B), O'Bryan, Radtke, and Prescott
Ha'Penny Bonnie Brodie (D), Duller
Ha'Penny Apple MacIntosh (D), Fleischman
Kayne's Thunder Road (D), Schulz
Mistmor Magic Moment (D), Carmejoole
Oak Mdws Gailejend Hollyhock (B), Mickelson
Orora's Humphrey (D), Schneider and Rubenstein
Revel's Reflection (B), Allensworth
Tekla Emerald Dancer (B), Brown

4/86 Artisan Emperor Waltz (D), Van Fleet and Witte
Bosque's Gucci D'Al De Bear (B), Lazar
Cauldbrae's Challenger (D), Morrison
Clarion Honky Tonk Rmblin'Man (D), Kyle
Glen Eire Crystal Magic (B), Giangregorio
Ha'Penny Blossom Too (B), Fallon and Lott
Lochengar Tamlyn Miss Brogue (B), Clark and Conro
Traleigh Unicorn's Amber Star (B), Mcclaran and Gaffney
Unicorn-Aellen's Duncan Sun (D), Colavecchio

5/86 Cameo Classic Lancia (B), Davis
Gai-Lejend Jonquil (D), Nakata
Ha'Penny Daw-Anka Mocha D'Lite (B), Maxwell
Raggmopp Raving Beauty (B), Kratz and Gold
Rich-Lin's Carrington Blue (D), Nootbaar
Surfsong's Amber Thistledown (B), Fournier
Till's Diamond Lil O'Em Shire (B), Till

6/86 Aellen-Traleigh It's Kismet (D), Finley and McClaren
Arrochar's B.C. Of Princeton (D), Shoemaker-Olson and Olson
Beagold Storm (D), Tabler and Larizza
Braemar Beau Blue At Meg Mel (D), Cross
Fox Lane's Enchanter (D), Lovett
Jande Brandy Alexander (D), Masters
Lochengar Great Affection, C.D. (B), Landro and Conro
Maccorkindale's Tawny Rogue (D), Swan
Oakengate's Sugar And Spice (B), Johnson and Steger
Wenloch-Arcadia Virginia Dare (B), Shannon and Lemons

7/86 Aellen's Traleigh Beau Django (D), Swarts
Arcadia's Twenty Two Kt Gold (B), Carroll
Bosque's Coco Chanel (B), Rawlins
Braemar Just A Gigolo (D), Thomas
Briery Knob Rainbo's At Hyatt (B), Shroeder
Chaniam Sorcha (B), Bailey
Edmar Trouble Bruin (D), Moe and Kent
Ha'Penny Braecan Maccrae (B), Peterson
Haute Ecole's Callander Girl (B), Dewitt and Cline
Jande Rosemary (B), Masters
O'Kelidon's Chimney Sweeper (D), Zaiger
Shiloh Tales of Romsey Abbey, C.D. (B), Barnicoat and Ellington
Shorelane's The Blackpearl (B), McKenna
Walkoway's Yum Yum O'Scotdale (B), Frey and Walkowicz
Wenlock's Winston Of Arcadia (D), Russell and Price

8/86 Arcadia Wildwood Foxglove (B), Stepankow and Bannon
Arcadia's Coco Ribe (B), Shook and Haarsager
Artisan Minute Waltz (B), Eppinger and Witte
Crisch Cover Girl At Dunrobin (D), Winnie
Daw-Anka Ha'Penny Maxwell (D), Hahn and Jameson
Greysteel Jomram (B), Freedland

11/86	Braemar-Glenmead Macgyver (D), Thomas
	Chesrite Treasure Of Dunwich (B), Farrington and Thomas
	Crisch Midnight Braid (D), Tuck
	Knightsbridge Gogetem Grace (B), Hobe
	Lochengar Master Of The Game (D), Leeper
	Mistymor Silver Shadow (B), Carmejoole
	Parcana Prime Time (D), Sutter and Parker
	Pembroke's Molly Pride of Jenn (B), Chelik and Murdock
12/86	Alashaws Mystical Night (B), Moran
	Applewood's Lord D'Arcy Cameron, C.D. (D), Canham
	Arcadia's Whiskey on Ice (D), Bauchat
	Artisan Merry Widow (B), Wright
	Brigadoon's Tara Terrific (B), Hanigan
	Cameo Somerset Samantha (B), Finks
	Cauldbrae's Challenger (D), Morrison and Thurston
	Classical's Silver Cloud (B), Sawka
	Donbarien's Try-Me Jaime, T.D. (D), Ardito
	Dunwich First Edition (D), Davies and Farrington
	Gladenmead Blue Heather (B), Farrington
	Jande Mary Louise (B), Parker
	Kweo's Flint Fireforge (D), Kaye
	Maywood Summer Dawn O'Aellen (B), Colavecchio
	Leannakay Baby Sophie (B), Clifford
	Osmart's Hi Yall A'M Copper Chania (D), Bailey
	Stonybrooks Amber Delight (B), Martin
	Windcache A Daisy A Day, C.D. (B), Haaland and Thomas
9/86	Alashaw Sat Night Special (D), White
	Classical's Paris Original (D), Pflum, Albarano, and Sawka
	Ha'Penny Daw-Anka Bedlam (B), Marth
	Ha'Penny Silver Morn Lindsay (B), Rayano
	Jande Bleuetiful Blue (B), Masters
	Jande Lucky Lucy (B), Robinson and Masters
	Jande's Nathan Detroit (D), Harrington
	Jocala Ebony Wizard Of Omega (D), Thompson and Lamb
	Montagne's Joker Wild (D), Prescott and Cline
	Stonehaven Dandy Duncan (D), Hopkins
	Stonybrook's Chocolate Rose (B), Thieberger and Larizza
10/86	Crisch Ebony and Ivory (B), Barton and Schaefer
	Crisch Echo At Windhill (B), Baumgartner and Schaefer
	Dearlove's Renegade (D), Einbinder
	Destiny's Forever Krystle (B), McClaran and Finley
	Scotdale Mahogony O'Walkoway (B), Shaw
	Sweetwater Sweet Basil (D), Garrett

	Mistymor Ode Gris Hombre (D), Pirone
	Parchment Farm' Silver Wraith (D), Mahigian
	Prospero Laird of Macphunn (D), Christel and Chapman
	Trillium Ragg Mopp Resumt (B), Layng
	Unicorn-Aellen's Cocoa Chip (D), Moss
	Walkoway's Darthmouth (D), Price
	Windfiddler's Warlock (D), Albarano
1/87	Arcadia's Nashville Kat (B), Shannon
	Ha'Penny A And P Artful Dodger (D), Marini
	Kythings Bobby Sox (D), Ashley
	Parcana's Princess Daisy (B), Parker
	Traleigh's Image Of Destiny (D), McClaran
	Windsor's Phil O'Dendron (D), Brask
2/87	Chaniam Tegan At Ruffhouse (B), Kennedy
	Colwellmaner Grey Steel From Osmart (D), Osloond and Freedland
	Everblu's Trace Of O'Kelidon (B), Zaiger
	Gladenmead's A Bit Like Becky (B), Greco
	Gunnstock Paint It Black (D), Gunn
	Ha'Penny Black Castle Of Sky (B), Fleischman and Green
	Ha'Penny Daw-Anka Brave Willie (D), Peddle
	Ha'Penny Mercedes O'Stonehill (B), Hoesten and Schneider
	Inverness Antique Silver (B), Fuller
	Lanmar's Cassandre Of Ha'Penny (B), Rubinstein
	Mistiburn's Meagan Murdock (B), Murdock
3/87	Arcadias Cherry Coke (D), Bannon
	Braemars Marathon For Stuart (B), Kline
	Crisch Charcoal Brackette (B), Hyman
	Dearlove's K-Nine (D), Lynn
	Greysteel Ballantree Mirage (D), Cowen
	Ha'Penny Daw-Anka Jeremy Slate (D), Swiedler and Chriss
	Ha'Penny Daw-Anka Jonathan (D), Jackson
	Midnight Blue Of Dundee (D), Cowles
	O'Kelidon Inverness Diplomat (D), Knapp
	Rooban's Buttons N'Bows (B), Nelson
	Stonehaven's Super Trooper (D), Carson
	Time's Rob Roy Of Bonnie Brae (D), Ober
	Wildwoods Imperial York (D), Stepankow and Shannon
4/87	Briaridge Blue Rock Of Brahmin (D), Morrison
	Cauldbrae's Crystal Gael (B), Stuart
	Classicals Up And At 'Em Hattie (B), Croucher
	Glen Eire Misty Megan of Caira (B), Garber
	Parcana Lord Corwin (D), Williamson
	Tiburon Cool Breeze At Holm (B), Capra and Haarsager

CBCC Match competition.

CBCC Match competition.

"Owd Bob"

By Alfred Olivant (1898)

"Should you, while wandering in the wild sheep land, happen on moor or in market upon a very gentle knight, clothed in dark grey habit, splashed here and there with rays of moon; free by right divine of the guild of gentlemen, strenuous as a prince, lithe as a rowan, graceful as a girl, with high king carriage, motions and manners of a fairy queen, should he have a noble breadth of brow, an air of still strength born of right confidence, all unassuming; last and most unfailing test of all, should you look into two snow-clad eyes, calm, wistful, inscrutable, their soft depths clothed on with eternal sadness—yearning, as is said, for the soul that is not theirs—know then, that you look upon one of the line of the most illustrious sheepdogs of the North."

Above: English and American Ch. Chauntelle Limelight. Owners, J. Richard Schneider and Dr. Thomas Davies.

Left: Australian, American, Canadian Ch. Beardie Bloody Mary. Owners, Jan and DeArle Masters.

Below: Ch. Gaymardon's Chesapeake Mist, at eight and a half years of age. Owners, Gail and Don Miller.

Pedigrees

The study of pedigrees is fascinating—and never more so than when a breed can be traced back to its modern "roots." In addition to Jeannie and Bailie, several working dogs were registered in the 1950s. In today's pedigrees, all lines lead back to the Beardie "Adam and Eve," through breeding to the Bothkennar dogs.

Besides Jeannie's sire, Baffler, and her dam, Mist, and Bailie's sire, Dandy, there were many working dogs that contributed to modern Beardies. Britt and Bess of Bothkennar (the latter a working dog) were part of the Bothkennar breeding program. Bess was sired by Bobby out of Bett. Britt, who captured two CCs, was sired by Jock out of Mootie.

Mrs. Willison also utilized Jennifer of Multan, Newtown Blackie, and Mirk, the sire of Ch. Bobby of Bothkennar. Mister, Craig, Fly, Ranger, Symphony, and Brasenose Bonnie, other branches of the Beardie tree eventually bred to Bothkennar stock, contributed to the Beardies of today.

Following are two earlier pedigrees tracing the foundation upon which the breed is built, and two modern pedigrees.

Further information can be obtained through the *Bearded Collies of Great Britain Partial Studbook*, compiled by Gail Miller and available through the Bearded Collie Club of America.

Jeannie of Bothkennar and Bailie of Bothkennar, with first registered litter. Left to right: Bravado, Buskie, Bruce, and Bogle. Owner, G. Willison.

```
                                             Jock (black)
                                 Britt of Bothkennar (black)
                                             Mootie
                     Balachan of Bothkennar (black)
                                             Bailie of Bothkennar (black)
                                 Bra'Tawney of Bothkennar (red-fawn)
                                             Buskie of Bothkennar
         Blimber of Bothkennar (black)*
                                             Bailie of Bothkennar
                                 Bruce of Bothkennar (brown)
                                             Jeannie of Bothkennar (brown)
                     CH BRONZE PENNY OF BOTHKENNAR (brown)
                                             Unknown
                                 Jennifer of Multan
                                             Unknown
CH BRAVO OF BOTHKENNAR (black)**
                                             Dandy
                                 Bailie of Bothkennar
                                             Unknown
                     Bravado of Bothkennar (black)
                                             Baffler
                                 Jeannie of Bothkennar
                                             Mist
         CH BEAUTY QUEEN OF BOTHKENNAR (red-fawn)
                                             Newtown Blackie
                                 Ridgeway Rob (black)
                                             Briery Nan of Bothkennar
                     Baidh of Bothkennar
                                             Bailie of Bothkennar
                                 Bra'Tawney of Bothkennar
                                             Buskie of Bothkennar
```

* Also from this litter are Ch. Benjue, Bristly (black), Burnetta (brown), and Ch. Benji (brown)

** Also from this litter are Ch. Bosky Glen (black) and Beauty Box (dam Bobby's Girl)

```
                        Unknown
            Unknown
                        Unknown
     Newtown Blackie
                        Unknown
            Unknown
                        Unknown
  Ridgeway Rob (black)
                        Bailie of Bothkennar (black)
            Bogle of Bothkennar
                        Jeannie of Bothkennar (brown)
     Briery Nan of Bothkennar
                        Bobby (Dan x Lassie)
            Bess of Bothkennar (tricolor)
                        Bett (Baldie x Meg)
CH WISHANGER'S BARLEY OF BOTHKENNAR (black)
                        Unknown
            Dandy
                        Unknown
     Bailie of Bothkennar
                        Unknown
            Unknown
                        Unknown
  Bra'Tawney of Bothkennar (red-fawn)
                        Dandy
            Bailie of Bothkennar
                        Unknown
     Buskie of Bothkennar*
                        Baffler
            Jeannie of Bothkennar
                        Mist
CH WISHANGER'S CAIRNBAHN (red-brown)
                        Unknown
            Jock
                        Unknown
     Britt of Bothkennar
                        Unknown
            Mootie
                        Unknown
  Wil'owisp of Willowmead (black)
                        Newtown Blackie
            Ridgeway Rob (black)
                        Briery Nan of Bothkennar
     CH WILLOWMEAD BARBERRY OF BOTHKENNAR
                        Bailie of Bothkennar
            Bra'Tawney of Bothkennar
                        Buskie of Bothkennar
CH WILLOWMEAD MY HONEY (brown)
                        Unknown
            Mirk
                        Unknown
     ENG/S AFR CH BOBBY OF BOTHKENNAR (black)
                        Bailie of Bothkennar
            Bond of Bothkennar (blue)
                        Bess of Bothkennar
  Merrymaid of Willowmead
                        Newtown Blackie
            Ridgeway Rob
                        Briery Nan of Bothkennar
     CH WILLOWMEAD BARBERRY OF BOTHKENNAR
                        Bailie of Bothkennar
            Bra'Tawney of Bothkennar
                        Buskie of Bothkennar

  * Also from this litter are Bogle, Bruce, Bravado, and two unnamed females
```

Ch. Willowmead Barberry of Bothkennar. Owner, Suzanne Moorhouse.

Will O'Wisp of Willowmead. Owner, Suzanne Moorhouse.

```
                                CH BRACKEN BOY OF BOTHKENNAR
                    Rowdina Gray Fella
                                CH WISHANGER CRAB TREE
                CH EDENBOROUGH BLUE BRACKEN
                                CH OSMART BONNIE BLUE BRAID
                    Blue Maggie from Osmart
                                Westernisles Loch Creran
            AM CAN BER ENG CH EDENBOROUGH GREY SHADOW (black)
                                Wil'owisp of Willowmead (black)
                    Ruaridh of Willowmead (black)
                                Sweetheart of Willowmead (black)
                Broadholm Christina (black)
                                CH BOBBY OF BOTHKENNAR
                    Bobby's Girl of Bothkennar (black)
                                Beauty Box of Bothkennar (black)
    Heyescott Jack Tar (black)
                                CH BRACKEN BOY OF BOTHKENNAR
                    Rowdina Gray Fella
                                CH WISHANGER CRAB TREE
                CH EDENBOROUGH BLUE BRACKEN
                                CH OSMART BONNIE BLUE BRAID
                    Blue Maggie from Osmart
                                Westernisles Loch Creran
            Josanda Melody Blue (blue)
                                CH BRAVO OF BOTHKENNAR (black)
                    INT CH OSMART BLACK BERRY
                                Westernisles Loch Creran
                Osmart Black Panache (black)
                                Blue Streak of Bothkennar (blue)
                    Prunella of Jupiters Oaks (brown)
                                Jenny of Jupitersoak
CH EDENBOROUGH QUICK SILVER, ROM (blue)
                                CH BRAVO OF BOTHKENNAR
                    CH BRACKEN BOY OF BOTHKENNAR
                                CH BLUE BONNIE OF BOTHKENNAR
                Rowdina Gray Fella
                                CH WISHANGER CAIRNBAHN
                    CH WISHANGER CRAB TREE
                                Wishanger Celendine
            CH EDENBOROUGH BLUE BRACKEN
                                CH BRAVO OF BOTHKENNAR
                    CH OSMART BONNIE BLUE BRAID
                                CH BLUE BONNIE OF BOTHKENNAR (blue)
                Blue Maggie from Osmart
                                Westernisles Brad of Bothkennar
                    Westernisles Loch Creran
                                Westernisles Wishanger Clematis (black)
        Tamboras Penny Black (black)
                                Ridgeway Rob (black)
                    CH WISHANGER BARLEY OF BOTHKENNAR
                                Bra'Tawney of Bothkennar (red-brown)
                CH WISHANGER CAIRNBAHN
                                Wil'owisp of Willowmead (black)
                    CH WILLOWMEADS MY HONEY
                                Merrymaker of Willowmead (black)
            CH EDELWEISS OF TAMBORA (brown)
                                Ranger
                    Bausant of Bothkennar
                                Symphony
                Burdock of Tambora
                                Banter of Bothkennar
                    Amberford Bracken (brown)
                                Musical Maid of Willowmead
```

Ch. Edenborough Quick Silver, R.O.M. Owners, Jim and Diann Shannon and Chris Walkowicz.

```
                                CH BRACKEN BOY OF BOTHKENNAR (black)
                    Rowdina Gray Fella (black)
                                CH WISHANGER CRAB TREE (black)
            CH EDENBOROUGH BLUE BRACKEN
                                CH OSMART BONNIE BLUE BRAID, ROM (blue)
                    Blue Maggie from Osmart (blue)
                                Westernisles Loch Creran (black)
        CH EDENBOROUGH HAPPY GO LUCKY, ROM (black)
                                CH WISHANGER CAIRNBAHN (red-brown)
                    Marilanz Amber Gleam (brown)
                                Broadholm Anne-Marie (black)
            Davealex Dawn Reign (brown)
                                CH BRACKEN BOY OF BOTHKENNAR
                    Rowdina Peach-A-Boo (black)
                                CH WISHANGER CRAB TREE
    CH ARCADIA'S PAPRIKA (red-brown)
                                Rowdina Gray Fella
                    CH EDENBOROUGH ADVENTURE, ROM (black)
                                Broadholm Christina (black)
            Rich-Lins Rising Son (black)
                                CH EDENBOROUGH BLUE BRACKEN
                    CH JASETON PRINCESS ARGONETTA (black)
                                Edenborough Queen Bess (black)
        CH RICH-LINS MOLLY OF ARCADIA, ROM (black)
                                CH BRACKEN BOY OF BOTHKENNAR
                    Rowdina Gray Fella
                                CH WISHANGER CRAB TREE
            Edenborough Full O'Life, ROM (black)
                                CH OSMART BONNIE BLUE BRAID
                    Blue Maggie from Osmart
                                Westernisles Loch Creran
CH WALKOWAY'S BRYN MAWR, CD
                                Rowdina Gray Fella
                    CH EDENBOROUGH ADVENTURE, ROM
                                Broadholm Christina
            Rich-Lins Rising Son
                                CH EDENBOROUGH BLUE BRACKEN
                    CH JASETON PRINCESS ARGONETTA
                                Edenborough Queen Bess
        CH RICH-LINS WHISKERS OF ARCADIA, ROM (black)
                                CH WISHANGER BARLEY OF BOTHKENNAR (black)
                    CH WISHANGER CAIRNBAHN
                                CH WILLOWMEAD MY HONEY (brown)
            AM/CAN CH HOOTNANNY OF BENGRAY (black)
                                Braelyn Broadholme Crofter (black)
                    CH BRECKDALES MERRY MAID OF WILLOWMEAD (black)
                                Breckdales Calasona River Danube (blue)
    CH ARCADIA'S MARCY OF RICH-LIN, CD (black)
                                Rowdina Gray Fella
                    CH EDENBOROUGH ADVENTURE, ROM
                                Broadholm Christina
            Rich-Lins Rising Son
                                CH EDENBOROUGH BLUE BRACKEN
                    CH JASETON PRINCESS ARGONETTA
                                Edenborough Queen Bess
        CH RICH-LINS MOLLY OF ARCADIA, ROM
                                CH BRACKEN BOY OF BOTHKENNAR
                    Rowdina Gray Fella
                                CH WISHANGER CRAB TREE
            Edenborough Full O'Life, ROM
                                CH OSMART BONNIE BLUE BRAID
                    Blue Maggie from Osmart
                                Westernisles Loch Creran
```

Chris Walkowicz with Walkoway's Bryn Mawr.

"A grey dog and a black-faced ram engaged in fateful duel."